The Ut Pictura Poesis Tradition
and English Neo-Classical Landscape Poetry

Flemming Olsen

The Ut Pictura Poesis Tradition and English Neo-Classical Landscape Poetry

UNIVERSITY PRESS OF SOUTHERN DENMARK 2013

University of Southern Denmark Studies in Literature vol. 57

© Flemming Olsen and University Press of Southern Denmark 2013
Set and printed by Narayana Press, Gylling
Cover design by Donald Jensen, UniSats
ISBN 978-87-7674-663-6

Printed with support from
Landsdommer V. Gieses Legat

University Press of Southern Denmark
Campusvej 55
DK-5230 Odense M
Phone: +45 6615 7999
Fax: +45 6615 8126
Press@forlag.sdu.dk
www.universitypress.dk

Distribution in the United States and Canada:
International Specialized Book Services
5804 NE Hassalo Street
Portland, OR 97213-3644
USA
www.isbs.com

Distribution in the United Kingdom:
Gazelle
White Cross Mills
Hightown
Lancaster LA1 4 XS
UK
www.gazellebooks.co.uk

CONTENTS

INTRODUCTION   7

CHAPTER ONE
THE PARALLEL   9

CHAPTER TWO
THE PARALLEL IN THE NEO-CLASSICAL AGE   11

CHAPTER THREE
NEO-CLASSICAL AESTHETICS   27

CHAPTER FOUR
LOCUS AMOENUS AND THE PASTORAL LANDSCAPE. EARLIER LANDSCAPES   45

CHAPTER FIVE
NEO-CLASSICISM AND LANDSCAPES   55

CHAPTER SIX
SOME OBSTACLES TO THE EMERGENCE OF THE LANDSCAPE POEM AS A LITERARY GENRE   65

CHAPTER SEVEN
FACTORS FAVOURING THE EMERGENCE AND ESTABLISHMENT OF THE ORTHODOX NEO-CLASSICAL TYPE OF LANDSCAPE POEM   73

CHAPTER EIGHT
FROM TOPOS TO GENRE 87

CHAPTER NINE
**THE INGREDIENTS OF THE
NEO-CLASSICAL LANDSCAPE POEM** 97

CHAPTER TEN
**SOME EXAMPLES ILLUSTRATING THE NEO-CLASSICAL
LANDSCAPE CONVENTION IN POETRY** 121

CHAPTER ELEVEN
THE CRUMBLING OF THE CANON 165

CHAPTER TWELVE
THE LANDSCAPES OF JAMES THOMSON'S SEASONS 201

CONCLUSION 217
BIBLIOGRAPHY 235
NOTES 261
INDEX 271

INTRODUCTION

This book investigates some assumptions within Neo-Classical aesthetics that were derived from the recognized parallel between painting and poetry as epitomized in the Horatian dictum *ut pictura poesis*. It analyses the application of the principle to one genre, viz. the poetic description of landscape, with particular reference to the period approximately 1680-1730.

Those years witness a twofold change of convention or "taste", as the Neo-Classicists themselves would have put it: artistically as far as the theme of landscape description was concerned, and psychologically in regard to the acceptance and understanding of it.

The year 1680 has been chosen as one of the two lines of demarcation – allowance being made for some background information and one or two earlier specimens of landscape poetry, among them, of course, the two versions of Denham's *Cooper's Hill* – because it is around that year that theoretical preoccupation with criticism and with what literature "ought to be" gains in solidity. Leibnitz said that "finis seculi novam rerum faciem aperuit",[1] the last quarter of the century witnesses the beginning of a new order of things, heralded by the influence of French critics like Rapin and Boileau. Between 1680 and 1684, there were no less than four English translations of Horace's *Ars poetica*. Some of the translators accompanied their versions in the vernacular with comments on, and elucidation of, the thoughts of the original, which means that they had to make up their minds about the implications of the Horatian precepts, among them *ut pictura poesis*.

The year 1730 has been chosen as the other limit because by then James Thomson's *Seasons* had been completed. The tendencies and developments to be analysed in the following pages did not come to a stop in 1730, but *The Seasons* – to which full justice will not be done in this book – is, besides being several other things, a brilliant perfection of the Neo-Classical landscape genre.

The term Neo-Classicism is used as the common denominator of a number of attitudes and tendencies, which will be discussed later in the book, rather than as a designation of a clearly delimited period of time.

The book's thesis is that some characteristics of the Neo-Classical landscape poem can be accounted for in terms of the aesthetics of the age, an important aspect of which was the *ut pictura poesis* axiom. Neo-Classical landscapes are not only far more inclusive than those of other traditions, which tend to be selective because they are frequently little more than stylized stereotypes. They are also far more attentive to colour than earlier landscapes. The fact that they are often more photographic does not prevent them from being social and political analogues.

The subject of the book is one corner of the *ut pictura poesis* tradition, not an exhaustive history of its treatment and development. Nor is the book a description of landscape description as such.

It is an almost exclusive literary undertaking; the art of painting will only sporadically be referred to, also because Neo-Classicist poets, critics and theorists make very scant reference to concrete paintings or names of painters.

CHAPTER ONE

THE PARALLEL

There are several reasons why, from early Antiquity and down through the centuries, critics and theorists have felt it natural to draw a parallel between poetry and painting.

For one thing, they are both imitations, and they both appeal to the intellect *and* the eye, which would make a parallel between literature and music less obvious. Accordingly, such parallels are less frequent.

Besides, both literature and painting speak to related areas of feeling – in many cases it was possible to point to thematic identity – which is why architecture is less appropriate as a parallel. Architecture can demonstrate greatness, power, defiance, elegance and grace – but very seldom, if ever, human love or jealousy.

Also, in the cases of music and architecture, there is an intermediate step of explanation (in words!) to be taken when those arts "speak to" the feelings or the intellect. Poetry and painting, on the contrary, make their impact immediately. Thus, it is easier for a picture or a poem to moralize than it is for a building. And, as Neo-Classical literature shows, texts can be "heightened" as well as canvases, ie made to convey more than their purely descriptive value. Thus, it was common knowledge that paintings could "reflect" a moral, eg if they depicted heroic or mythological scenes.

Also in terms of structure, similarities were near at hand. A poem and a tragedy are, like a picture, a framed thing. The plot of a tragedy equals the design of a picture, words fulfil the same function as colours, and problems in a text correspond to clair-obscur in a picture.

CHAPTER TWO

THE PARALLEL IN THE NEO-CLASSICAL AGE

1

Neo-Classicism is a conceptual rather than a temporal characterization. The word implies a respect for, a harking back to, and a preoccupation with, ancient Greek and Roman tenets and ideals, an agglomeration of attitudes and tendencies that are often subsumed under the heading of "the classical canon" or "the rules". The prescriptions by which Neo-Classicists worked had been formulated and, in the case of some of them, generally agreed upon, before 1680, and the period of their most widespread acceptance was circa 1670-1695.

Neo-Classicism dislodged the three words *ut pictura poesis* from their Horatian context, and their treatment of the Latin critic's dictum is not a comment on, or analysis of Horace's use of it.

The parallel was adopted with enthusiasm by Neo-Classical writers and critics. The age saw art mainly in mimetic terms, and its paradigm within the arts was normative and rule-obedient. Classification was a key concept, and the preoccupation with representation – which was, incidentally, one of Rapin's two main divisions of all literature – would naturally lead to an interest in "showing". Order was more relevant than development, which may be one reason why a preponderantly static genre like the landscape poem found acceptance.

Classical precedent secured the validity of the parallel, which came to be an established part of the Neo-Classical canon. In accordance with the spirit of the age, critics would naturally be inclined to seek their models in Antiquity. But there was the obvious snag that Greek and Roman painting was known only in scattered fragments. However, Pliny had written in some detail about the artists of the Ancient World (and, incidentally, he had given a prominent place to the landscape painter), and, besides, Neo-Classicists were satisfied that it was possible to make inferences in regard to the Classics' intentions and tendencies on the basis of the specimens of Greek and Roman sculpture that were extant. One thing that English Neo-Classicists cannot be accused of is xenophobia: they did not mind obeying a set of pictorial rules ultimately stemming from Antiquity expounded by modern French critics like Chambray (*L'idée de la perfection de la peinture*) and by members of the French Academy from the 1660s, eg Le Brun (*Conférences*). An important reason why *ut musica poesis* would be a less obvious parallel was that music had no critical tradition from the Renaissance to build on.

Neo-Classical pictorial theory never became an impressive edifice in England. When the Neo-Classicists tackled painting, their expectations conditioned their findings: painting was assumed to be a smooth-fitting branch of the system, which of course it proved to be. The various types of pictures were made to fit into a hierarchical matrix, just as was the case with literary "kinds", as the Neo-Classicists called their genres. The ascription to a "kind" was determined exclusively by the motif of the picture and not by eg its technique. Thus a correspondent writes to Mr. Spectator (Steele) on Saturday, December 6, 1712 (*Spectator*, 555) that the English certainly have good reason to be proud of the stage which "*Portrait* or *Face* Painting" has reached in their island. The correspondent concedes the first place to "History-Painting", but makes no attempt to grade the other categories, which seem to be of equal worth. Interestingly, Oldham had been at pains to spurn landscape painting in his version of Horace's *Ars poetica*, which came out in the early 1680s: such pictures are the result of the mediocre skill of "a common dauber".[1] There is no basis in Horace for Oldham's diatribe against that "kind", and the fact that he goes out of his way to stress the inferiority of the genre may be due to a feeling of personal dislike. However, it may also be taken as evidence that a "low" genre was beginning to become a contestant that it was increasingly difficult to ignore. In his Epilogue to Granville's "Dramatick Poem", *The British Enchanters: or No Music Like Love,* Addison had criticized pictures that lack dynamism:

> Scenes of Still Life, and Points for ever fixt,
> A tedious Pleasure on the Mind bestow.²

Pictorial as well as literary "kinds" were credited with almost ontological status. That attitude sometimes produces astonishing results where portrait painting is concerned: what is extolled is not the resemblance of the face, the expression of the eyes, or the magnificence of the posture, but, more generally and more vaguely, comments centre on whether the product is a true and dignified member of the *genus* portrait, for which implicit rules seemed to exist.

2

The stated purpose of Charles-Alphonse Dufresnoy's treatise *De arte graphica,* which was published in 1668, is to illuminate and underline the sisterhood of the arts. He strove to do for painting what Horace had done for literature. The four first words of the book are a verbatim quotation from Horace's *Ars Poetica*. After that, Dufresnoy proceeds:

> Similisque poesis
> Sit pictura....muta poesis
> Dicitur haec, Pictura loquens solet illa vocari (ll. 1-3)

Dufresnoy makes the Horatian dictum a maxim of general validity, and the structure of the book borrows the tripartite division that Vida had inaugurated for literature: invention, design, and colour. The first forty lines of the treatise substantiate the axiom of the sisterhood of *pictura* and *poesis:* the subject matter of the two is identical, the nature/art dichotomy applies to both of them, the rules are valid within both, and genius is required of the performer within both painting and literature.

Dufresnoy is not a cogent or consistent thinker. His poem contains a bewildering heap of advice to the practising painter, and he did not scruple to borrow a good deal from his predecessors; yet the book is more than a rehash of the ideas of earlier theorists. It is the fruit of a long time of pondering, combined with a mature and well-informed person's assessment of what he had read and seen. It is alright to say, as Laurence Lipking does,[3] that any painter who used his common sense would have been able to do what Dufresnoy did, viz. compile a series of commonplaces with moral prescriptions added. But the point is rather that Dufresnoy is the man who did it, and seen with the eyes of a contemporary observer, the treatise is not just a collection of truisms. *De arte graphica* is composed according to a pattern that the Neo-Classicists liked: thus, the book ends with a list of evaluations of, and tributes to, outstanding painters of the past. And Dufresnoy's formulations suggest an effort to establish a set of rules that had stood the test of time because they were based on exemplifications from actually existing paintings, ie the procedure is analogous to that followed by Aristotle for tragedy. The Frenchman's style, which is compact and elliptical, enabled him to say something, which has the characteristic Neo-Classical ring of finality.

Thanks to the translations of it, *De arte graphica* became instrumental in spreading interest in, and respect for, painting, and it attracted enlightened readers' attention to the interdependence of the two arts. The poem, in the French version of it made by Roger de Piles, was translated into English in 1695 by no less a person than Dryden. Even though it was with some reluctance that he agreed, at some friends' suggestion, to shoulder the burden – he had to squeeze Dufresnoy in between the translations of Vergil, with which he was very busy at the time – Dryden was not blind to the merits of "this useful work".[4] Dufresnoy not only supplies "the best and most concise instructions for performance",[5] the rules of painting being presented "methodically, concisely, and yet clearly".[6] More than that, Dufresnoy can "inform their (sc. his readers') judgement", and he enables them to "know when nature was well imitated by the most able masters".[7]

Even if there are some mistakes and misunderstandings in Dryden's version, which is, after all a translation of a translation, a reader who is no expert but genuinely interested in painting will get a reasonably precise idea of Dufresnoy's theories through Dryden's "paraphrase" of his text. Dufresnoy's treatise can hardly be called an *Everyman's Guide to the Art of Painting*, and neither Piles nor Dryden changed it into an essentially popular work. The natural target group would be readers having aesthetic interests, *virtuosi* and *connoisseurs* (which latter word appears in Piles' version, and which Dryden renders as "best judges".[8] Such readers appreciated it: Pope called the work "a small well-polished gem" in some lines he wrote to Jervas about it. And Jervas was so captivated by it that he was persuaded to look through the second edition of Dryden's translation before the publication of it in 1718.

3

The dictum was a case of a parallelism, not identity. It did not imply a wish of making literature mere decoration. But it was generally agreed that the genesis and creative process at work in painting and poetry ran along similar lines, and that the same criteria of quality applied to both arts.

Interest in the *commune vinculum* was widespread. Pictures came increasingly to be status symbols and sources of investment. As Jeffrey Spence points out, English art of the former half of the 17th century contained numerous stimulants to a "growing emphasis on the visual",[9] emblem books, masque scenery, woodcuts, etchings, and engravings. And many people were not unfamiliar with graphic representations of outdoor scenes: they might see them on their journeys abroad, or know them from engravings at home.

As the 17th century wore on, the prestige of painting was buttressed by the achievements of contemporary science, for, like the scientist, the painter was dependent on his eye, and science was analysing that *natura naturata* which painters like Claude and Poussin had made their object. Interest in painting was becoming one of the criteria of good breeding, and collecting pictures became a fashionable taste for other people than those who were immensely rich such as Charles I and the Duke of Buckingham, who were great collectors of art. Travellers saw pictures (and landscapes!) abroad, and they brought some works home from eg Italy to decorate the walls of their estates. Wealthy people would have picture galleries in their homes, as Pope did, and landowners would not only "distribute" the grounds surrounding their houses according to the prevalent taste within landscape gardening; they would also, not infrequently, dabble in painting in the hope of immortalizing their status symbols. The quality of such pictures – and some of them were probably pretty inferior – is less important than the fact that those who painted them were inspired by the idea that actual views and panoramas were worthy of pictorial representation. That is also proved by the considerable number of prospects that professional painters were commissioned to produce. As early as 1652, Sir Daniel Fleming had numerous pictures painted of the views from his house.[10]

The ties between the Sister Arts would be strengthened by the warm friendships that existed between many of the performers of *pictura* and *poesis* respectively. Congreve, Dryden and many others addressed commendatory poems to Sir Geoffrey Kneller, the portraitist, and the case of Pope is so illustrative as to deserve more detailed comment.

An anonymous biographer from 1744 assures us that, as a schoolboy, "Mr. Pope used to amuse himself with Drawing, and such like improving and rational Accomplishments" while his schoolmates were playing in the breaks between lessons.[11] One of the happiest periods of his life was the eighteen months, in 1713-14, that Pope spent as an apprentice to his friend, the painter Charles Jervas. The latter was especially famous for his portraits, a genre at which Pope, in his own estimation, was fairly adept:

> I find my hand most successful in drawing of Friends…insomuch that my Masterpieces have been one of Dr. Swift & one of Mr. Betterton,

he confides to Caryll in 1713.[12] However, in that period he was busily occupied by literary concerns, and he probably had to drop his apprenticeship in Jervas' studio in 1714 because he had committed himself to the translation of Homer.

In a letter to Caryll, probably from 1712,[13] Pope calls himself "a lover of Painting". We know that on the walls of his Twickenham estate he had numerous paintings (among the "8 Land Skips"), and the terminology of painting and metaphors from the language of the Sister Art permeate his writing from the earliest stages. Norman Ault has made an inventory of the numerous colours Pope uses in his works; thus, for "red", he has not only derivatives like redder, redden, but also vermilion, scarlet, cochineal, ruddy, sanguine, rust, ruby, rubric, rosy, roseate and crimson Therefore, it is probably true to say that the almost monochrome colour scheme of *The Dunciad* is functional and symbolic. The dominating colours are brown and black, modulated by occasional touches of blue, gray, or dirty yellow. That can be seen as a satirical inversion of the colours that Pope himself appreciated, and which appeared in the canvasses of his favourite painters, Raphael and Corregio. And when Dullness ultimately triumphs, colours disappear entirely, and Universal Darkness buries all.[14]

Pope developed "a painter's eye" when looking at nature, and he was responsive to the pictorial potential of a given scene, its "picturesqueness": "The decay of the Year", he wrote to Digby on October 10, 1725 is

> the best time...for a Painter; there is more Variety of Colours in the Leaves, the Prospects begin to open thro' the high Canopies of Trees to the higher Arch of Heaven: the Dews of Morning impearl every Thorn, and scatters Diamonds in the verdant Mantle of the Earth: the Frosts are fresh and wholesome: what wou'd ye have? The Moon shines too, tho' not for lovers these cold Nights, but for Astronomers.[15]

Pope's interest in the Sister Art was no passing whim, and his approach to it is remarkable, perhaps also unexpected. In matters pictorial, he largely ignores a possible substratum of coherent theory. He does not look upon painting in terms of an assessed hierarchy of genres, and "rules" are never taken into consideration. The object of painting, as he sees it, is *delectatio* pure and simple;

the *instructio* aspect is somehow felt to be irrelevant, and he has no qualms about dispensing with it. Also, we never find in Pope a serious discussion of the concept of imitation within painting. He seems to have enjoyed the study and practice of painting in a relaxed and "untheoretical" way. It would be misleading, however, to say that his preoccupation was entirely unreflecting, for he shows some interest in eg the powers of colours, and he devotes some pages to a discussion of the best means to produce an effect in the beholder. This concern for the response of the recipient is by no means unusual in Neo-Classical critics of either of the two arts.

Critics tended to overlook the possibly restricted validity of the parallel and to supply analogies that were not only un-Horatian, but also inherently improbable: thus Dubos advanced a theory to the effect that "les grans Peintres furent toujours contemporains des grans Poëtes",[16] a statement that would seem to be in need of some substantiation.

Equally, it was not unusual for literary performances to be called paintings: Pope considered Homer's *Iliad* a huge painting, and Locke described La Bruyère's *Caractères* as "an admirable piece of painting".[17] Waller's *Instructions to a Painter* (1666) is an invitation to a painter – no name is suggested – to depict on canvas the naval battle in June 1665, in which "His Majesty's forces at Sea" defeated the Dutch. The event is described in great detail in Waller's poem. The subject is heroic, ie worthy of being the theme of an epic poem, and the painting is to be in the same style as a heroic poem. Waller shows no great awareness of the technical differences between *pictura* and *poesis*, but a significant point is that it was thought natural to suggest that a great event could be expressed with equal success and justification in the two media.

Literary critics provide illustrations of the principle (both in heroic poetry and heroic painting the hero is placed at the centre of events), in a few cases surprising applications of it, but hardly ever anything like an analysis of the tenet itself. "La conciliation est facile sur le plan des idées vagues ", says Pierre Francastel.[18] Fénélon spoke on behalf of critical opinion when he wrote in *Lettre à l'Académie* in 1714:

On a enfin compris, messieurs qu'il faut écrire comme les Raphaël, les Carrache, et les Poussin ont peint, non pour rechercher de merveilleux caprices et pour faire admirer leur imagination en se jouant du pinceau, mais pour peindre d'après nature.[19]

The painters quoted belong to different ages and schools, and the motifs of Raphael and Poussin are not immediately comparable, so Fénélon's reference must be to what Mario Praz calls the *ductus*[20] of the painters in their imitation of nature, ie their avoidance of what is exaggerated and abnormal, and their rendering of typical aspects of human existence.

For the fact is that some critics were uneasy about the juxtaposition of words and colours: in his *Complete Art of Poetry* from 1718, Gildon says

> ... I must allow, that Colouring being a Part of the *Painter's Imitation*, has a better Claim to Excellence than the *Diction* or *Language* in poetry; which is no Part of the Imitation.[21]

One of the very few treatments that attempt to go beyond mere commonplaces is an article in *The Free-Thinker* (Monday, October 27, 1718), which has as its epigraph *ut pictura poesis*. The early passages recommend that painters draw inspiration from the reading of poets' works and advise poets to proceed similarly. That is nothing out of the ordinary; however, the writer is aware that

> there is not the least Resemblance between Words and Colours, as there is between different Languages: And therefore, it requires a strong Faculty of Imagination, and just Manner of Thinking, to be able to translate out of one into the other without losing the Spirit.[22]

This is one of the very few critical statements from the period that takes the difference of medium between *pictura* and *poesis* into account. Also, the writer recognizes that the process of transference, which is compared to an act of translation, requires the co-operation of rational and irrational factors, but no further clue is given in the article to analyse the operation of either "Imagination" or "Thinking".

The point about words and colours is touched upon elsewhere in the article:

> It seems equally difficult to paint in Words or in Colours, so as to impose the one upon the Reader and the other on the Beholder, for Realities. The Great Poet and the Great Painter think alike, but, they express their Thoughts by very different Powers. The Painter's Language is his Colours: The Poet's Colours are his Diction.

In terms of Neo-Classical critical writing, that is a statement of considerable acumen: the thinking – which probably refers to a combination of what ancient rhetoricians called *inventio* and *dispositio* – is identical in the two arts, but the realization depends on the medium. Yet the difference of the "Powers" is no more than just stated. It will also be seen how the aesthetic approach predominates: the "Spirit" should be preserved, irrespective of the material or form used by the artist, and the product should seem "real", ie respect verisimilitude and not be against nature.

Later in the same essay we are informed that

> The Poet and the Painter may mutually improve one another, by judiciously perusing each other's Works. The Similitudes, the Descriptions, and the Metaphors of one; the Landskips, Figures, and Postures of the other, equally tend to regulate, and enliven the Imagination.[23]

That is a typical Neo-Classical attempt to detail the parallel; both the thought and its "dress" are symptomatic. The passage may say something that is true, but it has very little information value for the uninitiated: the items compared are not on the same epistemological level, similitude being an aspect of style, landscape being a genre. And there is a good deal of begging the question in the formulation: a true artist – be he poet or painter – will know when to "enliven" and when to "regulate" his imagination; he does not have to seek support in a Sister Art.

A more interesting statement occurs later in the same essay:

The Perfection of a Master Painter is, to be able to perform the same Wonders by Colours, which the Poet commands by his Language.

4

The fact that *pictura* and *poesis* were acknowledged to be sisters does not mean that they were awarded parity of esteem. In accordance with the Neo-Classical approach to artistic theory, the two arts were carefully balanced and assessed against each other.

In *Timber: or Discoveries…*, which was first printed in the Folio of 1640, Ben Jonson details the various ingredients of painting and the debts owed to it by other arts and sciences:

> *Picture* tooke her faining from *Poetry:* from *Geometry,* her rule, compasse, lines, proportion, and the whole *Symmetry*…From the *Opticks* it drew reasons; by which it considered, how things placed at a distance and a farre off, should appear lesse; how above or beneath the head, should deceive the eye &C.[24]

In Jonson's opinion, then, painting is a derived art, composed of discrete and identifiable contributions from the sciences and literature. Over and above the inherent interest such an inventory may possess, it is significant that no such declaration of contents is ever established for literature.

Others awarded the palms to painting. In *The Paraphrase of the Book of Job* from 1700, Blackmore writes:

> Sometimes the Lord of Nature in the Air
> Spreads forth his Clouds, his sable Canvas, where
> His Pencil, dipt in heavenly Colour bright
> Paints his fair Rain-bow, charming to the Sight.

It is true that the somewhat infelicitous formulation of the passage caused the authors of *Peri Bathous* to incorporate the lines into their pretendedly innocent selection of memorable passages.[25] Yet, more interesting is the use Blackmore makes of the Renaissance *argumentum ex universo*, which saw God as the supreme artist: to a Neo-Classicist it was natural to make the Creator a painter.

The Lawyer Thomas Flatman wrote a small piece (published in *Poems*, 1682) *On the Noble Art of Painting*, which, from the outset, looks upon his own poem, and poetry in general, in terms of a picture:

> Strike a bold stroke, my Muse, and let me see
> Thou fear'st no colours in thy poetry,
> For pictures are dumb poems; they that write
> Best poems do but paint in black and white.[26]

Throughout the poem, Flatman does not doubt where to cast his vote: were not the Gods made "ever-living"

> But from those portraitures the painter made? (l. 9)

Flatman elaborates on the motif of the sun as the most magnificent of painters (ll. 44-47) before he ends the poem on a note of pictorial assertiveness:

> But all my lines are rude, and all such praise
> Dead-coloured nonsense. Painters scorn slight bays.
> Let the great command itself, and then
> You'll praise the pencil and deride the pen (ll. 71-72).

Because it only works in terms of black and white, *poesis* cannot do justice to its motifs and is incapable of using painting "after his desert": motifs require colours, and *pictura* can only be judged by its own criteria.

In Flatman's poem, the preference is stated without any explicit argumentation. Yet we find latent in *On the Noble Art of Painting* two points that later criticism exploited in order to establish the superiority of painting, viz. its appeal to sight, the queen of senses, and, as a corollary, its universal intelligibility – the aspect that Lessing was to stress in the middle of the 18th century.

Also earlier critics had realized that the assertion of the preeminence of sight could be profitably harnessed to a claim that painting was superior to poetry. According to Leonardo, the poetic imagination is inferior to the bodily eye of the painter, which apprehends directly the rich and wonderful variety of the external world, which the inner eye of the poet is unable to do.[27] No literary critic seriously disputed the gist of Leonardo's statement. Dryden, quoting Bellori, admits in his *Parallel* that words are inferior to colours because "sight is stronger than the force of words".[28]

Dubos gave the idea a typical Neo-Classical twist: since painting appeals to the noblest of senses, it influences us more strongly than poetry. By the same token, Dubos regards tragedy as the foremost literary "kind" because, being performed on a stage, it appeals directly to the eye. Besides, Dubos had an interesting approach to the aspect of understanding: poetry uses "des signes artificiels", which painting does not, for which reason the latter becomes immediately and universally intelligible.[29] But Dubos does not embark on any coherent theory of signs, nor does he explain in what way letters are more "artificiels" than colours.

The reason for the pre-eminence of colour was not only respect for the Horatian precept, but also that, as in the Renaissance, *mens picturans* was considered an empirical fact. Here it is relevant to point to the Neo-Classicists' interest in mirrors and their effect, and to the frequent occurrence of the word "reflexion" in its literal as well as its figurative sense. Reading literature and looking at pictures were considered pursuits that stimulated the image-producing faculty of the perceptive and *engagé* recipient.

Dubos epitomizes the attitude: the "stile de la Poësie" must be

> Rempli de figures qui peignent si bien les objets décrits dans les vers que nous puissions les entendre sans que notre imagination soit continuellement remplie des tableaux qui s'y succèdent les uns aux autres, à mesure que les périodes du discours se succèdent les uns aux autres. Il faut donc que nous croyions voir pour ainsi dire, en écoutant des vers: *Ut pictura poesis*, dit Horace.[30]

Dubos takes the comparison in the sense of picture-creating (presumably metaphorical) language as a poetical desideratum.

The noteworthy thing is that critics felt free to apply the parallel to varied and highly idiosyncratic purposes: to Aristotle, the two arts were sisters because they were both imitations. Horace saw the juxtaposition as a matter of equal distance between the work of art and the reader or beholder. Especially one parallel was frequently postulated, viz. between epic poetry and portrait-painting. The most distinguished "kind" in literature, viz., "the Epick", would of course be matched by an equally impressive pictorial genre. Already Aristotle had compared tragedy and portrait-painting.

5

However, for all the immediacy of appeal, there was widespread agreement, at least among literary critics, that there were respects in which painting was clearly deficient. As John Hughes exclaimed in *The Supplement: or A Picture in Verse*:[31] "Painter give o'er, for how wilt thou describe th'immortal part?"

Actually, colours are of little avail:

> Colours are but the Phantoms of the Day
> With what they're born, with that they fade away;
> Like Beauty's Charms, they but amuse the Sight...
> Then what are these t'express the living Fire,
> The Lamp within, that never can expire?
> That Work can only by the Muse be wrought,
> Souls must paint Souls, and Thought delineate Thought.

Here, the sense-dependence has become a liability: colours are ephemeral, and the highest purpose of art is to describe, and appeal to, the workings of the mind. For that, "the Muse", which Hughes seems to deny to Painting, is required. Hughes' attitude had been anticipated by Ben Jonson, who said in *Timber* that

> of the two, the Pen is more noble than the Pencill. For that can speake to the Understanding, the other, but to the sense.[32]

Neo-Classicism ranged "senses" lower than "understanding". Painting was considered an essentially manual art, hence less profound than its philosophical sister, poetry.

The majority of those who wrote theoretically on the subject of aesthetics were men of letters by profession. It is true that more than a handful of them had painting as a hobby and counted painters among their closest friends, but still aesthetic and artistic standards would most frequently be synonymous with literary standards, for the painters of the age seemed to be less interested in the theory of their art. Jonathan Richardson said that "the painter should have the talents requisite to a good poet",[33] and according to Shaftesbury the good painter should be like the good poet. If he treats of common and well-known subjects, he should endeavour to order his material in such a way that "his work itself becomes really new and original".[34] Dryden has a fairly long passage in his translation of Dufresnoy in which he attempts to prove to what extent the unities are applicable to both arts and should be respected by the performers of either.[35]

In accordance with the Neo-Classical predilection for pigeon-holing and system-building, the free interpretation of the maxim paved the way for a new and hitherto unrecognized "kind", viz. the poem that describes a concrete and recognizable landscape. A poem was given its name after the location it described: *Grongar Hill* and *Windsor Forest* are cases in point. The landscapes that 17th century critics had in mind and sometimes explicitly referred to were narrative (in the vein of Lorrain) or fantasy-inspired (emulating Salvator Rosa); but they were also, and that goes for the topographical descriptions as well, stylized and idealized. All of them were social, political or moral analogues.

6

In the *paragone* between the two arts, which never got beyond a peaceful, although at times fairly animated, exchange of views, Neo-Classicism evolved some convictions that were, of course, shaped by the fact that literary critics were more numerous and articulate than their pictorial counterparts. Admittedly, painting was acknowledged to hold a trump card in its possession of colours, yet painting was generally held to be inferior to poetry when it comes to descriptions of mental operations and states of mind, apart from the most schematic ones. Of course that deficiency was bound to be a heavy liability in an age that came to be so intensely preoccupied with all manner of *motus animi*. In moments of grandiloquence, poets would pay the compliment to the practitioners of the Sister Art that they had managed to give more than exterior likeness and to show their models' attitudes and thinking processes.[36]

CHAPTER THREE

NEO-CLASSICAL AESTHETICS

1

Neo-Classicism did not use the word "aesthetics"; the term was coined by Alexander Baumgarten in 1735, ie after the period dealt with in these pages. Instead they talked about "criticism" or, since their starting-point was usually literature, they discussed what "poetry" – by which they mean "literature" – should be. Neo-Classical "criticism" was a house with many mansions: it included, besides evaluations of works of art, elements of literary theory, history and morals.

The Neo-Classicists had a peculiar technique of argumentation: whereas they believed that they proved a point, they would most often do little more than confirm an acknowledged axiom or quote venerable precedent. Genuine causal explanations are virtually non-existing. The writer of a passage of criticism stops when he has exhausted the potentialities of an almost mechanical process. Critics' theoretical pronouncements – contrary to what they seemed to be convinced of – were not analyses as we understand the word; they served as illustrations or exemplifications. Their rules were held to be based on reason, but that does not mean that items of the Neo-Classical canon could be proved empirically or by means of what we would call a chain of argumentation. Therefore, much "critical" writing is actually a tribute to the magnificence of the edifice rather than an attempt to get to grips with the problems presented by the work of art.

Orthodoxy prevailed, also in the sense that it was not at all a question of mapping virgin territory or reaching new understanding. The evidence that writers and critics used to corroborate their statements usually boiled down to a quotation from another critic, preferably one of the church fathers, Homer, Horace and Aristotle. That is why conventional Neo-Classical theory so often becomes tautological in its demonstration. Of course not all critics say the same thing, but even approaches that pretended to be unconventional would very seldom venture off the beaten track.

The Neo-Classicists had no doubt that the rationality of the Supreme Being, who created the universe, was reflected in a comparable rationality of His creation. Man's endeavour to comprehend the world, then, was also an act of worship. To facilitate the grasp of the human understanding, the Neo-Classicists would resort to "methodizing", as they called it.

Vertically their methodizing is evident in the hierarchies they established for the genres of literature and, to some extent, painting. Horizontally, their systematization led them to consider all the arts to be members of one family. Comparisons and cross-references were not only legitimate, but obvious. Thus, there came to be an extensive common ground of vocabulary: in landscape poetry, for example, we find literal and figurative use made of terms from architecture (pillar, column), music (consort, harmony) and painting (colour, frame, prospect).

So, the popularity of the parallel between painting and poetry was due to the fact that it was eminently adaptable to, and consonant with, essential aspects of Neo-Classical thinking.

2

In their origin, rules – an obvious instance of "methodizing" – were not just arbitrary laws laid down by an authoritarian literary elite. Thus, the unities of the drama can be seen as a reaction against the unrestrained liberties in regard to time, action and place to be found in many 16th century dramas. The Neo-Classical age showed considerable solicitude for quality, and the rules were seen as a means of establishing some standards within the province of art.

The rules were said to hark back to Horace's *Ars poetica*, but that work was neither planned nor executed as a collection of prescriptions. Thus, there is no one equivalent for the word "rule". Instead we find terms like "norma" and "aptum", which are aesthetic rather than structural injunctions. That also goes for the series of recommendations in the subjunctive ("Let not Medea slay her children before the audience", etc.) and the numerous axiomatic statements ("there are no dolphins in woods"). From a formal point of view, *ut pictura poesis* is on a par with many other prescriptions in the *Ars poetica*.

The basis of the Neo-Classical canon is the idea that Reason is permanent and universal, and since Reason was the parent of the rules, the latter were equally permanent and universal. The Neo-Classicists were satisfied that their aesthetic edifice was based on an unassailable foundation, yet a modern reader will often find the language of their criticism empty on account of the vague denotations and the implied connotations.

Observance of the rules guaranteed a certain overall structure of the work of art. That means that they served as a tolerable crutch for a mediocre artist. Geniuses, however, could not only fill the frames satisfactorily, but would also know to what extent they could transgress them.

3

"To imitate is instinctive in man from his infancy", said Aristotle in his *Poetics*.[1] Imitation is a key concept in *Poetics*: "The poet (is) an imitator, like the painter or any other artist of that kind".[2] Literature could imitate the actions of men, he said. But he cast his net wider:

> Epic, poetry, tragedy, comedy, dithyrambics, as also, for the most part, the music of the flute and of the lyre – all those are, in the most general view of them, *imitations* (his italics).[3]

Imitation is a *sine qua non* if the finished literary product is to be successful:

If the poet has undertaken to imitate without talents for imitation, his poetry will be essentially faulty.

Even more, imitation in art is beneficial for the recipient's mental health: if we saw "certain objects as if real, we could not see them without pain".[4] The idea of imitation as a wholesome pursuit is also met with in many Neo-Classical critics.

Aristotle is not very explicit about the object or objects of imitation. With a parallel displacement, the same can be said about the Neo-Classical writers, to whom imitation was an essential requirement. They extol Homer and Vergil, but practically never specify *why* they admire them. Imitation of the two ancient writers is mandatory, but whether it is the stories they tell, the moral they inculcate, or the technique they use that seduce the Neo-Classicists is never made clear. That means that Homer and Vergil become household words. The tribute to them is obligatory – most often only their names are mentioned. They are above criticism, and they come to personify an undefined homage to ideal perfection in literature.

For the purposes of landscape poetry, another aspect of imitation is relevant: owing to the achievements of science, the world had proved to be explicable in terms of reason. For art to imitate that reality was considered legitimate, even honourable. However, it was not a matter of mere copying; Aristotle had taught the Neo-Classicists that that was away from the purpose of art. Any description or imitation is unavoidably subjective, which means that it is selective as well as corrective. To Aristotle, imitation of eg *natura naturata* is an act of creation, an emulation of nature, an implementation of her unrealized intentions – and a correction of her mistakes. The artist's talent will enable him to eliminate what is transient and particular and to reveal the essential features of the object. Aristotelian *mimesis* "dis-covers" the form towards which an object tends, but which it hardly ever reaches.

Mimesis urges the poet to dig beneath the outward aspect of things and explore the inner structure on which the external phenomenon depends. That view could easily be incorporated in the moralizing function of art. Aristotle said that authors of tragedies should follow skilful portrait painters who, while they express the particular lineaments, and produce a likeness, at the same time improve upon the original.[5]

When *natura naturata* was imitated according to this theory, it was ordered and stylized in the process, or "heightened" as the Neo-Classicists would call it. *Natura naturata* was held to be the work of the Supreme Being, and since one of the outstanding attributes of that Being was intelligence, nature, too, could not be unduly chaotic and wild. Accordingly, views and prospects of actually existing landscapes would be slightly idealized; we hardly ever find a "pure" topographical description, let alone a weed or a working-scene, in the Neo-Classical landscape poetry.

Such an idealized picture was generally referred to as "la belle nature", a term coined by the French critics Piles and Batteux.[6] One reason for the popularity of the tragedy was that its hero was a "la belle nature" specimen of mankind. What artists imitated, then, was that "idea or fore-conceit of the work", as Sidney called it.[7]

How the "idea" came into existence, and how it was activated in the creative process, was passed over in silence. The complication was that if the "idea" is postulated to be located in the artist's mind, the consequence is that the work of art imitates something within the artist. To avoid the risk of art becoming a purely subjective phenomenon, critics found it necessary to combine the "idea" in the individual mind with the universal "ideas" of the world pattern, traces of the divine archetypes being imprinted on the individual artist's consciousness. That is of course pretty vague, but it is consonant with the deductive reasoning of orthodox Neo-Classicists.

Locke's theory that ideas are formed inductively, on the basis of sense impressions, was a serious blow to the whole "belle nature" theory, which had also suffered because it was impossible to reconcile with one very popular Neo-Classical artistic genre, viz. portrait painting.

4

"Nature" is the word that appears with the greatest frequency in Neo-Classical literature and criticism. It was a Protean term: whenever a Neo-Classicist said "nature", he would refer to a set of political, scientific, social, aesthetic, and ethical ideas.[8] The concept of nature and its multifarious and diffuse interpretation enjoyed enormous prestige.

Nature could refer to an empirical reality characterized by permanence and order: "quod semper, ubique et ab omnibus…". Dennis has a pertinent statement to the effect that the larger concept of order has a twofold manifestation, viz. Reason inside the individual, and Nature outside him.[9] "General nature" was a reality to the Neo-Classicists, who had no doubt that the order of nature was reflected in the rules.

Neo-Classicism particularly emphasizes one aspect of nature, viz. the fear of the non-rational, including the shunning of extremes. So, rules were healthy since the unpredictable freedom of the human spirit had to be curbed.

"Nature's road" is the golden mean, which is within everybody's grasp:

> Take Nature's path, and mad Opinion's leave
> All states can reach it, and all heads conceive;
> Obvious her goods, in no extreme they dwell…

wrote Pope in *Essay on Man* (IV, ll. 29-31).

In this sense, nature is a moral absolute. But it was also an aesthetic key concept; it could mean "the universal and immutable in thought, feeling, and taste…usually connected with the assumption that the universally valued is also the objectively beautiful".[10] That must be what Dryden had in mind when he wrote, in 1677: "… those things which delight all ages, must have been an imitation of nature".[11] That is why nature could become, in Pope's words, "At once, the Source, and End, and Test of Art".[12]

That attitude explains the age's idolization of Homer and Vergil. Neo-Classicists saw this aspect of nature personified in their works. Poets and critics were agreed that "Nature and Homer are the same".¹³ The identification does not seem to be immediately obvious since neither Homer nor Vergil established or conformed to any rules. Nor could they be said to shun extremes.

One of the numerous ramifications of the concept of nature was that it could be used in a sense that comes very close to mean an artist's talent. Inevitably, then, the question arose about the relative positions of art and nature, or, to put it differently, talent and rules. In line 408 of *Ars poetica* Horace had posed the question

Natura fieret laudabile carmen an arte;

however, he did not want to commit himself: he irons out the difficulty by saying that you will find that, as the subject varies, it calls for the assistance of one or the other and reconciles the two without any trouble.

Practically all Neo-Classical critics on the subject were aware that the rules were insufficient to teach or help a mediocre author to produce a masterpiece, and that the rules could not account for all the beauties of a work of art. Paradoxically, it was reason that made it clear to those men of letters that there was something "above" or "beyond" their reason-based canon. Equally paradoxically, they did not scrap the rules but agreed that Homer and Vergil were possessed of a specific talent that enabled them to achieve excellence, or even perfection.

That special gift was called *genius*, and there was a common consensus that it was unlearnable. "Poeta nascitur, non fit," said Horace. Rapin, who devotes several pages of his *Réflexions sur la Poëtique en général* to appreciatory comments on "le génie" calls it "a gift from Heaven".¹⁴ In that French critic's opinion, the qualities requisite to "faire un poète" are "le jugement et le génie" combined with "une imagination nette et agréable".¹⁵

Judgement is another undefined talent. On the one hand, it is a "natural" gift in a man of taste, but at the same time it functions as a controlling force so that even genius does not transgress the prescriptions of Horace and Aristotle. Judgement often comes to be identified with the "art" aspect of the pair nature/art, just as genius belongs under the category of "nature".

Judgement was a kind of pale cast of thought circumscribing the artist's talent, a conscious, healthy, and rational curb on the impulses that "nature" might think fit to put into the poet's head. Yet nobody said anything about how it worked, and it is noteworthy that it was primarily taken as a characteristic of the artist rather than of the critic. The existence of "natural" poets was not denied: Homer was universally agreed to have managed with *ingenium* alone. However, the prevailing opinion was that "true ease in writing comes from art, not chance",[16] ie the poet's "nature" would benefit from a careful familiarization with the tools of his trade. And, unlike genius, judgement was learnable, eg by looking to ancient precedent.

Both judgement and the rules were considered salutary balances of genius, as Rapin said, the rules are meant to help the poet to "sçavoir jusques où l'emportement doit aller".[17] The line would be drawn by *la bienséance*, another loan from French criticism. *La bienséance* did not admit of, for example, truthful renderings of everyday existence. Verisimilitude, not naked realism, was the key idea; an analogical approach is seen in Denham's warning to translators: it would be "a vulgar error, in translating Poets, to affect being *Fidus interpres*.[18] The wording is borrowed from the Horatian statement in *Ars poetica*, ll. 133-34: "nec verbo verbum curabis reddere fidus interpres".

In portraiture, poet and painter had to perform an act of tight-rope-walking: they would have to preserve, or modify, or abandon the variable features of a face – whereas they would be forced to preserve the permanent or essential features. Thus they could "improve" or "heighten" their model without doing violence to either likeness or characterization.

Already Roman critics had discussed the question whether it is possible to account exhaustively for the qualities of a work of art in terms of *a priori* principles. Both Cicero and Quintilian had made allowance for a *nescio quid*, an irrational element in art, independent of, and transcending, the more obvious schematization of rules. The *non so che* was eagerly appropriated by the Italian Renaissance, and to the Neo-Classicists, *je ne sais quoi* and its near-synonym, *grace*, became more and more of a desideratum in art. Rapin talks of de certaines choses ineffables, qu'on ne peut expliquer…Ces grâces secrètes…c'est un pur effet du naturel.[19]

Gradually, a distinction comes to be established between beauty and grace: beauty is the harmonious and proportionate relationship between the individual parts, and between those parts and the whole. Beauty is loosely associated with the observance of some rules. Grace is what goes beyond the precincts of rules, thus belonging in the realm of genius.

> La beauté ne plaît que par les règles, et la grâce plaît sans les règles,

as Roger Piles sums up the position.[20] Grace is something that evades precise verbalization, and that something is acclaimed by the very widespread use of the French formulation *je ne sais quoi*, also by English critics. With his marvellous gift for terseness, Pope managed to present the essence of a long tradition in less than one line: "a grace beyond the reach of art".[21]

As will be seen, elements of subjectivity were allowed, even by orthodox Neo-Classicists, to exist side by side with "rules mechanick". No discrepancy was found between order and *je ne sais quoi*.

Furthermore, "nature" might refer to that slice of empirical reality which covers the out-of-doors. In this use, nature might be a derogatory term, being synonymous with the rough or the uncouth, in which case art might be looked upon as a redeeming structural force that licks it into shape. Pope talks about "nature rising slow to art".[22]

However, "nature" might also mean that which was charmingly unspoilt, reminiscent of the immediate freshness of the Garden of Eden. "God the first Garden made, and the first City, Cain," Cowley asserted in his poem *The Garden*. And in an article from *The Guardian* (August 4, 1713), we find the following passage:

> The love of warmth makes my heart glad at the return of spring… How amazing is the change in the face of nature; when the earth from being bound with frost, or covered with snow, begins to put

forth her plants and flowers, to be clothed with green, diversified with ten thousand various dies; and to exhale such fresh and charming odours as fill every living creature with delight...

However, the "natural" state of the out-of-doors preferred by the Neo-Classicists was one that was more or less gently disciplined by man's art. To the majority of poets, admiration of the countryside is directly proportional to the security of distance. A form-conscious age like Neo-Classicism would never allow nature complete freedom, so its landscapes are always hemmed in, subjected, civilized. Influential writers like Pope and Sir William Temple come down emphatically in favour of gardens, but the very idea of a garden presupposes some degree of human interference and planning.

Neo-Classical landscapes as described in literature are always more or less "heightened" to fit in with the poets' idea of what a "landscape" ought to be. "Prospects" were discreetly arranged things, weeds were anathema, and grottoes were popular because they showed man's victory over nature. On July 23, 1679, Evelyn made the following entry in his diary in a reference to the "Grotto in Chalky Rock" at the Duke of Buckingham's estate at Clifden:

> The place altogether answers the most poetical description that can be made of a solitude, precipice, prospect, & whatever else can contribute to a thing so very like their imagination.[23]

The harmony so beloved by the age arises out of a delicate balance between nature and art. Nature is universally acknowledged to be "the first thing", to which, however, art served as an indispensable helpmate and advisor. Addison says in *Spectator* 414:

> We find the works of nature still more pleasant, the more they resemble those of art.

So, even if grace reaches beyond art, it is unimaginable without art. On the other hand, art could never be celebrated in its own right. But it could be used so gently that its effects would remain almost hidden: *ars celare artem* was a happy compromise to an age which was increasingly susceptible to the charms of *natura naturata,* yet feared nothing like chaos.

5

The pattern of knowledge had a strictly formal structure in the late 17th century. The Neo-Classical cult of order and regularity naturally led to a fondness for classification. That kind of "methodizing" took the form of the establishment of hierarchies. The acknowledgement of the existence of scales was an integral part of the age's concept of order: "Some are, and must be, greater than others", wrote Pope in *Essay on Man.*[24]

The principle was known from the Renaissance chain of being, and the inclination to "place" an artist in relation to his colleagues was not a Neo-Classical invention. It was known in the Renaissance, too: Dolce's *L'Aretino* originated in an endeavour to determine the relative merits of Michelangelo and Raphael, and in his *Réflexions sur la Poëtique d'Aristote* from 1674, Rapin gives a long list of commentators of Aristotle, containing not only names but also hierarchized evaluations.

There is quite a lot of humdrum in this classification bug, but it seems that a Neo-Classicist had not understood and appreciated an artist properly until he had pigeon-holed that artist on a scale.

However, hierarchies were not only applied to individual artists, but to the sister arts of painting and poetry as well. In 1669, Félibien made a "valued file" of pictorial genres.[25] Still-life is assigned the most humble position, and it is diametrically opposed to the most favoured genre, viz. heroic poetry: it is static, hence undramatic, and moral lessons can be deduced from it only with great difficulty. English critics, too, are unanimous in their depreciation of the still-life. Shaftesbury calls it "the last and lowest degree of painting".[26] The second lowest rung of Félibien's ladder is occupied by landscape, then follow animal paintings (animals being superior to landscape in that they are alive), and via the portrait painter we ascend finally to "le grand peintre", who depicts epic or historical scenes.[27]

Neo-Classicists conceived of literature primarily in terms of "kinds", which was the word they used for what we call genres. At least as much attention was devoted to such abstractions as to individual works, and concerns about kinds was a determining factor in literary criticism.

The Neo-Classicists showed considerable unwillingness to venture beyond the lines staked out by Aristotle and Horace and their Renaissance exegetes. They showed little or no theoretical interest in unconventional genres. A good work was one that could be fitted smoothly into the existing mould. Thus, quality came to depend heavily on correctness, which contained a strong element of pure formalism.

The ancient rhetorical *invention* idea was interpreted to mean "finding something" rather than "thinking up something". The Neo-Classicists preferred to find their stories or themes in ancient literature rather than being contemporary, let alone original in our sense of the word. As we have seen, imitation played a major part in aesthetic discussions. A consequence of that attitude was that the success (or failure) of the finished product came to depend – to keep within rhetorical terminology – on the *elocution* aspect. For that was where the author showed his skill – or his shortcomings.

In this connection it is important to remember that the Neo-Classicists hardly ever engage in analyses of stylistic features, rhyme schemes, or stanzaic structures. Their comments are not elaborately technical, and their concentration on verbal felicities makes their formal reflections both abstract and vague. Their favoured formulation "dress the thought" implies that the thought has been structured before it is uttered (*invention* had seen to that), or, to put it differently, that thought can exist independently of words. That is why the spate of *artes poeticae* published during the period would always contain page after page of purple patches. They are mere collections of quotations, torn out of context, not evaluations. Their justification resides not least in the fact that they point backwards: since such formulations had been used once they could legitimately be used again.

Horace had warned poets not to mix genres:

versibus exponi tragicis res comica non vult,[28]

and the Neo-Classicists paid lip-service to the principle of the separation of the genres. However, their practice belied their theory, for they admitted mock-heroic poems as well as pastoral dramas.

The bulk of their genre discussion is centred on tragedy and epic because they could point to glorious classical prototypes. Aristotle had spoken favourably of tragedy,[29] but *Poetics* leaves no doubt that the greatest of the Greek poets is Homer, the writer of epic poetry. And Vida's *De arte poetica,* which was published in 1527, inaugurated the cult of Vergil, for, in spite of its title, Vida's book is almost exclusively about epic poetry. Also French Neo-Classical theorists like Rapin and Bossu were far more preoccupied with epic poems than with tragedy, and English critics followed in their footsteps.

There were numerous reasons for the popularity of the "heroic poem", as the Neo-Classicists called the epic genre. For one thing, it was believed to imitate the whole of nature whereas other genres only imitated parts of it; accordingly, it was held to incorporate more aspects than tragedy, being now narrative, now dramatic, now lyrical, and now didactic.

Secondly, this wide range meant that more claims were made on the author of an epic poem than on a tragedian: he was expected to be in full command of a considerable amount of historic material, and to be well versed in both science and the arts so as to be able to enrich his fable with episodes. The result was – and that is a third reason – that epics were better suited for didactic purposes than tragedies.

The Neo-Classical cult of reason and fondness for didacticism made it natural for them to venture to introduce a non-Aristotelian element, viz. *the cause,* which held parity of esteem with plot and character. The reason for the age's preference for the *Iliad* rather than the *Odyssey* was that the "cause" of the former poem – the destruction of Troy – was more dignified than that of the *Odyssey,* which boils down to little more than the eviction of Penelope's suitors. By the same token, the *Aeneid* was universally respected on account of its "cause", viz. the creation of an empire.[30] It will be seen that, in Neo-Classical usage, "cause" borders on "moral".

Other "kinds" were cursorily referred to and given a very summary treatment. The position may seem confusing, for the Neo-

Classicists would maintain that epic and tragedy were at the apex of the "kind" category, implying, it would seem, that there was a gamut of genres below the two. However, that is not the case. The *plenum formarum* of the chain of being was not known within the hierarchy of literary genres. Comedy, for example, was relegated to a not specified, but decidedly inferior position because there was no classical prototype for it. Pastoral was assigned the lowest station in the file: it was placed among the "vulgar lays", its imitation being decidedly inferior to that of tragedy and epic, its register being what classical treatises would call the *stylus humilis*.

That is why the landscape poem found it difficult, at the beginning, to assert itself as a genre: it deviated from the stereotyped landscapes of the Ancients, it is almost static, and it does not tell a story with dramatic incidents, suspense and climaxes. On the contrary, it consists, on a superficial view, of "mere description".

Although the pictorial hierarchy is reminiscent of its literary counterpart in not being very comprehensive, only one parallel is maintained with any consistency, viz. that between heroic poetry and portrait painting. Apart from that, no consistent one-to-one correspondence developed between the Sister Arts within the province of genres. Thus, in the *Parallel*, Dryden deplores the absence of a "low" genre within painting to match the inferior literary genre of comedy.[31]

6

As was mentioned towards the end of the previous section, one of the reasons why the rating of the landscape poem was low in the early years of the Neo-Classical period was its lack of dynamism.

The Neo-Classical attitude to the pair stasis/motion was ambivalent and, at the same time, symptomatic. For all the different uses of the word, nature was considered immutable, reason was generally acknowledged to be permanent, and the fixity of the "kinds" was an established fact. Beauty was to be judged by unchanging criteria. No Neo-Classicist ever talks about development, and if he referred to motion at all, it was as a stepwise and calculated phenomenon.

In this area too, classical precedent could be invoked: Aristotle decreed that a tragedy should have a beginning, a middle and an end, and the rules of the epic required that it had a proposition and an invocation, followed by narration and *dénouement*. Besides, the individual incidents of an epic must cohere, and the work as a whole is expected to show a high degree of continuity. In his *De arte poetica* from 1527, Vida had supplemented the familiar triad *invention, disposition,* and *elocution* with a fourth ingredient, viz. *action*. The latter was a fundamental ingredient in the heroic epic. For the climax is not the only attractive thing; the before and the after of the situation that is reflected are equally significant. It is true that a portrait would give a momentary impression of the person portrayed, but he was depicted for the achievements that could be seen or imagined to lie behind or ahead of him rather than for the regularity of his features or the colour of his eyes. And the portraits were usually made of outstanding personalities, not of humble farmers or conventional housewives.

A consequence of the Neo-Classical concern with imitation was their absorption with reflection, both in the literal and the figurative sense. Mirrors and mirroring are a recurrent *topos* in the aesthetics of the age. Mirrors gave faithful and, to the perceptive beholder, suggestive images of the object or objects reflected. In this context, it is remarkable that the implication of the words following *ut pictura poesis* in Horace's poem, viz. "si propius stes" was never properly investigated. In spite of the increasing solicitude and demands of the consumers and collectors of works of art, nobody ever raised the issue to what extent the beholder's position vis-à-vis a painting might determine the benefit he drew from it, or whether contemporary texts should be treated differently from those of earlier ages.

Total inability to move was anathema, witness the age's aversion to still-lifes. What Neo-Classicism favoured was controlled dynamism: near-stasis, or momentary "frozenness" seem to have been considered a sublimation of movement. With some poets we are not far from an assertion that God ordained arrested movement for His creation to be properly worshipped. It is a token of peace and serenity for water in a landscape to flow so sedately as to serve as the poet's looking-glass and to show everything in its right place. Parnell is not the only poet who makes the "smooth expanse" of the river, which reflects "calm nature's image on its watery breast", symbolize a state of moral perfection.[32] Conversely, a torrential river in literature is a conventional emblem of moral or political unrest or chaos, and "rolling waters" in landscape poems are virtually always ominous.

7

The Neo-Classical attitude to the pair stasis/motion illustrates their fondness for moderation and balance. But, more generally, the individual items and their mutual discrepancy are indispensable for obtaining ultimate harmony and equilibrium. The idea of *concordia discors* goes back to Lucan's *Pharsalia*,[33] and the principle was smoothly incorporated into the Neo-Classical canon. The construction of the syntagm is significant: *discors* is the adjective, thus being an attribute to the major concept, *concordia*. So, the reference is to a uniformity which, having variation as an inherent and indispensable characteristic, ultimately resolves it.

8

Horace had taught that

> aut prodesse volunt aut delectare poetae
> aut simul et iucunda et idonea dicere vitae.[34]

Horace does not make it clear whether he is talking of literature in general or about the individual work. However, the Neo-Classicists combined the two functions that had been separated by Horace, and they aimed at both the individual work and literature and painting in general. They saw *instruction* and *delectation* as two aspects of the same stimulus.

To the Neo-Classicists, the Sister Arts were expected to be clearly didactic. Instruction was felt to be the common ground for both arts, but the teaching they were supposed to impart was never narrowly technical. Neo-Classical *artes poeticae* were not at all written with the purpose of making their readers competent versifiers. When the Neo-Classicists invoke the *prodesse* aspect, which they very frequently do, they aim at the duty of poet and painter to inculcate respect for the intelligent arrangement of the world. Comments on Vergil's *Georgics*, for example, express more than sheer unreflecting joy of nature; the commentators are also sensitive to the value of the general didacticism of Vergil's poem, over and above the practical advice given in regard to apple-growing, bee-keeping, etc. The latter points are never in the focus of the commentators' attention.

By the same token, the pleasure aroused by literary representations of *res creatae* would usually be blended with awe-struck, or even religious, sentiments, as is evident in the case of landscape poems. The noun "pleasure" would regularly be qualified by the adjective "rational", for pleasure was not a matter of easy-going hedonism. The ethical element of pleasure was very strong, and it would be satisfied by "images of virtue and vice". There was abundant evidence that such images could be given with the brush as well as with the pen. And of course, the moral of a work of art would stand a better chance of being heeded if it was part and parcel of a work that pleased.

Pleasure was not only rational and moral, it was also conservative. The Neo-Classicists abhor what they lump together as the non-natural because they felt that it obstructed God's intelligent design and could consequently teach them nothing – and, accordingly, convey no pleasure to them – so why bother about it? It was only with the onset of sublimity that ventures were made into what had hitherto been shunned and remained unmapped. The paradox is that sublimity, too, caused the Neo-Classicists to feel pleasure – a pleasure that is anything but rational, that is.

9

When isolated, the Horatian tag is at once categorical and susceptible of considerable interpretation. Neo-Classical writers and critics, to whom the phrase became a household expression, were fond of epigrammatic succinctness, especially such as could be shown to have ancient, or supposedly ancient, sanction. Yet they blandly disregarded the original context of *ut pictura poesis* and suggested numerous respects in which the parallel might be held to be valid.

The relationship can be a thematic or a conceptual one – and a good many other things. Mostly, they ignored the difference of medium – that which was Lessing's main point of attack. They did not stop to consider how arts working with different materials and forms could be reasonably subsumed under one aesthetic heading. The Renaissance had endeavoured to eliminate the difference of medium, and to a considerable extent the Neo-Classicists followed in its footsteps. Some of the similarities perceived were of course due to the fact that painting and poetry were arts, but others were rooted in what was believed to be features that were common to the two of them.

Ut pictura poesis, from being merely a conventional dictum, developed into an important aspect of Neo-Classical aesthetics. Like so many other Neo-Classical axioms the parallel was postulated rather than proved, which, however – and that is symptomatic of the Neo-Classical approach – detracted nothing from its significance.

In the orthodox Neo-Classical period, the arts were essentially deductive in their approach, adopting and commenting on some maxims that had been propounded by sometimes fairly remote predecessors, and showing a marked disinclination to move into uncharted waters.

The many *a priori* statements on which the Neo-Classical canon rested endowed it with the aura that surrounds the incontrovertible. Yet it was its very structure that made it vulnerable in an age that was beginning to regard with admiration the achievements of a science which questioned axioms that had hitherto been taken for granted.

Neo-Classical aesthetics is reminiscent of a closed circuit. However, the fact that it was to a considerable extent old wine put into not very new bottles did not exclude discussions of, and reflections on, problems that have engaged other ages, including our own.

CHAPTER FOUR

LOCUS AMOENUS AND THE PASTORAL LANDSCAPE. EARLIER LANDSCAPES

1

The landscapes of the *locus amoenus* and pastoral traditions are more stereotyped and less elaborate than those of the Neo-Classical type because their prime function is to serve as a backdrop against which a scene is performed. The landscape is not there in its own right.

The basic ingredients of a *locus amoenus* are a tree, a spring, a meadow, and a carpet of flowers; besides, there may be an overhanging rock and birds whose "sweet notes" mingle with sounds of wind and water.[1] Well-known instances are Homer's account of Calypso's grotto and Alcinous' garden. But many of the short idyllic nature passages in Neo-Classical poetry have evident points of similarity with this tradition. In the Garden of Eden (the prototype of a "pleasant place"), says John Hughes in *A Letter to a Friend in the Country*, there were "happy Woods", "warbling Birds, soft whisp'ring Breaths of Wind", "murmuring Streams" and "a green Plain".[2]

A *locus amoenus* scene – and that applies to the *hortus conclusus* as well – contains little, if any, realistic nature description. Colours are stereotyped and devoid of nuances, and the scene is idealized, not topographical. It is art rather than nature, although energetic attempts may be made to *celare artem*. Equally significant is the fact that there is no structuralization of the items and no attempt to reach an ultimate *concordia*, which means that such descriptions fall outside the Neo-Classical conceptualization of nature. Beside, a *locus amoenus* is not called a landscape, but a "place" or, very frequently, a "garden".

2

In the Preface to his Pastorals, printed in 1708, Ambrose Philips regrets that

> in an Age so addicted to the *Muses*...*Pastoral Poetry* comes never to be so much as thought upon, considering especially that it had always been accounted the most considerable of the smaller poems.[3]

In the Neo-Classical hierarchy of genres, pastoral was relegated to a definitely humble position. In 1677, Joshua Poole had given the following epithets as possible qualifiers of "pastoral": "low-stiled, humble-stiled, rustick, plain, pleasant, jolly, youthful, country".[4]

The rural scenes of poets' pastorals never reflect any deep-felt love of, or interest in, the country. In fact, pastoral was not necessarily associated with landscape. Gildon lists the recommended content of a pastoral as follows: "Philosophic Questions, Riddles, Parables." The following items may be included: "Vows, Praise, Promises, Complaints, Mirth, Joy, and Congratulations". By a "Pastoral Scene" Gildon understands "a simple Plot, Fable or Design".[5]

Pope, too, makes light of pastoral landscape; that appears from his *Discourse on Pastoral Poetry*, which was published several years later than his *Pastorals*, viz. in 1717. Description is obviously not a distinguishing feature: the form of pastoral is "dramatick, or narrative, or mix'd of both" – but not descriptive.[6] What little Pope has to say about the localization of pastoral makes the artificiality of the thing clear:

> In each of them a design'd scene or prospect is to be presented to our view, which would likewise have its variety. This variety is obtain'd in a great degree by frequent comparisons, drawn

from the most agreeable objects of the country; by interrogations to things inanimate; by beautiful digressions, but these short; sometimes insisting a little on circumstances; and lastly by elegant turns on the words, which render the numbers extremely sweet and pleasing.[7]

What Pope recommends is a *belle nature* landscape serving as a foil to stylistic sophistication.

In the pastoral landscape – and this is true also of pastorals written before the Neo-Classical age – we find water (crystal brooks, streams, floods, fountains), trees (oak, myrtle, cypress, "boughs"), verdant meadows (often including a mossy bank), grasses, some species of flowers, a shepherd (sometimes also a nymph) and some sheep. The setting is nondescript, and the function of the items is at the same time practical and conventional: for example, the air is sultry, hence shade is useful – shade being also an appropriate *locus* for the shepherd's reflections, philosophical thinking, or amatory dialogues. By the same token, grass serves for the grazing of the sheep, and the grass and the mossy bank are soft and agreeable for the shepherd and the nymph to recline on, at the same time enabling them to keep an eye on their "fleecy care".

It seems to be a basic characteristic of pastoral landscape that it is mediated, not directly apprehended. In actual fact, it is a vehicle for the description of something else, eg what love is, what town life is like, or the excellent qualities of a human being.[8] The prime function of the landscape is far from being a narrowly utilitarian one. Even if eg early 18th century pastoral writers were not blind to economic realities (thus, the sheep often figure as "milky dams"), they do not look upon *natura naturata* in teleological terms, which both the *hortus conclusus* tradition and the Neo-Classical landscape convention do. Nor is it the intention of pastoral landscape to celebrate nature's beauties. The items serve as a scanty sketch of the background that forms the setting of the real subject, which may be, for example, thwarted love. The pastoral landscape, which is part and parcel of the poetic diction of that genre, is actually a non-urban stage direction for the narrative, which is what matters. That is why the description of the scenery is usually found at the beginning of the poem, one or two items being cursorily referred to as the poem goes along.

Pastoral landscapes are sparing of details and show little variation: virtually the only month they know is May, just as the overwhelmingly predominant colour is green; other colours, let alone nuances, are reduced to a minimum. It is a static sunlit scene, reminiscent of the still-lifes of painting. There is never a "whole" landscape, the scene is anything but topographical, and the details are not structured because they are not meant to add up to any whole. Finally, and that is another basic feature, neither pastoral nor *locus amoenus* landscapes are contemplated or enjoyed by a detached observer who has come with the purpose of "commanding" it.

3

Pliny's description, in a letter to Domitius Apollinaris, of "my villa in Tuscany" is an interesting text in the context of the subject of this book[9] because Pliny anticipates not only the approach (a beholder surveying a segment of the out-of-door panorama) but also the wording that we shall meet again in Neo-Classical landscapes. One might ask the question whether Melmoth, the translator, has been influenced by the terminology of the prevalent English descriptive tradition so that he gives a paraphrase rather than a truthful version of the text. However, even if he had tampered with the exact wording of the Latin original, Melmoth would have been unable to alter the configurations of the landscape. But the fact is rather that the English verbal tradition is indebted to Pliny' vocabulary: thus Pliny repeatedly uses the formulation "prospectus habet" (eg ll. 40 and 93), and when, in lines 131-32, he wishes he could bring the whole villa before his friend's eyes, the Latin text has "totam villam oculis tuis subicere", the idea of which is analogous to the "commanding" posture which the Neo-Classical beholder assumes before the panorama. It is a topographical scene, the items of which are neither mythological nor symbolic, indeed, where botany and architecture are concerned, they are both concrete and specific. The vista is obviously a seen one: words like "aspect", "view", and "prospect" crop up again and again, and a view from above is recommended (l. 34). The horizon is made up of mountains (ll. 12-13), which limits the scene, conferring the likeness of a picture upon it (ll. 35-37). Pliny connects his landscape with the capital by means of the most famous river of the country (ll. 29-32). The Neo-Classicists followed suit with their predilection for the upper regions of the Thames valley.

Ben Jonson's poem *Penshurst*, from 1616, includes contemplated rural scenes, but everything is made subservient to the *ad majorem patroni gloriam* idea: the beautiful architecture, the elegant interiors, and the well-kept state of Penshurst are extensions of the sterling qualities of its master. Hence the panorama, though admittedly containing topographical details, is a background more than a structured landscape. The "mount" is not the centre from which all observations radiate, and there are no colours in the scene. The emphasis throughout is on the owner's profit and pleasure.

The first two lines of Milton's landscape description in *L'Allegro*

Streit mine eye hath caught new pleasures
Whilst the lantskip round it measures[10]

anticipate the technique of the Neo-Classical landscape poets: the narrator's "wandering eye" measures – which is probably a term borrowed from the science of surveying – the scene that spreads before him. He seems to be in an elevated position, and we are not allowed to forget that it is a contemplated panorama "(it sees...", l. 77). The objects are provided with precisely observed colours ("Russet Lawns and Fallows Gray", l. 71; "Daisies pide", l. 75). Some of the other epithets also testify to acute observation ("labouring Clouds" and "tufted Trees", l. 78). There are even intimations of the imagined mysterious or mythological drama that Neo-Classicists were fond of staging on the empty foreground: behind the "Towers and Battlements" that are "Bosom'd high in tufted trees"

perhaps some Beauty lies
The Cynosure of neighbouring Eyes (ll. 79-80).

The landscape of *L'Allegro* is not topographical, nor are the enumerated objects arranged as a whole, it is an indiscriminate marshalling rather than an exploitation of the moralizing and associative conventions attached to each of the items. The unity of the poem consists in its being the projection of a mood of happiness.

In *Paradise Lost*, IV, ll. 205-68, Satan beholds the Garden of Eden, and no wonder "this first grand Thief" is struck with awe and wonder, for what meets his eye is

> in narrow room Natures whole wealth, yes more,
> A Heav'n on Earth.

It is implied at the beginning that Satan is placed on a hill ("Beneath him...he views..." l. 205), but the observing subject is not referred to again in the long passage. The scene is an epitome of bliss, as could be expected when even the minutest detail has been designed by God. On the other hand, for a locality to be the sum of perfection undeniably imposes some limitations on it. Milton goes to considerable lengths to give Eden the appearance of a geographical locality, but many lines read as if taken out of a pastoral. A lake

> holds her crystal Mirror
> to the fringed Bank with Myrtle crown'd (ll. 261-63).

There are few colours, thus the flowers are dealt with as being "all of a hue" (l. 256). The objects are not elaborately co-ordinated, they are there to illustrate the glory of the Garden – they serve the *majorem Dei gloriam* idea. That means that the *concordia* is postulated at the beginning rather than implied at the end of the description as is the case with the Neo-Classical landscapes.

Marvell's *Upon Appleton House* was probably composed in the early 1650s when Marvell was private tutor to Mary Fairfax. Again, the procedure is that of extolling a man's qualities by praising his estate. The poem contains several stanzas of meditation, but we are also given a description of the estate itself and its surroundings. Marvell's poem is a tribute to "my Lord Fairfax", one of Cromwell's generals, who composed poetry himself. The advantage of Fairfax's house is that

All things are composed here
Like Nature, orderly and near.

True proportion holds – and ought to hold – between man and his surroundings. Houses should not be oversized, we are told in the second stanza. The theme of scale is of considerable relevance for Neo-Classical landscape poetry, as is also the following statement from stanza two of Marvell's poem: "No creature loves an empty space".

The estate accommodates itself to its lord and master like a living organism, and there is both literal and moral truth in the description of the house, which becomes an emblem of its owner's moderation. The happiness of rural retirement runs as an undertone through the poem.

The middle-aged Cowley, looking back to his younger days, wrote in 1665:

> I thought when I first went to dwell in the country, that without doubt I should have met there with the simplicity of the old poetical age, I thought to have found no inhabitants there but such as the shepherds of Sir Philip Sidney in Arcadia, or of M. d'Urfé.[11]

That is the impression many a mid-century town-dweller would have of "the country", not least owing to the condition of the means of communication and the forbidding hardships of travel.

In his poem *Solitude* Cowley outlines his own favourite landscape.[12] The setting of the short poem is anything but topographical; it is an imagined rather than an observed prospect – but still it is a prospect. It is true that there are "here"s and "Hail"s in the poem, but what the beholder contemplates is a dream landscape. ("A silver Stream shall roul..." reads more like a Homeric *epitheton ornans* than an acute observation). There is no overall structuring of the landscape, which reflects the poet's aspirations rather than being a tribute to the Great Design. The landscape serves as a vehicle for a metaphorical formulation of his attitudes: stanza one looks at nature in social terms (patrician trees and plebeian underwood), stanza two extols the happiness of rural retreat (ye country houses and retreat which all the Gods...love), stanza three touches on the art/nature dichotomy (Cowley was always a staunch defender of nature, "the wisest architect"), stanzas four and five see retreat as an ideal of happiness ("let me careless and unthoughtful lying" and see how the sunbeams smile and hear "how prettily they talk").

The opening lines of Katherine Philips' poem *A Country Life* run as follows:

> How sacred and how innocent
> A country-life appears
> How free from tumult, discontent,
> From flattery or fears!
> This was the first and happiest life
> When man enjoyed himself;
> Till pride exchangëd peace for strife
> And happiness for pelf.[13]

The country – a nondescript locality – is not only synonymous with guilelessness and freedom from discontent, it is also the nourisher of poetic inspiration and the sanctuary of pure feelings. It is a figurative meaning of "country" that is celebrated, not a literal one: Miss Philips describes some moral values rather than a series of sense impressions. And, nor surprisingly, the rest of the poem, which comprises 90 lines, launches a fierce attack on the narrator's arch-enemy, viz. the pomp and vanity of life in society.

Edmund Waller's poem, *On St. James' Park, As Lately Improved by His Majesty*, describes a specific locality, and there is a sufficient number of references in it – to Westminster Abbey, Whitehall and the Mall – to justify the title. But, once again, the intention is not so much to give a topographical account of the park as to use it for a different purpose, viz. to show it as an embodiment of the King's personality, as another example of his wisdom and benevolence. Waller uses the surveying technique known from Neo-Classical landscape poems without describing a landscape in the proper sense of the word, many landscape items having been replaced by urban landmarks.[14]

Even if Waller lays his fulsome praise of the King on with a trowel, and even if his poem describes a townscape rather than a landscape, it is not without interest on technical grounds: the observer is discreetly present in the early part of the text, and the items are arranged as what the Neo-Classicists would call "a varied prospect": the water, the trees, the birds overhead, and the Mall. The objects are tentatively ranged into level-like groupings: "Yonder the harvest" (l.49), "Here, a well-polished Mall" (l. 57), "Near this (ie the Mall) my Muse...sees..." (l.67). Equally important is the use of shifting views which Charles – and with him, the reader – has from the "oracular shade" in the "gallery of aged trees":

> His fancy objects from his view receives;
> The prospect thought and contemplation gives,

which comes very close to the Neo-Classicists' two-tier approach to a scene, viz. sensation followed by reflection. In the concluding couplet of *St. James' Park* Waller states the moral which has been implicit in the poem all along:

> Reform these nations, and improve them more,
> Than this fair park, from what it was before.

As in Denham's *Cooper's Hill,* the reference to actually existing localities triggers off considerations of a moral and political kind.

CHAPTER FIVE

NEO-CLASSICISM AND LANDSCAPES

1

According to the OED (1972), the word landscape was introduced as a technical term of painters. It is defined as "as picture representing natural inland scenery as distinguished from a sea picture, a portrait, etc.". There are two spellings of the word, landscape and landskip (or lantskip).The fact that it is originally a term designating a pictorial work of art is of considerable relevance for the later treatment of the word landscape and the landscapes of *natura naturata* given in poems.

Pictorial critics began early to tackle theoretical issues connected with landscape. Thus, the author of the anonymous *A Short Treatise of Perspective*, which was published around 1600, establishes a distinction between "natural" landscapes (such as woods, hills, and valleys), and "artificial" ones (eg towns and castles). And there are intimations of the technique used by later "epic painters", who would tend to reserve the foreground for a dramatic or mythological incident, in the author's advice that the foreground should be kept apart from "the rest of the lantskip for the standinge of such as are principall in the historie".[1]

Henry Peacham's book from 1606, *The Art of Drawing with the Pen and Limning with Water Colours*, besides giving some advice to the prospective painter, enumerates some features of a landscape painting which more or less take the form of rules: the panorama should be closed by a "fair Horizon", the sky should be overcast or clear, perhaps showing sunrise or sunset, "over some hill or other".[2] The light should make the items of the landscape stand out without distorting their forms, and a "landscape" is a compound of scenery, buildings, and figures:

> You shall please very well, if you shew in the same, the faire side of some goodly Citie, hauen, forrest, stately house with gardens,[3]

but the scene may also show "through the woods, the ruines of Churches, Castles &c".[4]

The popularity of the book is proved by the fact that, by 1661, it had appeared in four editions, and the 1612 edition provides a significant supplement, viz. a chapter about the "Fairest and Most Beautifull Landskips in the World."

The tentative theorizing in Peacham's and Edward Norgate's books (*An Extract and Compendious Discourse concerning the Art of Miniatura or Limning* from 1625 and the amplification and revision of the book in 1649, *Miniature, or the Art of Limning*) move along lines that will be familiar in Neo-Classical criticism: the work of art as a source of pleasure, and the structure and verisimilitude of the artefact.

2

The landscape shown in pictures is a framed and limited panorama, a scene which can be grasped in its entirety by an observer from a fixed stand, which is also a vantage point. A locality is made an artistic object, and, to Neo-Classicism, the artistic treatment could be pictorial as well as literary. The widening of the content of the word landscape is another illustration of the *ut pictura poesis* idea: besides being "a picture representing inland scenery", the word comes to mean also a limited segment of the extensive panorama of *natura naturata*, whether actually seen or imagined, and made the object of literary description, which could conceivably be contained within the frames of a picture and which provokes a certain kind of response in the beholder. The link with painting may become tenuous in the use some Neo-Classicists make of the word, but it is never entirely severed. The affinities with the Sister Art may be seen in the "paintability" of the scene as well as in its overall structure.

There had been literary landscapes before Neo-Classicism, of course. Both the *locus amoenus* and pastoral traditions, which were dealt with in the previous chapter, had "a place" as their setting, but a genuine Neo-Classical landscape is easily distinguishable from the classically inspired "pleasant place" and Arcadian idylls.

The first non-pastoral and non-*locus amoenus* landscapes in literature dating from the early and the middle part of the 17th century treat the locality as no more than a necessary background – in accordance with one of the OED definitions of "landscape": "a background of scenery in a portrait or figure-painting". The last recorded instance of that meaning is from 1676. Ben Jonson's poem *Penshurst* from 1616 might serve as an example, the "foreground portrait" being that of the owner of the estate of Penshurst.

The next stage is an awareness of the potentialities of the "place", a tendency which becomes discernible towards the latter half of the 17th century. Cowley's *Dream of Elysium* from 1637 mingles "pleasant place" attributes with features of an observed scene: there is a "spotless Lillie" and a "blushing Rose", and mythological figures like Bacchus, Jove and Nectar make their appearance. But there is also an anticipation of the Neo-Classical technique of surveying:

> How many objects charm my wandering eye,
> And bid my soul gaze there eternally.[5]

The landmarks that catch the observer's eye are actual streams and trees, even if the setting is a dream, and the idea of "shifting views" is conveyed by a fair sprinkling of "here"s in the following passages. However, the spectator vanishes after 15 lines, and the description is carried on by its own impetus, so to speak, exploiting the associations prompted by owls and nightingales.

Shortly before the turn of the century, poets begin to concentrate on the landscape for its intrinsic value and for the reflections it evokes. However, approaches to that technique are made before

1690 by Denham as well as Chamberlayne, and of course the trend continues far beyond the period analysed in these pages. The reason why Neo-Classical poets considered landscape an appropriate object of study and treatment in its own right may be the one given by Ambrose Philips in 1708, when he attempted to take up the cudgels for pastoral:

> For, as in Painting, so, I believe, in Poetry, the Country affords the most entertaining Scenes and most delightful Prospects.[6]

"Landscape" referring to a literary description occurs already before 1700. Burnet wrote in 1689:

> I will not describe the Valley of Dauphiné, all to Chambéry, nor entertain you with a Landskip of the Country, which deserves a better pencil than mine.[7]

And in *Remarks on Prince Arthur* form 1696, Dennis pays tribute to the author of the *Aeneid*:

> Vergil, after he has terrified his Reader with the Description of that wonderful Tempest which we find in the Beginning of his Poem, takes care to refresh him, by the pleasing Landskip of the place where Aeneas has landed.[8]

3

However, it was not any tract of land that qualified for the Neo-Classical designation landscape. In order to get a better grasp of what a Neo-Classical landscape was, we must look at the age's conception of parts and wholes.

In his poem *To Sir Godfrey Kneller*, from 1694, Dryden praises the portraitist for his sense of proportioning: "Of various parts a perfect whole is wrought".[9] The recognition of discrete stages is a characteristic and pervasive phenomenon in Neo-Classical thinking. There is abundant evidence from eg the spheres of physics, psychology, and aesthetics to show that the Neo-Classicists were fond of focusing on the singleness and the individualness of things. But they were equally preoccupied with the susceptibility of an item of being incorporated into a larger whole.

Probably on the analogy with the cosmic order that had been demonstrated by Newton, Neo-Classicists favoured the idea that harmony more or less presupposed a comprehensive whole. The individual ingredients were indispensable for obtaining the ultimate equilibrium even though they were mutually discrepant. Leibniz considered harmony the highest metaphysical truth: harmony was achieved as a result of the interplay of incompatible differences. Each part was assigned a place by divine decree, and divergences served an ulterior purpose. On the other hand, exclusive concentration on particularity was seen as a movement in the direction of chaos: when a particular item was given disproportionate emphasis, disorder was bound to ensue.

One of the Neo-Classical wholes was indivisible and irreducible, viz. God. In all other cases their wholes were made up of distinguishable parts, yet somehow they were more than a mere sum of the parts. The Neo-Classicists did not hesitate to apply the physical principle of a whole and its parts to other areas, where it was supposed to be equally valid. In fact, "uniformity amidst variety" is one of the most frequently used formulations to account for the Neo-Classicists' view upon problems within science as well as the arts. The theory of artistic creation is a clear illustration of the attitude.

Division into smaller parts meant manageability, classification meant clarity; those ideas were of paramount significance to the age. The Neo-Classicists recognized and appreciated the individual item and its inherent value, at the same time seeing a given item as a part of a whole by which it is coloured (thereby sometimes acquiring a symbolic meaning), and which is, in its turn, coloured by its constituents because the latter were carefully selected. A Neo-Classical synthesis, then, will usually be the culmination of a stepwise and accumulating progression. That was the way reason was supposed to work.

Analysis followed by synthesis was believed to be a characteristic of the operations of the human consciousness, both in its self-analysis and in its scrutiny of what was outside the ego.

Blackmore personifies the mind and describes its activities as follows:

> As she can reckon, separate, and compare,
> Conceive what order, rule, proportion are,
> So from one thought she can still more infer,
> Maxim from maxim can by force express,
> And make discover'd truths associate truths confess:
> On plain foundations, which our reason lays,
> She can stupendous frames of science raise.[10]

Locke's theory of the processing of sensual impressions to ideas is another instance of stepwise progression. And his theories of association and contiguity are based on a clear conception of a delimited body. Science, too, was preoccupied with what bodies were and how they could and should be placed in relation to each other. The discussion is of some relevance to pictorial technique. Painters, landscape poets, scientists, and theologians were all equally loth to recognize such a thing as "pure space". Characteristically, when attempts were made to come to grips with the concept, familiar analogies were resorted to: according to Blackmore, pure space is that "which knows no height, or depth, or middle space",[11] ie a terminology indebted to the "levels" of painting. By the same token, Locke is slightly uncomfortable when he is to define infinity: he advises his readers to add foot to foot, "and the power of enlarging his idea of space by farther additions remaining still the same, he hence takes the idea of infinite space".[12]

In all areas, the procedure was not to stop at inferior or intermediate stages, but to add them up, move beyond them, and, preferably, find a larger structure, a design. The technique was sanctioned by rationalist religion: in His infinite wisdom, God had articulated the world, but He had taken care to make a wonderful pattern out of the sum of the parts. Also, contemporary literary terminology is illustrative: the current formulation was not that a given poem was eg an elegy, but that it belonged to the "elegiac kind". Locke's partiality to general truths[13] and the Neo-Classical conviction that there was such a thing as "general nature" are evidence of the same way of thinking.

This principle of "articulation" also appears in landscape poetry: the beholder does not see blurred outlines or a vague totality. Items are arranged with great deliberation, and there is a subtle interchange between the parts and the aesthetic synthesis which is the whole.

Lucan coined the phrase *concordia discors*,[14] and the Neo-Classicists appropriated the term – or substituted an English equivalent, viz. uniformity amidst variety – as well as the idea. The variety aspect implies that there are discrete and different phenomena, and the uniformity aspect implies that those phenomena are felt or postulated to have certain qualities in common. If not, a degree of uniformity was of course difficult to obtain.

Katherine Philips intimates in her poem *L'Accord du Bien*, published in 1674, that discord has an inherent urge towards harmony:

> Thus all things unto peace do tend,
> Even discords have it for their end.
> The cause why elements do fight
> Is but their instinct to unite.[15]

An important aspect of Neo-Classical optimism was its conviction that particular items by their very nature would tend to move towards harmony and order. In some cases, a state of perfection had been reached, eg in the marvellous pattern of *natura naturata*. In other areas, eg the classification of works of art and the evaluation of the achievements of artists, harmony was a permanently sought but rarely attained ideal. It was the Neo-Classical endeavour to determine the place of any individual item within a larger structure that naturally led to the establishment of hierarchies where artists were pigeonholed as being superior to some and inferior to others.

4

The landscape we meet in Neo-Classical poetry is an application of the principle of *concordia discors* to *natura naturata*. The components are there in their own right – what is shown is actually a slice of non-urban scenery – but not for their own sake. The artistic unity of the "kind" has an aesthetic as well as what might be called a semantic ingredient: the items have been selected for their connotations as much as for their denotations, and the combination of them arouses pleasure at the same time as it teaches a moral. The landscape poet takes the reader by the hand, so to speak, and gives him an experience of an ordered progression, not a ritualistically rigid one, but still one that is perceptibly different from a helter-skelter enumeration of more or less incompatible details. The unity of mood achieved by such a poem is created by the poet's admiration of the Great Design and his concomitant satisfaction with the way things are.

Locke had said that the natural and inevitable movement of the human mind is from the particular to the general.[16] Ratiocination favoured a movement towards greater abstraction, a "going upwards", one might say. It is no mere coincidence that the landscape poet must climb a hill before he is able to draw his generalizing conclusions: elevation of body precedes all-embracing moral reflection. The hilltop is the point of vantage from where parts are seen in their true proportions as being independent and, at the same time, "placed" in the whole, or interdependent. The frequent references to perspective are not difficult to account for since a beautiful and meaningful whole cannot possibly be made up of a chaotic jumble of details. And the wonders of that whole are conveyed by the observer's state of elation when taking in and adding up the details.

The landscape is a moral, political and social analogue. Accordingly verisimilitude is a *sine qua non,* and certain requirements have to be met for a tract of land to be recognized and exploited as a landscape. Even though the constituent parts were both contrary and complementary, they would still belong to the same conceptual field, their common denominator being, for example, plausible contemporaneous occurrence in a natural landscape. Thus a tree and a hill would have a recognizable *commune vinculum*, the river often serving as a copula on the concrete level. But wildly incongruous ingredients would be incapable of leading to ultimate harmony. Horace had warned poets not to place dolphins in woods (*Ars poetica,* l.30).

What is represented in poems of the landscape "kind" is neither an idealized Arcadia of the past nor a Utopian Golden Age scene of the future. Landscape denotes something that is neither town nor wilderness, nor the barren sands of the desert. It is neither an account of a family outing nor a working scene full of bustling activity. Denham's landscape in *Cooper's Hill* is a typical specimen. The landscapes are artefacts, slightly arranged versions of what was given, "heightened ", in order to meet the requirements of the genre. That becomes evident if we consider for a moment what Hoskins has to say about the actual appearance of the countryside in the Neo-Classical age:

> Towards the end of the 17th century, landscape was very different from today: there were more trees, and heaths and commons often extended for a dozen miles or more, only rough and narrow tracks crossing them, so that travellers feared the sudden onset of bad weather or the premature falling of darkness …[17]

> Over large tracts of the country, especially in the west and the north, and to a considerable extent in the south-west also, the pattern of field and hedgerow, hamlet and farm, road and lane, had established itself pretty much as we know it.

> But over millions of acres between the Yorkshire and the Dorset coast, the country scene was still largely medieval. Farming was carried on in open fields that had not changed basically since the 13th century, and beyond the arable fields and their meadows lay large tracts of common pasture. Much of it covered with gorse and furze, rising in places to moorland and mountains.[18]

No wonder that the landscape poets had to be fastidious in their choice of locality: their predilection for the Thames region becomes understandable in the light of Hoskins' information. But even scenes that qualified for inclusion were not allowed to remain unadorned. It was, as Roger de Piles put it, a matter of making "la nature sortir de son chaos".[19]

From the second decade of the 18th century and onwards, the landscapes of nature and art ride on a wave of popularity: the salutary effects of the country, the pleasures of retirement, the utility of gardening, and the privilege of being a landowner are referred to again and again, and with increasing fervour, by poets and critics.

CHAPTER SIX

SOME OBSTACLES TO THE EMERGENCE OF THE LANDSCAPE POEM AS A LITERARY GENRE

1

It was a slow and laborious process for the landscape poem to find its own feet and win recognition as a genre. One reason was the imitative theory that Neo-Classicism inherited from the Renaissance, according to which both poetry and painting fulfil their true function only when imitating human life and nature in their abstract or "highest" form. Plato had taught that *natura naturata* is nothing but a reflection, hence unworthy of imitation. What artists ought to imitate, in order to get closer to perfection, was accordingly not what was before their eyes, but rather a mental form, an idea. It is obvious that adherents of that theory would look askance at a type of literature basing itself on the contemplation of a slice of the actual scenery.

The theory of the Idea held a strong position for at least two reasons: when forming in their minds an example of superior beauty, artists would feel convinced that they actually imitated the procedure of the Creator, who, as also the Hermeneutic philosophers maintained, is pure mind and contains within Himself the ideas, or archetypal patterns, of all created things.[1] Secondly, the hypothesis contributed to the strengthening of the ties between the arts since all of them were supposed to have their source in, and to be determined by, the Idea in the artist's mind.

> A painter must raise his head beyond what he sees, and form a model of perfection in his own mind which is not to be found in reality; but yet such a one as is probable and rational,

wrote Jonathan Richardson in *The Theory of Painting* (1715).

It will be seen that the theory of "Idea" is connected with the concept of *la belle nature* as cause and effect. The idealized picture of nature favoured by *la belle nature* also disparages "reality" for the benefit of a mental abstraction, and even if the landscape poets did not work with abstractions to the same extent as *la belle nature*, the latter was to prove the most formidable enemy to landscape poetry. Though it was somewhat diluted in the first decade of the 18th century, the *belle nature* ideal was never totally discarded, and the landscape poets never managed to extricate themselves entirely from the abstracting and generalizing pull of "the best nature", as the Neo-Classicists frequently called it.

2

Such critical discussion as there was in the years 1675-1700 virtually always went along lines suggested by the Ancients or focused on postulates read into them by modern French exegetes like Rapin, Boileau, and Bossu. Somehow, the critical idiom seemed unfitted to cope with types of literature that had not been commented on by Aristotle or Horace. The latter's *Ars poetica*, which was a "conversation piece" devoid of fanaticism and doctrinaire obstinacy, came to be looked upon as a storehouse of universal literary and critical truths. Even though the prevalent conception was that the *Ars poetica* was an unsystematic collection of precepts – Roscommon said that "the work lacks regularity"[2] – that did not diminish its prestige: the Neo-Classicists considered it the Fifth Gospel. They quoted its statements profusely and made cautious and reverential attempts to construe them, but never questioned its basic assumptions.

In the heyday of Neo-Classical orthodoxy it was asking for trouble to ignore or disobey its rules. Theoretical discussion was kept entirely within the bounds prescribed by the canon, and since neither Aristotle nor Horace had seemed to know a "kind" called the landscape poem or devoted any noticeable energy to the theoretical discussion of landscape description, the latter subject fell outside conventional classifications. Consequently, some suspicion, or even opprobrium, would be attached to it almost *a priori*, and it was rarely judged on its own merits.

The most eminent genre theorist of the third quarter of the 17th century was the Frenchman Rapin, who published some seminal works of criticism in the 1670s and 1680s, beginning with *Réflexions sur la Poëtique d'Aristote* from 1674. In its composition, the work set the example also for numerous English Neo-Classical treatises on literature and the *beaux-arts:* it consists of a theoretical and a practical part. The former is the first attempt to give a systematic and coherent account of the Neo-Classical canon, of which Rapin himself was one of the chief architects. The second part, *Tome des Comparaisons*, contains an evaluation of writers ancient and modern.

Rapin is mainly concerned with the epic, for which he lays down some fairly elaborate rules. Genres for which there is no classical precedent are treated with impatience, or simply rejected: the sonnet, the madrigal, the *rondeau*, and the *ballade* "ne sont que des espèces du Poëme imparfait".[3] The landscape poem is not even mentioned.

Rapin's *Réflexions* was translated into English by Rymer in the same year in which it was published (1674), and Rymer became popular and respected almost overnight. Dryden's statement from 1677: "Rapin...is alone sufficient, were all other critics lost, to teach anew the rules of writing"[4] epitomizes English critical opinion. The fact that Rapin was awarded the status of an authority meant that his tenets were adopted rather than analysed or criticized. English theorists from the 1680s were satisfied that Rapin gave them Classicism straight from the horse's mouth.

Another outstanding contributor to the establishment and propagation of the Neo-Classical canon, particularly with reference to the theory of genres, was Le Bossu, whose *Traité du Poëme Epique* appeared in 1675. It was translated into English in 1695, and up to 1710 Le Bossu was more quoted in England than any other French critic, Boileau not excepted.

The purpose of the *Traité* was to make the readers understand the Aeneid better,[5] and Le Bossu's theories were based on observations made in Homer's and Vergil's epics. He is a stern didacticist: "L'Utile...est une propriété essentielle à la narration épique, et... l'Agréable n'en est qu'une qualité ".[6]

Le Bossu did not have a grievance against descriptions as such. In a later passage he comments on the use and function of descriptions: they should definitely be subservient to the epic pattern; they must be short

> et, de plus, nécessaires et accommodées au caractère général du poëme, et au caractère particulier du Sujet que l'on décrit, autant que cela peut se faire.[7]

The gist of this not very informative statement is that descriptions should be assimilated into the plot and the tone of the poem. Only such descriptions merit praise as "ne sont que pour elles-mêmes",[8] ie they must serve other purposes by eg being allegorical. And other factors complicated the emergence of the landscape poem. It was not only that, concentrating on *natura naturata,* it would lack the "cause" that was part and parcel of epic didacticism. It was also that the landscape description was considered incapable of inspiring the reader with sufficiently dignified emotions, the result being that the *prodesse* element might be jeopardized.

That deficiency was made up for when the landscape poem reached maturity, but to critics of the last two decades of the 17th century, a landscape poem would have represented a grave breach of decorum. It might be argued that Denham's *Cooper's Hill* met with almost universal critical acclaim. However, to begin with, the poem was praised for its epic grandeur and for the lessons it taught, and only later for its landscapes.

Besides, there were formal considerations. The Neo-Classicists were very sensitive to form, and poets were expected to subject themselves to rigorous discipline in order to attain to that formal perfection that lent charm to the work of art and enhanced the reader's pleasure. However, there was not among the existing conventions of landscape description anything comparable with the sophistication of the epic, or with that "happy dramatic progression" which Boileau praised so warmly.⁹ One way out of the difficulty of characterizing the form of poems that we would consider reflective or descriptive was to range them under one or the other of the two main categories, epic and drama. That was, as just mentioned, what happened to Denham's *Cooper's Hill*.

3

In the early lines of the *Ars poetica*, Horace warns poets not to use descriptions where they are out of place. Roscommon translated the *Ars* in 1680 (*Horace's Art of Poetry*), and, like other translators of Horace working around 1680, he provided his English version with running comments. In the gloss on l. 23 ("Denique sit..."), he says:

> Descriptions which have no immediate relation to the Subject, corrupt and destroy them (sic). *Homer, Virgil* and *Sophocles's* Descriptions are all necessary and well-introduced.¹⁰

It is not that Roscommon is against descriptions as such. The point is rather, to use the formulation of one of his contemporaries, Oldham, who also translated the *Ars poetica* around 1680, that "though good elsewhere, 'tis here but foisted in".¹¹

In his remarks on l. 14 et seq. of the *Ars poetica* ("inceptis gravibus plerumque...") Roscommon construes the Latin text to mean that Horace objects to patched-up and consequently disorderly descriptions:

> From Grave and Serious Beginnings, which Promise Sublime and Marvellous Things, they descend into a shining Description of an (sic) wood, an altar of Diana, a River, the Rhine, the Rainbow. Their Descriptions are stitch'd together like Patch-work. Their Patches, indeed, are Purple, but are Childish and Extravagant, because ill-placed. Writers must never abandon themselves to such Digressions, let them be of what Nature soever, when their Design calls them elsewhere.¹²

Roscommon does not brief his readers in regard to the proper composition of a description, nor does he illustrate his warnings with instances, deterring or otherwise. The point he wants to make is that descriptions in inappropriate places, "going away" from the subject – "extravagant" has probably preserved its etymological sense – or composed of improper ingredients, are objectionable. The last sentence of the quotation about "Digressions" and poets' "Design" is an echo of several critics' intimation that poets were prone to resort to description when their epic inspiration was flagging.

What the early Neo-Classicists objected to, then, was the undue lingering on a detail which might take the form of rhetorical showing off. That was also what Horace was aiming at when he said, "Vir bonus et prudens...ambitiosa recidet ornamenta".[13] Characteristically, many early critics from the period talk about "mere ornament", a probable echo of Le Bossu's statement that *successful* descriptions "ne sont point de simples ornements".[14] Rapin put the matter succinctly: the judicious poet will only make use of descriptions "pour faire éclaircir les matières, et jamais pour faire paroître son esprit".[15]

When the word "description" is used in isolation, without any qualifiers, by the early Neo-Classicists, it is, in the great majority of cases, a technical generic term for the different figures of speech in which a poet might indulge. And it was against the abuse of that device that critics repeated their warnings. There is little doubt that some of the difficulties that the landscape poem had in making its breakthrough were due to the unpleasant associations clinging to the word description. For of course a landscape poem is, at first glance, "mere description", which is something quite different from eg a felicitously worded orchard scene in an epic.

It is here that influence from the Sister Art proved a potent, if not decisive, factor: it would have been preposterous for the pictorial canon to have banished "description", which, in painting, had no negative connotations. In his two pictures with motifs from Phocion's life, Poussin, *the* classic painter to Neo-Classicists, showed that descriptions could be determinant factors of an epic situation. His scenery is far more than background, and the rigid system of its structure proved that description was entirely compatible with rational reason, a fact that had also been illustrated by Rapin's *Jardins*.

Nor should it be forgotten that "landscape" was a genre within painting long before the Neo-Classical period.

CHAPTER SEVEN

FACTORS FAVOURING THE EMERGENCE AND ESTABLISHMENT OF THE ORTHODOX NEO-CLASSICAL TYPE OF LANDSCAPE POEM

1

During the Neo-Classical period, there were developments outside the literary field, eg within science, and in the attitude to gardens, that carried the conception of a beholder and of what was beheld in a certain direction. In their several ways those aspects underlie the assumptions that determine the framework and the content of the landscape poem. For instance, the moment order and harmony are pervasive powers in the Zeitgeist, some consequences for the questions of form and limitation are bound to follow; or, when sight is represented as the Queen of Senses, the status of an observer becomes of interest; or again, the fact that *natura naturata* comes to be looked upon as an intelligent construction on the part of the Supreme Being inevitably colours people's attitude to landscape.

Landscape poetry shows that Nature has assigned a place to each individual object and that obedience to this pattern, "knowing one's place" and "shunning pride", is a prerequisite of the smooth functioning of the whole. That was the way the Supreme being had ordained things to be. Thus was legitimized a social condition without equality, but with unprotesting inferiors and superiors that were not overweening in their arrogance: the item that "o'erarches" another also protects it, and shade is not inherently inferior to light, for they also serve who only stand

and wait. The Neo-Classicists' beloved maxim "follow nature" could very easily be given political and social connotations, and the achievements of contemporary science inevitably led to a moderate optimism: was the Great Machine not characterized by frictionless harmony? The landscape poem is *also* a paean praising the way things are.

2

In *The New Organon,* Bacon had written:

> And all depends on keeping the eye steadily fixed upon the facts of nature and so receiving their image simply as they are. For God forbid that we should give out a dream of our imagination for a pattern of the world.[1]

The belief that there exists an objectively existing nature which differs from the subjective extrapolations of man's imagination, ie the Cartesian dualism claiming that subject and object are two separate entities, was strongly held by the Neo-Classicists. It was accompanied by a conviction that man's eyesight enabled him to see nature "such as she is", and that man's mind could analyse it and his words describe it truthfully. That optimism seemed justified by the marvellous results achieved by scientists like Newton. Aspects of nature are worthy objects of study, for "All are but Part of one stupendous Whole", as Pope said.[2]

Incentives to an increased preoccupation with the concrete facts of *res creatae* and the concomitant disparagement of "mere speculation" were supported by the fact that The Philosophical Society, founded in 1645, changed its name and its activities, in 1662, to The Royal Society. Already in the last decade of the 17th century, the influence of The Royal Society and of eminent scientists began to permeate non-scientific fields of study. The analytical methods of science were brought to bear on the objects of the world, as well as on the observer of those objects. Truth came to lean more heavily on empirical facts – though the interpretation of the facts might of course be subject to idiosyncratic variation – than on dogmatic postulates. There is a significant shift from orthodox acceptance to independent inquisitiveness.

Those tendencies have some relevance for poets' treatment of, and attitude to, landscape. From being a vague localization on a par with a stage direction (witness the use made of it in pastoral), landscape acquires independent interest as a part of *natura naturata*, and it is contemplated as any object within philosophy or science was contemplated by the Neo-Classicists. The ego as a sentient being was balanced by, indeed presupposed, an object *in esse* or *in posse* of this being's analytical activities. Poets deal with the features of a panorama in the same way as Locke had dealt with the human understanding and Newton with planetary motion: they make empirical observations of individual items of reality, they add them up and make them form a whole, after which they proceed to make generalizations on a higher, more abstract level. The relationship between the parts and the whole is of crucial importance to Neo-Classical thinking and, accordingly, to landscape poetry. Pope's words from *Essay on Criticism*

> 'Tis not a lip or eye we beauty call,
> But the joint force and full result of all,[3]

might be used, *mutatis mutandis*, to explain the landscape poet's careful adding up of details.

3

Locke's *Essay Concerning Human Understanding* was published in 1690. His initial move is to separate analyst and object analysed, but he is perfectly aware that it requires "art and pains" to see the understanding "at a distance and make it its own object".[4] Next, he proceeds to reject innate ideas; nor can there be "certain principles, both speculative and practical…universally agreed upon by all mankind",[5] for fools and children do not know maxims like "whatever is, is" or "it is impossible for the same thing to be and not to be".[6] He recognizes himself that one consequence of his radical standpoint is that the idea of God cannot be innate,[7] and it is imaginable that it was such intimations of heresy that caused him to delay the publication of his *Essay*, which probably had a gestation period of several years.

Locke works on the assumption that when a person is born, his or her mind is "a white paper void of all characters, without any ideas".[8] From where, then, does the mind get its material?

> From experience...from our observations employed either about external sensible objects, or about the internal operations of our minds, perceived and reflected by ourselves.[9]

That is a crucial statement, not only because it stresses the operations of the individual's senses and mind, but even more because, in this theory, knowledge is made dependent on sensory perception. And Locke does not lose courage half-way: he states that without sensation there can be no consciousness.

Locke had full confidence in the power of the senses. Although the knowledge they provide may not be as reliable as our intuitive inferences or as deductions made by our reason, "yet it is an assurance that deserves the name of knowledge".[10] And Locke clinches the matter:

> Nobody can, in earnest, be so sceptical, as to be uncertain of the existence of those things which he sees and feels.[11]

Locke's contemporaries shared his "naïve realism", and the problem about the character of the surrounding world is never brought up for serious discussion for the very good reason that nobody saw it as a problem.

The influence of Locke's epistemology is clearly perceptible within Neo-Classical landscape poetry. A given scene, or a segment of the panorama, only acquires meaning the moment it is conveyed to a human catalyst and mediated through his mind. Landscape presupposes a beholder, it is "country" in the etymological sense of the word, viz. "contra", opposite or facing someone. The structure of the "country" – which, incidentally, shows little variation from one poet to another – determines the direction and process of observation, and the spreading vista is not only looked at, but also experienced. The beholder uses the characteristic Neo-Classical inductive procedure to get at the total impression, and the two stages in the treatment of sense data termed by Locke "sensation" and "reflection" aptly characterize the course of the process in landscape poetry as well.

4

The poetical "landscape scene" is a reflection or an imitation of an order or harmony that is postulated to exist outside the poem itself. For the Neo-Classicists did not share the Puritan hostility to the world of the Fallen Adam. Somehow they saw the impact of the Fall as being restricted to man in town, whereas rural scenes were invested with almost prelapsarian perfection. Science, which was ancillary to religion and never went beyond it, had demonstrated that the universe and its operations were a marvellous illustration of God's design. John Ray's *The Wisdom of God Manifested in the Works of the Creation* reached its third edition in 1704. According to Ray, order and harmony were generally accepted to be characteristic features of the whole as well as the parts. A state of permanent balance and interdependence was supposed to prevail. Blackmore puts it as follows:

> Things sink and rise, a being lose or gain
> In a coherent, undissolving chain.[12]

The conception of *natura naturata* was teleological: nature was not a blind mechanism, for behind it there was a First Cause, which both scientists and philosophers were anxious to emphasize was not mechanical. Nature was made for man's understanding and delight, and more or less discreet pointers remind the observer – be he a scientist, the reader of a work on "natural philosophy", or the beholder of a landscape scene – that "God's in his heaven – All's right with world", as Browning was to say in *Pippa Passes*. Thus religion was objectivized, it tended to become a thing placed before people's eyes and entirely comprehensible to human reason. Moreover, a correspondence was postulated to exist between the design of *natura naturata* and the capacity of the human brain and heart to "read" the moral. That *rapport* becomes evident when the landscape poet on his hilltop regards "the spreading scene".

A recurrent motif, which may account for some of the popularity of the countryside, is town crowds and town pollution. According to John Hughes, the "Smoke and Clamour" of London made a poet unable to create anything at all.[13] Conversely, John Worlidge, Cowley's contemporary, looks upon nature as *locus meditationis*:

> This Country-Life improves and exercises the most Noble and Excellent Parts of our Intellect, and affords the best opportunities to the insatiable humane Spirit to contemplate and meditate on; and to penetrate into, and discover the obscure & hitherto occult Mysteries & Secrets of Nature...and to attain the Highest Perfections in Science and Art.

Granville sees the country as a haven of retirement and serenity, where genuine values are found:

> From Pulpits banish'd, from the Court, from Love,
> Forsaken Truth seeks Shelter in the Grove;
> Cherish, Ye Muses, the neglected fair,
> And take into your Train th'abandon'd Wanderer.[14]

Addison's statement to the effect that "a beautiful prospect delights the soul as much as a demonstration"[15] equals the result of beholding with the conviction carried by a scientific proof. And Shaftesbury enlists landscape in the religious speculation of the age: "Whatever in Nature is beautiful and charming, is only the faint Shadow of that First Beauty".[16]

5

Whereas Locke had analysed man's mind, Newton took aspects of the universe as his object, and this "mortal man" managed to "unfold all Nature's Law".[17] He showed that cosmos is answerable to its own laws, but he did not doubt that those laws had been excogitated by the Supreme Being. Consequently, the individual watching *natura naturata* "reads" the Work of God, just as in the Bible he reads the Word of God.

Who is so stupid as to doubt the evidence of his eyes? Locke had asked. Empiricism regarded sight as the Queen of Senses, not least because it was an indispensable instrument of the new Science: sight was active in the realization of objects as objects, whether the naked eye or optical instruments were used. "Our sight is the most perfect and the most delightful of all our senses," said Addison,[18] "perfect" because it was supposed to be able to give an exact rendering of reality, and "delightful" because it was a pleasure to contemplate that reality.

Newton's *Opticks* had been completed as early as 1692, but was not published until 1704. Newton was not interested in aesthetics, and there is evidence that he desired to be known as a theologian rather than as a physicist or mathematician. *Opticks* is an extremely theoretical work, consisting almost exclusively of drawings, figures, theses and axioms. But it was the method he adopted that caused Newton to be considered the embodiment of scientific genius:

> The main Business of natural Philosophy is to argue from Phaenomena without feigning Hypotheses, and to deduce Causes from Effects, till we come to the very first Cause, which certainly is not mechanical.[19]

It has been said that Newton gave colour back to poetry, which is probably at least partly correct; at least he inspired the landscape poets with an increased sensitivity to the effects of light, shade, and colour. But he also gave an impetus to contemporary engrossment with the difference between the world "out there" and the mind "in here".

The Free-Thinker devotes one of its essays (No. 125, Monday, June 1, 1719) to the multifarious pleasures to be derived from using and playing with "optical glasses", and about the same time we find evidence of the popularity of the "Claude glass" (named after the painter Claude Lorrain). It was a small curved mirror, with a toned surface, which was meant to be held above a person's head so as to enable him to see the landscape behind reflected in it. What appeared in the glass would be a scene similar to one in a landscape painting. The surface was toned down in order that the outstanding features of the panorama might be seen more clearly than the details, and thus a sense of perspective would be conveyed.

Perspective became the fashion during the second quarter of the 15th century, thanks to the influence of Brunelleschi. But artists first had to overcome some misgivings deriving from this "defiance of the barriers fixed by the nature of things between painting and sculpture".[20] Of course the popularity of the telescope (after *circa* 1615) made perspective even more challenging and fascinating. The point for landscape poetry is that the poet places himself aloof and at a distance from the scene, relying on perspective to make him the centre of the diminutive universe so as to enable him to relate the items to each other and to give them their just proportions.

From the hilltop, the observer's "wandering eye" surveyed the scene. Around 1700, surveying emerged as a science and as a hobby. The technique and procedure of surveying are of fundamental importance for landscape poetry: like surveying, landscape poetry presupposes, indeed necessitates, an observer plus the object of his observations, viz. a stretch of the surrounding country. The poet's eye when surveying – the frequency of this word in landscape poetry is remarkable – does not roll in a fine frenzy, but is comparable to a physical instrument. The surveyor was supposed to establish a "station" by placing himself on an eminence in the landscape from where he would proceed to "take sightings".

The landscape poet "dominates the scene", which implies both control and possession. It is a noticeable fact that the Neo-Classicists treat two of their favourite kinds of property, viz. women and land, in analogous ways. In landscape poetry, for example, we have the active artist versus the passive model, the wish to define its qualities, perhaps even a suggestion of seeing without being seen. Also, it is remarkable how often a woman's body is described in terms of a landscape.

6

The ideals of harmony, balance, and order beloved by the Neo-Classicists naturally underscored problems connected with limitation and form. The idea of limitation proved eminently compatible with science's attempts to make cosmos out of chaos; besides, it was inherent in the standards of beauty that were transmitted from the Renaissance. In his version of Lomazzo's *Trattato*, Haydock called form "a beautiful and limited thing",[21] perhaps with an allusion to the fact that the Latin word "formosus", which originally meant "the shapely", came to mean "the agreeable". To the Neo-Classicists, the concept of form was associated with healthy limitation. What is amorphous or unstructured, like weeds in landscape poetry or infinity in Locke's epistemology, is viewed suspiciously or accompanied by negative qualifiers.

The idea of limitation is a cornerstone in Neo-Classical thinking, permeating most spheres of human activity. The cult of limitation is an aspect of the age's predilection for making things manageable, pigeon-holing them, and determining their affiliation to categories. Also, of course, it is a way of avoiding extremes. Characteristically, one of the arguments adduced to justify the rules was their supposed capacity to "control" unduly soaring flights of the imagination.

> Hyperboles, so daring and so bold,
> Disdaining Bounds, are yet by Rules control'd,

wrote Granville in the didactic poem whose title contains a warning against unwarranted freedom of thought and style in poetry, *Essay upon Unnatural Flights in Poetry*.[22] The popularity of the epigram testifies to the fondness of the age for what is terse and succinct. And the idea underlying the construction of the "Claude glass" was that of "limiting" a landscape by "framing" it: the glass was supposed to be moved until the perfect vista stood out and was isolated from the larger view. Both religion and politics had shown the disastrous consequences of the transgression of bounds: "enthusiasm" within religion, and, in politics, the arbitrary sway of a minority, or even of one person. It is true that landscape gardening, which was a fairly late development in the Neo-Classical age, allowed nature a considerable degree of freedom. But it only became possible after people had familiarized themselves with the relative freedom of layout to be found in the English type of garden. And limitation continued to be established: the point of the so-called ha-ha fence was to make the explorer respond with an exclamation of pleased surprise or admiration at the unobtrusive elegance with which the line of demarcation had been drawn. So that kind of unbounded view was also part of man's design.

7

During the first two decades of the 18th century, garden descriptions and garden imagery became "the vehicle for some of the deepest feelings of the age, and some of its shrewdest comments on the human situation".[23] They are more or less influenced by man's attitudes, hence another instance of the subject/object relationship, a point of intersection for man's dominion and nature's, and they are spatial arrangements of *natura naturata*. And, over and above that,

> as the seeming planlessness of the garden is planned....so it might be with Man and his world; as the natural garden exhibits a wide range of diversity and prolific growth, so does the system of creation,[24]

said Pope, ie gardens may be able to teach us something about the deeper meaning of our own life and may be looked upon as an alternative chain of being with a *plenum formarum* and all its variety.

To the Neo-Classicists, preoccupation with gardens became a status symbol as well as a sign of a refined taste. A predominantly urban society sometimes chose to turn its back on the bustle, noise, and stench of London and went in search of what was outside the town walls. When Neo-Classicists refer to gardens, they do not mean a few square yards of allotment ground; a garden is an impressive arrangement, sometimes covering a considerable area of land. From the late 17th century and onwards, the vegetable kingdom was effectively incorporated into literature, and the fondness for observation and experimentation went hand in hand with a utilitarian concern with plants, trees, and soil.

Sir William Temple's essay *Upon the Garden of Epicure: or Of Gardening in the Year 1685*, which was published in 1690, is an informative and enthusiastic expression of an influential and widely respected Neo-Classicist's attitude to gardens. It is a handbook in the widest sense of the term, but it is anything but a pedantic inventory of the streaks of the tulips. Sir William was one of the finest exponents of the *virtuoso* spirit, in which the study of nature and fine arts went hand in hand with financial and moral pursuits, and the *virtuosos* were pleased to recognize that profit can be so delightfully acquired.

Sir William demonstrated that gardens contain marvellous restorative powers for the mind as well as for the body of man, and echoes of his attitude are audible in most Neo-Classical garden descriptions. The emphasis is on the "outer world" as one of the amenities of life, the element of work is not unduly stressed, and attention is focused at least as much on the atmosphere as on the ingredients. In Sir William's opinion, it is not to be wondered at that God Almighty placed Adam and Eve in a garden. Paradise, such as Temple describes it in the essay, is remarkably like a contemporary garden.

Some Neo-Classical garden designers found their inspiration in the formal arrangements so beloved by the French. Le Nôtre, who lived from 1613 to 1700, brought the French garden to perfection. It was symmetrical and radiated from the house, just as the French society of those days had an obvious and undisputed centre in the person of *le Roi Soleil*. The ensemble made up a huge symmetry, and the house was visible from any point in the garden because it was not surrounded by trees. Such gardens were evident manifestations that man had imposed his will on nature; they testified to the designer's cleverness and were a projection of the owner's power. The total effect was one of *concordia discors* – all the carefully separated enclaves were ultimately part of the same garden.

English *connoisseurs* increasingly found their pleasure (and sometimes also their profit) in a lay-out that differed from the French one in that it endeavoured to eschew the use of violence to the inclinations of nature: the configurations of the English landscape do not lend themselves willingly to the rigid schematism of long, straight walks, and the designers only lent a helping hand here and there; "consulting the genius of the place" became a catchword.

That does not mean that the "natural" English garden is a mere wilderness, it is definitely the result of human planning and more or less gentle tampering with the features of the landscape. It is "nature to advantage dress'd" and informal only in so far as it is less artificial than a French formal garden.

By the same token, the gardener's profession became one of enormous prestige. A gardener would often lay out the grounds in such a way that a visitor would be instructed to walk in a specific direction along a particular path so that his perambulations would have a "natural" beginning, middle, and end, with some arranged stops and calculated surprises on the way. That is why a correspondent to the *Spectator* (No. 477) could talk about "my compositions in gardening", and the poet Shenstone said that one part of his estate at Leasowes might resemble an epic or a dramatic poem.

Competent gardeners and designers would throw whole estates into garden-like arrangements, and later in the 18th century professional arrogance might cause landscape architects like eg "Capability Brown" to indulge in various idiosyncracies and whimsicalities.

A landmark in the field of Neo-Classical landscape gardening is Stephen Switzer's *Ichnographia Rustica* from 1718. The target group of the book was obviously the *nouveaux-riches*, dealers and merchants, who were in search of a profitable investment that could at the same time be a source of pleasure and a status symbol. Throughout, the book concentrates on the visual effects of the lay-out, and Switzer is not averse to the artificiality and segmentation known from the "French" garden. He obviously favours a picturesque effect: the views and surroundings that are detailed in the *Ichnographia* are eminently fit to be made the subject of a painting: the country is open, the woods are placed in strategic positions, and the beholder finds himself at a point of vantage. The different kinds of terrace suggested are similar to the divisions seen in many contemporary landscape pictures and poems: the whole expanse is split up into several horizontal levels, and there is an empty foreground in front of the landscape proper, a counterpart of the terrace that Switzer advises his gentlemen readers to place adjacent to the house so as to provide some breathing space before they plunge into the arranged scene.

Switzer does not conceal the inspiration that can be had from other arts, among them literature. Thus, when he advises landowners as to the placing of a stream in their estate, he does it because

> the Stream running exactly under the Hill is very beautiful & comfortable to the Songs of the Antient, and best of our Modern, Poets.[25]

In another passage he says that it is imperative that a designer should

> make himself Master of all rural Scenes. And the Writings of the Poets on this Subject will give him considerable Hints.[26]

Switzer never identifies his literary sources, nor does he quote their landscapes. Yet the important thing is that his readers were being accustomed to see a connection between the landscapes that poets – among them, some contemporary ones, it appears – had described and those that designers could arrange, or had arranged.

The phases in the lay-out of gardens that have been outlined in this section illustrate the change that man's attitude to nature underwent during the Neo-Classical period. In the pastoral, nature was ignored, or at best stylized so as to serve as an unobtrusive frame for an artificial genre. The Neo-Classical preoccupation with gardens owes its origin to man's rediscovery of *natura naturata* and his gradual realization of his own place in the Great Design. Gradually man comes to feel in a position that enables him to be generous, allowing nature a modicum of independence. Natural configurations begin to be considered inherently beautiful, and man's efforts are directed towards helping nature along instead of subjugating it.

The analogy with the procedure Aristotelian *mimesis* advises poets to follow in their treatment of reality is obvious. It is true that man never lets go his hold entirely – he shares Hamlet's misgivings before the "unweeded garden" – but "corrections" and "improvements" serve another purpose than proving man's superiority and control: they were performed with a view to provoking a response in the beholder. The intransigent formal garden was abandoned partly for patriotic reasons, but also because "the face of nature" came to arouse pleasurable emotions. The garden became a sum of forms that suggested meanings or started trains of sentiment.

CHAPTER EIGHT

FROM TOPOS TO GENRE

1

What we witness within landscape description in the years 1680-1730 is the development of a *topos* into a genre. A shift of emphasis becomes perceptible: poets begin to set the landscape free, so to speak, and a literary genre becomes static and spatial. Epic poetry, centred on action, is characterized by a dynamism that sometimes becomes breath-taking, but landscape, lacking the epic fable, moves at a sedate pace, and, incidentally, landscape poems respect the unities of time, place, and action to a far greater extent than do epics. Epic movement is replaced by the movement of the observer's eyes. The change necessitated a new technique: the emphasis came to be on the observations to be made from one fixed point – just as a scientist would find a point of vantage from where to make his analyses.

The Neo-Classical "kinds" were more than mere taxonomic categories in which works sharing certain features were placed. They tended to influence the artist's material to a considerable extent because their requirements determined the structure and frequently also the formulation of what he wrote. They became imperatives for poet and reader alike – a set of instruction to the poet for the kind of total effect to aim at, and a set of directions to the reader for the way the work was to be read. Thus, the expectations and emotions aroused in the reader were largely predictable as were the boundaries laid down for the poet.

"Kinds" were separated according to criteria of subject, style, and effect on, or calculated response in, the recipient. Those points have some similarity with the triad *inventio, dispositio,* and *elocutio,* the three stages known from classical rhetoric. Horace had voiced the opinion that the division of literature into genres is based on the assumption that there is a particularly suitable way of presenting a given theme, and the considerable number of *artes poeticae* and treatises on style dating from the Neo-Classical period bear witness that no little importance was attached to the way the thought was dressed. Such books explicitly state that the choice of a given formulation is not only dependent on the author's genius, but is also a device which the competent craftsman exploits for the benefit of his reader.

The "kind" theory never became a perfect system with a definite place assigned to each type of literary work. Actually, below the two highest, the epic and the tragedy, it was pretty much of a muddle, some genres being vaguely relegated to an inferior position without further specification. The first decades after 1700 show a considerable willingness to admit new additions to the fold, without critics necessarily proceeding to make a rigid definition or classification of them. The landscape poem is a case in point, the class is not very copious, and several specimens are fairly short; the type never became a massively dominating "kind" rivalling others for supremacy.

The landscape poem distinguishes itself from the epic in that, in the epic, there is a hero who is *in* the poem, which is an account of his achievements. The epic writer would usually "invent" – in the Neo-Classical sense of "find" – his material in Holy Scripture as well as in mythology or ancient or more recent history. The landscapes of pastoral and the formalized settings of *locus amoenus* and *hortus conclusus* are inconceivable, or even impossible, for botanical, geological, or climatic reasons. The landscapes of the *ut pictura poesis* tradition are always *vraisemblables*, to use Roger de Piles' term, though not necessarily *vrais* throughout, deviations from camera-like fidelity being instances of conventional *licentiae poeticae* sanctioned by decorum. The response stimulated in the beholder is not, as in the *hortus conclusus* tradition, one of mystical elation; the *ut pictura poesis* landscape is not exclusively homiletic, which does not mean that it is merely hedonistic: the poet always reads a religious, political, or social moral into his observations. The *dispositio* of pastoral differs from that of the genuine landscape poem in that localization is not a *sine qua non*. Pastoral does not dwell on the landscape for its own sake, which appears, for instance, from the restricted use it makes of colours.

2

The movement described in this chapter is not a smooth chronological one in which one decade shows a larger number of relevant genre features than the immediately preceding one. Different traditions co-existed peacefully. Thus Cleveland's *Upon Phillis walking in a morning before sunrise* with its exploitation of pastoral technique, is roughly contemporary with Denham's pioneer work *Cooper's Hill*. And we know that John Cleveland was extremely popular, also after his death in 1658: there were no less than 25 editions of his poetry between 1647 and 1700.

Still there are perceptible differences between the treatment of a landscape as given by an early 17th century writer and one who wrote in the second half of the century. To become aware of the change, we can compare Ben Jonson's poem *Penshurst*, which is from 1616, with Waller's *On St. James' Park As Lately Improv'd by His Majesty*, from 1661. Both pieces are written in the tradition in which a poet pays homage to a landowner by celebrating his estate, the point of course being that the excellence of the rural seat are a reflection of the sterling qualities of its owner. Waller's poem is far more of a topographical account than Ben Jonson's. Such surroundings as the latter describes might be found in many other estates than Penshurst, but there is no mistaking of the localization of Waller's poem, even apart from the title, and *On St. James' Park* is far more sensitive to the spatial arrangements of the grounds than is *Penshurst*.

The difference is even more striking if we compare a short *topos*-scene from Shakerly Marmion's poem *Cupid's Courtship, or the Declaration of the Marriage between the God of Love and Psyche* from 1637 with a detailed landscape description from William Chamberlayne's heroic poem *Pharonnida* from 1659.

Marmion's work is a complicated mixture of legends, mythology, and incidents from the world of everyday life. Book I opens with a description of the Golden Age:

> No sickness nor infection did appear,
> No sullen change of season did molest
> The fruitful soil, but the whole year was blest
> With a perpetual spring, no Winter storm
> Did crisp the hills, or mildew blast the corn:
> Yet happier far, in that it forth did bring
> The subject of this verse whereof I sing.[1]

This passage is part of a much larger context. It could not possibly exist independently because it is essentially tied to something that the poet (and perhaps the reader) considered far more important, viz. the story itself. This description, little more than a *topos*, is there to furnish a background, and that means that it has little intrinsic interest or value.

The descriptions we find in William Chamberlayne's *Pharonnida*, which was published in 1659, is far more interesting. The poem is an epic, running to more than 15.000 lines, and love, the main theme, is interwoven with accounts of the religious struggle between Turks and Christians. However, what actually happens is pretty obscure – Saintsbury confessed that it took him three years to get a reasonable grasp of the plot[2] – because there are innumerable digressions and subplots.

Here are the surroundings of the castle of Ariamnes, the male protagonist:

> Ere at his castle they arrive, which stood
> Upon a hill, whose basis, fringed with wood,
> Shadowed the fragrant meadows; thorough which
> A spacious river, striving to enrich
> The flowery valley with whatever might
> At home be profit or abroad delight,
> With parted streams that pleasant islands made
> Its gentle current to the sea conveyed.
> In the composure of this happy place

Wherein he lived, as if framed to embrace
So brave a soul as now did animate
It with his presence, strength and beauty sate
Combined in one...³

The castle on its hill dominates the surroundings: elevation of locality equals elevation of status; it is a clearly framed scene, and there is a correspondence between the owner and his estate (the *Penshurst* motif again). No other human habitation is visible, and the *locus amoenus* tradition is almost verbatim referred to ("happy place"). However, the scene shows that we are on the way towards a genuine landscape description, where the river, for example, serves the twofold purpose of creating pleasure and yielding profit. Everything breathes harmony.

In Book II, Canto IV, ll. 144 et seq. occurs a description that might very well be made into an independent poem. It is a remarkably long *excursus* in an epic, although it tends to become inconspicuous in the enormous number of lines that the poem comprises. However, even if it is contingent, the description makes use of many of the devices of the fully-fledged landscape genre. It is an account of the surroundings which the King gives his daughter Pharonnida:

         Nor was she in domestic beauty more
(145)   Than prospect rich – the wandering eye pass'd o'er
         A flowery vale, smooth as it had been spread
         By nature for the river's fragrant bed.
         At the opening of that lovely angle met
         The city's pride, as costlier art had set
(150)   This masterpiece of wit and wealth to show –
         Unpolish'd nature's pleasures were below
         Her splendid beauties, and unfit to be
         Looked on, 'less in the spring's variety:
         Though from the palace where in prospect stood
(155)   All that not art or plainer nature would,
         If in contention, show to magnify
         Their power, did stand, yet now appeared to vie
         That prospect which the city lent; unless
         Diverted from that civil wilderness

(160) The pathless woods, and ravenous beasts within
       Whose bulk were but the metaphors for sin
       We turn to view the stately hills, that fence
       The other side 'o the happy isle, from whence
       All that delight or profit could invent
(165) For rural pleasures, was for prospect sent.
       As nature strove for something uncouth in
       So fair a dress, the struggling streams are seen,
       With a loud murmur rolling 'mongst the high
       And rugged cliffs; one place presents the eye
(170) With barren rudeness, whilst a neighbouring field
       Sits clothed in all the bounteous spring could yield.
       Here lovely landscapes, where thou might'st behold
       When first the infant morning did unfold
       The day's bright curtains, in a spacious green
(175) Which nature's curious art had spread between
       Two bushy thickets, that on either hand
       Did like the fringe of a fair mantle stand,
       A timorous herd of grazing deer, and by
       Them is a shady grove, through which the eye
(180) Could scarcely pierce, a well-built lodge, from whence
       The watchful keeper's careful diligence
       Secures their private walks; from hence to look
       On a deep valley, where a silver brook
       Doth in a soft and busy murmur slide
(185) Betwixt two hills, whose shadows strove to hide
       The liquid wealth they were made fruitful by
       From full discoveries of the distant eye.[4]

These regal grounds repay closer scrutiny, for here we are approaching the real thing. First of all, the landscape is evidently a viewed scene, the beholder is not Princess Pharonnida herself, but the writer pointing things out to the reader, sometimes leading him by the hand ("we", l. 162), or urging him to investigate on his own ("thou", l. 172). The landscape is *seen*, witness the numerous occurrences of "eye", "view", "look", and "behold". And the observer's eye follows the features of the scenery ("wandering eye", l. 145, "we turn to view", l. 162, "one place", l. 169, "here",

l. 172), occasionally stopping on the way ("the struggling streams are seen…", l. 167). The observer's position is somewhere in or near the palace (l. 154), which is placed on a hill.

The landscape shows all possible ingredients and configurations: river (l. 147), brook (l. 183), woods (l. 160), hills (l. 162), clifts (l. 169), a field (l. 170), and a valley (l. 146), but the only sign of human presence is "the watchful keeper's lodge" (ll. 180-81); the keeper himself is suggested, but not seen. The sum total makes up a prospect (ll. 145, 158, 165); it is partly closed by the hills ("fence", l. 162 and the two hills seen in the distance in ll. 185-87). The items are placed relative to other items: "between/Two bushy thickets", ll. 175-76), the thickets stand like a fringe on either side of the green (ll. 176-77), the brook slides between the hills that cast their shadow over the water (ll. 183-86); the streams are struggling among the cliffs (ll. 167-69), and there is a "neighbouring field" (l. 170). Landscape features are contrasted: cliffs and fields (ll. 169-70), pathless woods with ravenous beasts as against "all that delight or profit could invent" (ll. 160-64). The contrast is also one of forbidding impenetrability versus pleasant fertility. Besides, on a larger scale, there is emulation between the prospect of the city and the prospect of the countryside, and it is the latter that engages all the observer's attention.

The view from the palace, presenting both town and country, is a rivalry between nature and art. They are "in contention" (l. 157), and even though art is conventionally qualified as "nice" and nature as "plainer" (l.155), still it is nature that captivates the beholder's attention. Nature is somehow responsible for the arrangement of the scene: the "vale" of l. 146 seems to have been "spread" by nature between two bushy thickets. Altogether, the scene breathes an atmosphere of gentle adaptation and designing. Art is admittedly "costlier" (l. 149, sc. than nature), but it is cold and static. Nature is "unpolished" (l. 151), and only worth looking at in the variety of spring. Yet nature has her own "curious art" (l. 175): the postulated talent of adapting her own configurations. And nature is dynamic, working according to the principle of *concordia discors* (ll.166 et seq.). Security – the watchful keeper's eye – industry, and profit are discreetly hinted at, but it is not a working scene.

The panorama also contains "lovely landscapes" (l. 172); in this context the word means a slice of the surroundings such as they might appear, or have appeared, in a painting. The big landscape contains replicas in miniature of itself, replicas whose features, if detailed, would be similar to those of the larger canvas. And many of the epithets are such as will occur again and again in Neo-Classical landscape poetry: deep valley, silver brook, shady grove and stately hills.

It is true that it is a kaleidoscopic scene, which is not clearly divided into recognizable horizontal or vertical levels. Yet it is a far cry from the catalogues devoid of perspective that Chamberlayne's predecessors (and some of his contemporaries) would indulge in, for there is an unquestionable attempt, on Chamberlayne's part, to structure the prospects. It is also true that the scene is far from being *vrai*, indeed it is hardly *vraisemblable,* in that so many good things seem to be gathered in one place and that fertility and barrenness are rubbing shoulders. Chamberlayne's exterior is more *belle nature*-like than those of his successors. Also, his picture is colourless, which is a major difference between the view from Pharonnida's castle and later views. On the other hand, Chamberlayne's concern is primarily with landscape as such, and not with the possible allegorical or mythological allusions of the items. By the same token, the moral is not so much attached to the individual components (mountains symbolizing elevated status, etc.) as to the *tout-ensemble*. This "happy isle" – island implying seclusion and boundaries at the same time – is in a state of perfection because discord is found on a lower level only: the "dress" is fair enough, although it may cloak "uncouth strife" (ll. 166-67). The sense of perfection is also conveyed by the merging of stasis and gentle movement: the grazing deer are standing still, no animal or human being crosses the stage, and the gamekeeper remains within his lodge. The only dynamic element is the flowing of the water, but the "struggling streams" (l. 167), even though turbulent, are not allowed to inundate the idyllic landscape. They are kept in their proper domain by worthy opponents and helpers. And the silver brook (l. 183) slides along so softly (yet not lazily) that it presents no danger: on the contrary, it is a source of fertility to the growths on the adjacent hills, which – the motif of reciprocity again – attempt to shade the brook, either to protect it from the heat of the sun (which is not referred to) or to screen it from the unduly inquisitive eye of the distant beholder.

Perhaps a little unexpected, the royal premises also accommodate a shepherd (II, iv, ll. 210 et seq.), whose environment and occupation are entirely those of a conventional pastoral: the brook, the mossy bank, and his innocent playing of the pipe. The limitation and sequestration of the place is referred to repeatedly (II, iv, ll. 217 et seq.) and are ascertained by an observer. Lines 231 et seq. depict the mountain on which the palace stands:

> The stately mount, whose artificial crown
> The palace was, to meet the vale stole down
> In soft descents, by labour forced into
> A sliding serpentine, whose winding clew
> (235) An easy but a slow descent did give
> Unto a purling stream; whose spring did live,
> When from the hill's cool womb broke forth, within
> A grotto; whence before it did begin
> To take its weeping farewell, into all
> (240) The various forms restrictive Art could call
> Her elemental instruments unto
> Obedience by, it courts th'admiring view
> Of pleased spectators – here, exalted by
> Clear aqueducts, in showers it from high
> (245) Supporters falls...[5]

Apart from the strikingly miserable versification, the passage is remarkable for the way the items are made to play together: the mountain strives to "meet the vale" (l. 232), gently and secretly, as if going to a lovers' rendez-vous. Nature endeavours to reconcile her own opposites; the mountain sends a spring down its sides as an emissary, the spring having its origin in the hill's "cool womb" (l. 237). However, before it is allowed to follow its natural bent, it is intercepted by human devices which force it into submission. Art overtops nature – the palace is on a hilltop – but it also restricts nature, forcing its elements into "unnatural" submission. The inference is that nature ought not to be tampered with: the mount is stately in itself and could very well do without the "artificial crown" (l. 231) of the castle. But unsympathetic spectators take pleasure in the ingenuity of the arrangement and are inclined to connive at the violence committed to nature. Chamberlayne does not say much about profit and utility in these lines. What he does dwell on, however, is the fact that, owing to human interference, nature is prevented from eliminating her own contrasts and fulfilling her true purpose. The spring of the stream is found in that compromise between art and nature, a grotto. Part of the water, it seems, is subjected to the constraining influence of art and is "exalted" (l. 243) by the aqueducts.

The landscape descriptions to be found in Chamberlayne's *Pharonnida* are at least as detailed and varied as those of Denham. But his unspeakable prosody detracts from the beauty of the scene. A benevolent interpretation might suggest that his unconventional rhythm and bold enjambements testify to an endeavour to virtually eliminate the line as a unit. However, since such experiments were practically unheard of in the middle of the 17th century, a more likely explanation is that Chamberlayne was a hopeless versifier with a deficient ear for scansion; indeed quite a number of lines in his huge epic read as if they were intended as a parody – which they were not. However, although he was no great artist, Chamberlayne does give a representative assembly of the landscapes that were "possible" and permissible, and in his types of landscape older patterns exist side by side with more modern approaches. Denham and Chamberlayne show an unprecedented interest in landscape *per se*. It is appropriate to call attention to the fact that there was at least one later edition of *Pharonnida* in 1689. The poem was perhaps given a favourable reception because its descriptions of landscapes would be palatable to an audience of the late 1680s and the early 1690s.

CHAPTER NINE

THE INGREDIENTS OF THE NEO-CLASSICAL LANDSCAPE POEM

1

R.G.Collingwood states that, between the 16th and the 19th centuries, man's central intellectual effort was devoted to "laying the foundations of natural science", and during those centuries, "philosophy took as its main theme the relation of the human mind as subject to the natural world around it as object".[1] It is one of the salient characteristics of the Neo-Classical landscape poem that the subject/object relationship is always present, explicitly or implicitly. Dyer's formulation from *The Country Walk*, "A landscape wide salutes my sight"[2] epitomizes the position.

The use of a first-person observer and narrator was not a Neo-Classical invention, but the poets of that age were extremely fond of that approach when dealing with *natura naturata*. The narrator faces nature (and figuratively speaking, *vice versa*), and he gives an account of a concrete or imaginable, hence plausible, experience. The mood becomes one of immediacy, familiarity, and sensitivity.

The beholder is purely functional – neither his age, social background or education are ever referred to. He is there because landscape deserves or needs to be described and enjoyed. And the beholder obeys the rules of that game.

The idea of reciprocity has affinities with contemporary epistemological thinking. What Locke does to the understanding is, according to his own words in the first chapter of the *Essay*, to see it at a distance and make it its own object.³ And Newton said in *Principia*

> For from the position and distances of things from any body consider'd as immoveable, we define all places.⁴

The beholder is always alone, never engages in conversation with any other human being though his observations are obviously aimed at a recipient. In his *Ars poetica*, Horace had touched upon the problem of distance where contemplation of works of art was concerned; actually he had seen the parallel between painting and poetry as residing in the fact that, in both, proper enjoyment depended upon the correct distance:

> Ut pictura poesis erit: quae si propius stes
> te capiat magis, et quaedam si longius abstes.⁵

Although the beholder of the landscape scene repeatedly moves his head, he never expresses the wish of getting closer to the ingredients of the scene, let alone touching them or plunging "into" them. The hilltop he has chosen ensures the appropriate extent of space, and his attitude to the landscape is neither that of the "improver" nor that of the proprietor. He stands aloof, and his position enables him to get the components into their due proportions so that scale is safeguarded, and the moral overtones are not lost sight of. Perhaps under the influence of Berkeley's *New Theory of Vision*, from 1709, which treated, among other things, of the third dimension, the beholder is engrossed with the relative position of the ingredients, and he makes ample use of words like "here", "there", "yonder", "behind", "beyond", distant", and "nearby".

"The beholder" is an apt designation for the narrator of the landscape poem, for his sight is activated over and above the other senses. The singing of birds is not an indispensable feature of a landscape poem, and, generally speaking, references to hearing as well as to smell, are of decidedly secondary importance. What very often happens is that the beholder becomes cognizant of the quiet of the scene, which means that what he notices is rather the absence of sounds. And in any case, aural impressions are not so detailed and specified as the visual ones.

The beholder's vision is not initially the synoptic apprehension of *Gestalt* psychology, but one that, in typical Neo-Classical fashion, is carefully and meticulously established by a stepwise progression so as to allow the impressions to sink in, prompting the appropriate speculation. The beholder's discovery procedures are identical with those he uses when he wants to find his bearings in the world at large, and he moves his head in order to convey the feeling that the prospect is not "for ever fixt". In the end, he does arrive at a total comprehension of what he sees, and the landscape becomes a vehicle for abstract reflections of a political, social, or moral kind.

2

The current expression "the visual field" testifies to man's habit of seeing the world around him as something framed and limited. The scene described in a landscape poem is a spatial structure, a "picture" also in the sense that the horizon is clearly perceptible or implicitly recognized, and that it contains features discreetly suggesting frames analogous to those of many pictures.

The view was early thought to give food for thought: Waller writing in mid-century, says about King Charles surveying his masterpiece the park from "a gallery of aged times":

> His fancy objects from his view receives,
> The prospect thought and contemplation gives.[6]

Heaven forms the "roof" and is taken for given; it is always blue, and the sun is only there as a foil to the ever-present shade. Hills or undulating mountains serve as a line of demarcation between the visual field and what is beyond, which is never exploited. The poem is not a description of an explorer's longing to get away from where he is. The horizon is not conceived as an obstacle to the imagination or a challenge to the visionary power. The hills in the background are generally vaguely sketched and not individualized and surrounded with an air of finality. They are seen in terms of helpers rather than trammels: they protect the scene from strong winds, and they contribute to the creation of an atmosphere of serenity and security. Dennis is of the opinion that "Nature design'd them (sc. the Alps) only as a mound to enclose her Garden Italy".[7] The formulation found in *The Guardian* from Tuesday, August 4, 1713, is symptomatic:

> I could trace the maze for some miles, until my eye was led through two ridges of hills and terminated by a vast mountain in another county.[8]

There is nothing in the rest of the essay to suggest that the narrator is annoyed at having his vision "terminated" so categorically. However, the mountains or hills closing a conventional scene were far from always "vast"; more often they were "gentle" or "undulating" so as to mark off the field of vision without obtruding unduly upon the view. Hughes tells us that "misty hills the far horizon join",[9] which is another *topos* of the landscape genre: clods on the ground and clouds in the sky – the two words are etymologically identical – were hard to tell apart in the distance, but it did not really matter since they were part of the same pattern.

Once more, a parallel with epistemology naturally suggests itself. In the early pages of his *Essay,* Locke deplores that so far we have been prone to "let loose our thought into the vast ocean of being", but his intention is to become cognizant of "the horizon ... which sets the bounds between the enlightened and dark part of things".[10] So "horizon" was an acknowledged term for a dividing line. In a later passage Locke says that the human brain can only with difficulty contain the idea of "space infinite"[11] (although he adds that he is inclined to believe that space is infinite). It is probably owing to its vastness and boundlessness that the sea is only cursorily referred to in Neo-Classical landscape poems.

3

In the Neo-Classical landscape tradition, trees were regarded with affectionate awe. "A tree is a nobler object than a prince in his coronation robes," said Pope to Spence in 1728.[12] Some poets use trees for purely ornamental purposes, but more often than not they are functional, viz. serving as the vertical frames of the scene. They usually link several features of the landscape, and sometimes a moral is read into their structure, growth, and strength. On this point, too, Neo-Classicists preferred the civilized and manageable aspects of *natura naturata*. What they celebrate in their poems is, characteristically, not a forest but a grove, and the latter term is not just a term of poetic diction for any area of woodland. A grove can be a group of trees deliberately planted or arranged in a definite pattern by a human designer, but it can also be a decorative adaptation of the landscape made by the Greatest of all designers. In either case, it is a source of pleasure and a haunt "for contemplation fit". A tree can be an oak, an elm, etc. but, with all its branches and leaves, it can also be an epitome of order or unity of design, where all components "concur in *one*, are Parts constituent of *one* Whole," to use Shaftesbury's phrasing.[13] The trees which occur in landscape poems are such as are found in woods and "natural" surroundings: there are no apple trees, etc., which means that the idea of utility recedes into the background.

Roger de Piles advised landscape painters to make scrupulous studies of trees. In his opinion, trees are among the most important ornaments of a landscape picture. Trees should be distinguished according to their kind, he says, and the varying density and colour of their foliage give scope for "des changes agréables". There should be old trees alternating with young ones, pointed ones and round-topped ones, indeed, even the colour of their bark should be clearly discernible; bark is normally grey, Piles adds by way of instruction.[14] Claude, Poussin, and other landscape painters would often make compositional use of trees: they are "wings", framing one or both sides of the picture or the foreground centre, where the action, such as it is, takes place; or they are landmarks showing where one horizontal level ends and another begins. Trees never seem to be dropped accidentally on a canvas.

Taking their cue from landscape painters, or at least finding support in a congenial procedure, Neo-Classical poets integrated trees smoothly into the *tout-ensemble*. There are always trees in a described landscape scene, often both single ones and in clumps. Their use and function are analogous to those found in pictorial representations. Landscape trees co-operate with other items: they "o'erarch" a plain or "o'ershadow" a river, and the light and colour effects they create are invariably referred to; the "trembling leaves" and the "soft gliding" of the river are stock devices to counteract stasis. By virtue of their height and density, they are awe-inspiring and can symbolize soaring ambition as well as praiseworthy staying power. The shadow they create are a favourite place of mediation as eg in Waller's poem *On St. James' Park:*

> Here Charles contrives th'ordering of his states,
> Here he receives his neighb'ring princes' fate.

And Marvell wrote in *Appleton House:*

> How safe, methinks, and strong, behind
> These trees have I encamp'd my Mind.[15]

Shade had been a stock ingredient of pastorals. It had the task of protecting the shepherds against the scorching sun and, by implication, of providing coolness for intelligent dialogue or reflection. It is interesting that even pastorals purporting to be located in England persist in including this legacy from the classical pastoral, where the shade can be said to have some justification because the "scorching sun" can be anything but a cliché in Italy or Greece.

There is shade in virtually all Neo-Classical landscape poems. It is not a permanent state but occasioned by the wafting of the breeze in the leaves or by the sailing of the clouds. The opposition between stasis and motion is safeguarded. The funny thing is that the sun never occurs – it is seen only in terms of its effect, viz. shade. On the whole, weather phenomena are of decidedly peripheral interest: it never rains, and movements of the air are never gales, but breezes. The season is never made explicit, but the description points to summer.

The two main functions of shade are to provide a play of light, frequently of a *clair-obscur* type since shade is the antipode of light, and to cater for man's spiritual or recreational inclinations. Switzer recapitulates a long deliberation on trees and groves as follows:

> 'Tis here the wearied Traveller and laborious Rustick seek for Shelter and Refreshment, and (*sub die*, as the Latins term it) to stretch their wearied Limbs, and enjoy that sweet Repose, and those meridian Naps, appointed for the Recruit of Nature in the recessive Intervals of a sultry Day. 'Tis here the indefatigable statesman reads over and considers the several Governments of the World, and makes such observations as are for the Service of his Prince and Country: 'Tis here the learned Divine oft forms his elegant and pathetic Orations, and the Poet his never-dying Poems.[16]

The beams of the sun, their different refractions and momentary exclusion, give a rich spectrum of colours. "Glade" is another word with a high rate of frequency, not only for the obvious reason that it forms a convenient rhyme with "shade", but also because it is so intimately connected with impressions of light, shade, and colour. For, in the Neo-Classicist poet's usage, a glade is not so much "a clear open space or passage in a forest", as the OED defines it; rather, it is any place to which light can momentarily penetrate. It forms a contrast to the overhanging trees whose leaves, set in motion by the gentle breeze, now permit the rays of the sun to penetrate, now exclude them, the result being the "chequer'd shade", which is virtually part and parcel of the poetic diction of landscape poetry.

Shade in Neo-Classical landscape poetry is more than the shadow of one or more trees. It is any place with a diminished intensity of light, such as the slope of a hill, the lower part of a valley, a section of the forest floor, or the inside of a grotto.

As their predilection for *concordia discors* shows, Neo-Classicists were not averse to juxtaposing seeming incompatibles, witness also their fondness for the punning of "wit", and their partiality to composite genres like the mock-heroic poem. The idea that, in order to be perfect, a picture ought to contain tensions of light and shade became very widespread indeed, and it was considered natural to apply the principle of reconciled opposites also to "pictures in poetry", and, more generally, to other spheres of life. In *Essay on Man*, Pope parallels the pair pain/pleasure with the contrast *clair/obscur*:

> The lights and shades, whose well accorded strife
> Gives all the strength and colour to our life.[17]

4

One of the OED definitions of a prospect is "an extensive sight or view; the view of the landscape from any position". That definition is applicable to the Neo-Classical landscape prospects: the "extensive view" tends to be both far-reaching and wide, and the view is always taken from an elevated position:

> Nor are the Hills unamiable, whose Tops
> To Heaven aspire, affording Prospect sweet
> To human Ken,

sang John Philips in *Cyder* (1708).[18]

The point about the Neo-Classical prospect is that it establishes reciprocity between a beholder and what is beheld at the same time as it suggests man's lordship over nature. The beholder's eye would travel swiftly towards the outstanding landmarks of the panorama, just like a surveyor's eye taking "sightings". Prospect of course implies view, but it also comprises ingredients – poets often talk about a prospect "of" something, but a prospect has no division into levels, and it is not unequivocally three-dimensional. Hence the "paintability" aspect is toned down because the very rapidity of the movement of the eye would tend to ignore effects of light, shade, or colour. The eye may be arrested for a moment on the way, barely registering what met it, but it would travel quickly on to rest on some distant spot, such as a church spire (an actually existing locality may often serve as a landmark), which would hold the spectator's attention. It is not so much a *tour d'horizon* as an effort to get to the limits of the field of vision of the particular direction in which the poet is looking, thus assuring visual control of the scene. Each turn of the head would give the poet fresh prospects, for a "prospect" never becomes a "landscape", indeed, the landscape generally includes several prospects. Shenstone's distinction between the two terms, though written in the 1730s, is valid for most Neo-Classical landscape descriptions as well:

> Prospects should take in the blue distant hills; but never so remotely, that they are not distinguishable from clouds...Landskip should entertain variety enough to form a picture upon canvas.[19]

Accordingly, a prospect rarely makes up a whole poem since, in a prospect, movement takes precedence over description.

> As when our Eyes some Prospect would pursue,
> Descending from a Hill, looks round to view,
> Passes o'er Lawns and Meadows till it gains
> Some fav'rite Spot, and fixing there, remains:

Those lines, in which Granville metaphorically records how his "transported Muse" chooses a "bright Theme",[20] contain a prototype of what a prospect is. Neo-Classical man seems to have been pleased with the role of *homo prospiciens* because prospects were at one and the same time stimulating to his moral sense and flattering to his sense of domination.

Prospects could be both topographical and ideal. The view from Richmond was reputed to be one of the finest in England. Pope took up his residence in the immediate neighbourhood, at Twickenham, whose "cluster of houses and historic church rested gracefully in a broad bow of the river as it curled down through its 'matchless vale'". Pope remarks that the sight of such scenes (eg also the localities described in *Cooper's Hill*)

> is apt to give the Mind a compos'd Turn, and incline it to Thoughts and Contemplations that have a Relation to the Object.[21]

Like other items of the landscape poem, prospects were incorporated into current Neo-Classical cosmology and morality. Thus, a prospect was supposed to be able to give the beholder an immediate and overwhelming illustration of God's benevolence. From the top of a hill, says Hughes, it is possible to see

> Where Nature's hand....
> ... far around in beauteous Prospect spreads
> Her Map of Plenty all below.[22]

That is probably what Addison had in mind when he declared that "a beautiful prospect delights the soul as much as a demonstration",[23] and Bosworth was the first of many writers to use the term, in 1651, about the seductive features of a woman's body, another instance of the lavishness of "Nature's Hand".

Stephen Switzer advises the landowner to familiarize himself meticulously with the actual configurations of his possessions before he proceeds to commit his intentions to design. Thus he will develop a clearer eye for

> the natural Advantages of Levels...the proper Places to sink Pits, or to raise Mounts, to view and diversifie the Prospect.[24]

But he is anxious to emphasize that though a prospect could be easily arranged by art, a "natural" one is a godsend. The proprietor should pay heed to

> the exterior Beauty of a Seat: Such are the Prospects of any noble Vale, Lawn or Surprising Hills of Wood, and, in short, any Prospect that is accounted valuable .... there ought to be as open a view as possible.[25]

The *discors* element is so much part and parcel of the prospect that qualifiers like "variety" and its derivatives and synonyms are almost predictable whenever a prospect is referred to.

> The greatest part of the town stands upon a hill, and has its view bounded on all sides by several ranges of mountains, which are,

> however, at so great distance, that they leave open a wonderful variety of beautiful prospects,

says Addison in a passage from his account of his crossing of the Alps.[26]

A prospect, then, was a good thing, indeed it was treated by some critics as being inherently moral:

> The Pleasure in our sensible Perceptions of any kind, gives us our first Idea of *Natural Good*, or *Happiness*; and then all Objects which are apt to excite this Pleasure are call'd *immediately Good*...Thus *Meats, Drink, Harmony, fine Prospects, Statues* are perceived by our Senses to be *immediately Good*.

The words are from Hutcheson's *Inquiry*.[27]

It was possible to free the term prospect of its subjective element and to treat is as an aggregate of landscape features. When a landscape poet objectivises what is before his eyes, he not only recognizes its independence of himself, he also makes an effort to describe it such as it is, or rather, such as, in his opinion, it ought to be. There is a good deal of Aristotelian *mimesis* in the poets' treatment of landscape.

In order to give the beholder of a landscape painting and the reader of a landscape poem a "realistic" impression of the relative size and position of the items, some knowledge of perspective was required of painter and poet alike. Once more we see a movement that seems to confirm the Horatian dictum *ut pictura poesis*: poetry borrows a device from the Sister Art, transforming it slightly so as to adapt it to a different medium: for example, the river is often made to form a middle ground of a poem, a centre around which the scene displays itself.

5

The pleasure which Neo-Classicists found in views and prospects necessitated a "high place" to be fully enjoyed. That led to a reappraisal of hills and, to some extent, mountains.

> High objects, it is true, attract the sight; but it looks up with pain on craggy rocks and barren mountains, and continues not long on any object, which is wanting in shades of green to entertain it,

wrote Dryden in the dedication to *The Indian Emperor*. That statement from the middle of the 1660s – the play was printed in 1667 – epitomizes the attitude of the 1660s and 1670s to mountains: mountains are slightly frightening; they can serve as visual boundaries, but then they are at a safe distance. Hills, on the contrary, are far more appealing, almost friendly. Hills are essential in Neo-Classical landscape poetry: they are the base where the beholder takes up his position. Hills and mountains are complementary in that they form the starting-point and the limit of the panorama, and they frame and determine the scene at the same time. Hills and mountains are active participants of the scene, forming contrasts to valleys and plains, and having an intricate relationship of reciprocity with rivers. Besides, with their sloping outlines and undulating configurations, they counteract the predominant vertical and horizontal lines of the panorama.

There was, of course, venerable precedent for respecting elevation of place: the Biblical prophets ascend a mountain in the landscape, and salvation is believed to come from the mountains. During the Neo-Classical period, the attitude to mountains became gradually less reserved: owing to their height, they naturally became symbols of the moral greatness to which Longinus attributed the sublime in art. Mountains were held to have a *je ne sais quoi* quality, and the capability of the human mind to rejoice at mountain scenery is taken by Longinus as evidence of the greatness of the soul itself. Some writers eg Thomas Burnet (*Theory of the Earth*) considered mountains to be remains of a better world.

Another reason for the incipient popularity of mountains can be found in pictorial theory. In 1692, John Ray said that mountains must be pleasant to look at since "the very images of them, their Draughts and Landskips are so much esteem'd".[28] Roger de Piles devotes some chapters of his *Cours de Peinture par Principes* from 1708 to *Roches* and *Des Lointains et des Montagnes*. According to him, mountains are "d'un agrément infini", indeed they may even become "de quelque sorte sociables".[29]

Neo-Classicists had always found hills more "sociables"; they were smoothly incorporated into a man-centred philosophy of utility: they gave shelter and protection against the strong winds, they were the places where rivers and brooks had their origin, they supported the downward meandering of the water, they gave nourishment to woods and groves, and in their sides were found fascinating grottoes. Finally, they were the artefacts of a well-intentioned Creator, visible manifestations of His greatness, and obvious moral analogues.

In his poem *Cyder* from the first decade of the 18th century, John Philips voices the general utilitarian opinion of hills:

> Nor only do the Hills exclude the Winds:
> But, when the black'ning Clouds in sprinkling Show'rs
> Distill, from the high Summits down the Rain
> Runs trickling; with the fertile Moisture chear'd,
> The Orchats smile; joyous the farmers see
> Their thriving Plants, and bless the heav'nly Dew.[30]

Lady Winchilsea repeatedly expresses her fondness for the hill she has in the garden of her estate at Eastwell. She nicknamed it Parnassus, but it was far from being a vertiginous thing. She regretted that it made her feel "so little of the poet, that I am still restrained from attempting a description of it in verse," even though "the agreeableness of the subject has often prompted me strongly to it".[31]

Hills and mountains were necessary for the operations of the cyclic pattern of nature such as the Neo-Classicists conceived it, and the epithets attached to them point to their role in the landscape scene. Besides showing various nuances of colour, they are "lofty" or, very commonly, "rising", because their interaction with the low-lying river or the plain where they are "planted" (by the Great Designer) is never forgotten.

Cliffs and rocks have different connotations from hills: rocks are "huge" or "impending", cliffs are "steep" or in other ways inaccessible. Rocks and cliffs never invite climbing, and before the cult of the sublime sets in, the attitude to them is guarded. A "tumbling rock" is often one of the discordant elements required to set off the silence and ultimate harmony of *natura naturata*.

Mountains are generally more "vast" and impressive than hills, and poets find it a comforting thought that they are safely placed in the distance.

6

The kinds of water we meet in landscape poetry are neither roaring cascades à la Salvator Rosa nor the fathomless depths of the sea. Water means spring, brook, stream, rivulet, and, very often, river. All the waters are soft-flowing and anything but turbulent, for water, too, is adapted to the world view of the age.

The brook serves a variety of purposes in a landscape poem. Its movement runs counter to the many vertical lines; it encloses the foreground of the scene, thus furnishing a rough division into horizontal levels, between which it serves as a connecting link. The stream is very often in the middle ground, at a convenient distance from the observer, but not so far away as to be hardly distinguishable. Of course it never runs in an undeviatingly straight line: it is "winding" or "meandering" among "smiling meads". The tension established between the ultimately straight drive of the stream and its many curves on the way illustrates the principle of uniformity amidst variety. The bends of the river – and Neo-Classicism was not averse to allowing nature to abhor straight lines – are also exploited to suggested depth in the "picture". At the same time, the wilful meanderings of the water are tokens of "a grace beyond the reach of art".

The river is "soft-gliding", thus introducing an element of gentle dynamism in the otherwise fairly static landscape scene. It was perhaps owing to the stagnancy of their water that lakes were less popular. But the river, in its motion,"conducts" the beholder's eye because it touches or skirts, and, ultimately, connects the central ingredients of the landscape. It is essential that the speed should be moderate, and preferably the flow is unhindered by human interference. The ideal movement is so slow that the water, which is of course unpolluted and "silvery" becomes "limpid" or "crystal", creating a marvellous play of colours when the sun shines on it, or when it is momentarily hidden by the clouds. The movement is due to the river's own forward drive, hardly ever caused by the ruffling of the breeze on the water's surface, which is remarkable considering the poet's preoccupation with the effects caused by the light wind stirring the leaves of the trees.

Frequently, the water functions as that favourite device of the age, a mirror, reflecting the stability, prosperity, and harmony of the surrounding scene and, by implication, of *natura naturata*. For, like many other periods, the Neo-Classicists "found books in brooks": Dyer's approach in *Grongar Hill* is a case in point.

The view of the gliding water inspires the landscape poet with reflections on the utility of rivers. The water fertilizes the country through which it streams; besides, it is a useful means of transportation (exportation and importation are mentioned or implied in a good many poems), and the fish with which it naturally abounds provide food for man's table and pastime for his rod and line. Once more, it is the familiar pattern of *prodesse* and *delectare*, and several writers cite the river and its multifarious connotations as evidence of God's benevolence. Early 18th century utilitarianism is a combination of down-to-earth reality and acts of religious worship.

Finally, the river is exploited to illustrate a principle of reciprocity on several levels. Most hills have brooks or rivulets running down their grassy sides; the spring of such waters is found pretty high up, often in a grotto. The rivulets nourish the waters of the larger river underneath, with which they merge. They enter into a quasi-marital state, the adjective "uxorious" being not infrequently used to qualify the smaller of the two streams. The recompense given by the river to the hill is the fertilization of its soil so as to ensure luxuriant vegetation. The hill, in its turn, shades and protects the river; its "feet" are solidly planted very near the water's edge, bidding defiance to anyone who would be presumptuous enough to disturb the course of the water.

Blackmore describes the interaction as follows in Book I of *Creation*:

> See how the mountains in the midst divide
> The noblest regions, that from either side
> The streams, which to the hills their currents owe,

May every day along the valley flow,
And verdant wealth on all the soil bestow.³²

The reciprocity works on other levels as well: rivulets falling into the river are held to "pay tribute" to one greater than themselves. It seems pretty obvious that the economic and social overtones of the word tributary were present in the poets' and readers' minds. One instance is the incident in *Windsor Forest* where the Thames keeps state like a monarch, graciously accepting the allegiance of the less important streams.³³

The main river is itself a tributary to the sea, and once more we have an instance of reciprocity. Stanzas XI and XII of Katherine Philips' poem *To Lukasia, in defence of declared friendship* (Lukasia is a person often addressed by Miss Philips) are illustrative:

And as the river when it once has paid
    The tribute which it to the ocean owes
Stops not, but turns, and having Curl'd and Play'd
    On its own shores, the shore it overflows.

So the soul's motion does not end in bliss
    But on herself she scatters and dilates,
And on the object doubles till by this
    She finds new joy which that reflux creates.³⁴

Miss Philips exploits the river/sea relationship to characterize the working process of the soul: like the waters of the river, the soul is incessantly moving, and, again like water falling onto the sea, it "dilates" and returns with renewed impetus to the "object" of its activity. The process generates joy, which serves as a dynamic impulse driving the soul along. The idea is akin to the vortex theory, which was popular with late 17th century philosophers, and according to which the generative principle of the universe is comparable to the circular motion of a turbulent vortex.

It is with the sea as with the mountains on the horizon: their existence is recognized, but they are not objects of study in their own right. Neo-Classicists obviously found it difficult to grasp what actually happened when the water of the river merged with that of the sea: they were loth to accept the idea of the river losing its identity, and there are numerous allusions to a more or less mysterious "reward" on the part of the ocean, allowing the water – which has been somehow ennobled and purified by the contact with the "brine" of the sea – to flow back, in a recognizable though not identical state, and fertilize the banks with renewed vigour. Neo-Classicists were anxious to underline that minor changes of a more or less accidental character did not imply fundamental transformations, not to say loss: stability was a characteristic of the natural order of things.

The sequence of "inspire", "nourish", "fertilize" and "reward" is used both in river and non-river contexts, it being illustrative of the *cliens/patronus* relationship obtaining not only between river and sea, or river and hill, but also between poet and patron, or between the poet and his muse. Katherine Philips, for example, uses the sequence in the poem in which she pays tribute to the composer Henry Lawes: his "lyre" "rewards" the wit "it did at first inspire".[35]

The Thames greatly exceeds all other rivers in popularity and esteem. Like the Tiber, which was popular with classical Roman writers, it waters a capital city, and, like its Italian counterpart, it is surrounded with a halo of historic and patriotic associations. Already Cowley refers to the Thames as "the best of rivers". The most favoured stretch was the vicinity of Richmond, where the river winds among low hills covered with leafy trees, and both Denham and Pope were captivated by the charms of that region. Both Cowley and Denham use the flow of the river to characterize a poet's style:

> His candid Style like a clear Stream does slide
>   And his bright Fancy all the Way
>   Does like the Sunshine on it play;
> It does, like *Thames*, the best of rivers, glide.[36]

7

The kinship of hill and water was further strengthened by the fact that on hill-sides would often be found grottoes, and the brook or the rivulet would often have its source in a grotto.

Grottoes fascinated the Neo-Classicists, particularly those writing after 1710, mainly, it seems, because they provided excellent opportunities for ingenious combinations of art and nature. Usually, in the lay-out of grottoes, art was made to "improve" nature, the result being that, on the one hand, the end product would look wilder and more mysterious than nature had been able to make it look, but that, on the other hand, the artificiality of the ting was unmistakable: the grotto proved man's superiority. Neo-Classical man would make a good deal of play with the idea that he was fond of wildness – provided that it was disciplined, of course. The grottoes of later Neo-Classical poetry were often pretty artful constructions, and much ingenuity and lavish sums of money were spent to make them as "natural" as possible. Paradoxically, several landscape poets qualify grottoes by the epithet "artless".

A grotto became an indispensable ingredient in landscape gardening. It is a well-known fact that Pope spent a considerable amount of time, money, and ingenuity on the arrangement and accessories of the grotto of his Twickenham estate. Landed proprietors would carry their grottomania to considerable lengths, which provoked the satiric ridicule of *The Spectator*.

A correspondent writes a letter to Mr. Spectator, dated 30 November, 1714, in which he brings up the question of ladies' pastimes. In a recent issue, the correspondent says

> you...recommended to your Female Readers, the good old Custom of their Grandmothers, who used to lay out a great Part of their Time in Needle-work.

But the advice is different to "the poetical ladies":

> There is a very particular kind of Work, which of late several
> Ladies here in our Kingdom are very fond of, which seems very
> well adapted to a Poetical Genius:
> It is the Making of Grottos.[37]

The correspondent happens to know a lady who possesses of a very beautiful specimen, "composed by her self, nor is there one Shell in it not stuck up by her own Hands".

However, such grottoes, evidence on a longing on the part of some *femmes savantes* to parade a status symbol are not the ones we find in landscape poetry. The latter have not degenerated into mere toys, and the associations surrounding them are richly faceted. They are looked upon with awe because they are lonely places, suitable haunts for contemplation (the connection with Plato's cave is extremely tenuous, if at all discernible). They offer shade and perhaps also protection. Besides, they are of obscure, but decidedly primitive origin, a rather bizarre cog in the ingenious wheel. They convey a pleasurable horror, which made them even more popular with the advent of sublimity. They are welcome breaches of symmetry in the scene, and no matter how geometrically they are constructed inside, they offer an element of variety. Nobody ever explores a grotto, in print, at least, and it is never discussed where they lead, but sometimes there are speculation on the light effects that can be provided inside them. Pope had doors installed in front of his grotto at Twickenham so that he could control and alter the light inside.

8

There are ruins in the great majority of Neo-Classical landscape poems, and, like the other items, they are a mixture of object and symbol. The 17th century had been somewhat reserved in their attitude to ruins, mainly looking upon them as signs of ineluctable decay. In his *Sacred Theory of the Earth*, from 1684, Thomas Burnet had conceived of the world as a deplorable and irremediable ruin after the Fall. But orthodox Neo-Classical landscape poets exploited more than one connotation of ruins.

The state of ruins in 17th century paintings is generally a nondescript medium between incipient dilapidation and utter decay. They were factors that contributed to neutralizing the distinction between ideal and topographical landscape. As the landscape genre of poetry develops, the writer's point becomes more and more to make an aesthetic interpretation of ruins rather than a record of their exact state of decline. Though the ruins found on English soil were predominantly medieval, taste in ruins embraced both classical and Gothic specimens. But irrespective of their origin, ruins are obvious stimulants of reflection in *poesis* as well as in *pictura*.

The response was a composite one: astonishment at the legacies of a remote past, sweet melancholy at the conjecture of what life must have been like among those stones – "elles élèvent la pensée par l'usage auquel on s'imagine qu'elles ont été destinées;" as Piles said[38] – sadness at the inexorable evidence of *tempus edax rerum*, longing for a past Golden Age, and thrill at the mysterious and obscure connotations, some of which were religious, of the structure. Ruins "embody moral lessons about the transience of all human works", says Martin Price.[39]

A pithy summing-up of the Neo-Classical attitude to ruins occurs in a "letter" to *The Guardian* from a certain R.B. to Nestor Ironside, the *nom de plume* of the editor. Describing the pleasures of going out into the country and the enjoyment from being there, R.B. writes:

> The ruins of the several turrets and strong holds, gave my imagination more pleasant exercise than the most magnificent structure could, as I look upon the honourable wounds of a defaced soldier with more veneration than the most exact proportion of a beautiful woman.[40]

The tone of the "letter" is poles apart from the early 17th century shyness of, and aversion to, ruins. Ruins titillate the spectator's imagination for their imperfections are due to their having been in the "service" of passing time. Besides, as appears from the wording of the quotation, the new attitude is obviously inspired by ideas of sublimity, which taught that perfection is not synonymous with symmetry, and that beauty admits, even presupposes, some elements of horror.

Another item of fairly frequent occurrence in the landscape poem is the church spire. Breaking the horizon, it can serve as a landmark in a prospect. Also, churches provide shelter and are places of community still being used as against ruins, which are remains of former glory. But churches are not there for religious reasons. Feelings of awe or worship are inspired by the "great design" of the landscape rather than by a particular seat of religion. Such buildings as are admitted to the Neo-Classical landscape poem are often actually existing works of architecture, as for example Windsor Castle. But even in the "heightened" landscapes there are none of the classical temples known from landscape painting, and perhaps because Piles had dissuaded painters from showing peasants' hovels and shepherds' huts in their canvases, such edifices hardly ever occur in poetry.

9

The items mentioned in the previous sections may be supplemented by others, depending on the angle chosen: water mills or wind mills are sometimes modest background figures (a quiet reminder that even in an idyllic scene, work may be necessary), and the beholder of Tickell's *Oxford* contemplates libraries as well as domes. But trees, hills, and a river are the cornerstones of Neo-Classical landscape poems.

Peaceful fertility prevails without ever becoming obtrusive. Sheep – a pastoral reminiscence – graze the fields, and an occasional shepherd looks after his flock. If cattle are mentioned, they are not specified and on a decidedly lower level of interest than, for example, grottoes. The "silvery streams" are the abodes of the generic concept "fish", but, generally speaking, animals are not indispensable inhabitants of the scene.

Human activity is discreetly suggested but never comes to the fore. Yet, all the ingredients of the supposedly natural scenes are man-oriented and are accommodated to his likes and dislikes. The treatment awarded to weeds is symptomatic: weeds are plants that are useless, or even obnoxious, from man's point of view; they are signs that "unadorned nature" intransigently tries to assert her independence and challenge man's dominion. Accordingly, weeds are only referred to in passing, and they are always characterized by negatively loaded words. The Neo-Classical landscape poem to a considerable extent confirms Oscar Wilde's statement: "It is the spectator and not life that art really mirrors".[41]

The accomplishments of human effort are always discernible, eg in the path or the ruin. But those who are responsible for the serenity must be supposed to work, or to have worked, behind the scenes. There are few human beings in the landscape: the beholder commands the panorama in more than one way. A thin column of smoke in the distance may indicate human habitation, but, characteristically, the sight of smoke is just registered and the place of its origin only vaguely conjectured. Civilization never obtrudes, just as "raw nature" is kept in check, but, simultaneously, the very existence of signs of human activity confers a feeling of security on the observer: he is, in a way, *in medias res*, but *res* are circumscribable, and discreetly circumscribed, by the human will.

Whereas landscape painting regularly shows several groups of figures, the shorter landscape poems only occasionally feature a vaguely identified "wanderer", who does not seem to be heading for a specific goal, nor does he seem to be present with the same purpose as the beholder himself. The wanderer is "in" the scene, for which reason any communication between him and the beholder is out of the question. The wanderer is objectivised and depersonalized, the human figure becoming an item on a par with, though of markedly less interest than, the other components of the scene.

In the longer poems, there may be a hunting scene that the beholder conjures up and invites his readers to imagine. For a brief moment, some largely unidentified human beings invade the scene and disrupt the serenity. The climax of the scene takes place on a hilltop or in a stream, ie in localities that belong among the conspicuous parts of the whole. The victim may be for example a historical person who is made to suffer rightly or wrongly, or it may be an animal that does not usually appear in a peaceful and realistic landscape description, eg a stag. Besides introducing a change in the purely descriptive mode, such incidents have distinctly moral and symbolic overtones, eg the great one being pursued and killed by the smaller ones, or the tyrant suffering his well-deserved overthrow. It is remarkable that, once the hunt is over, harmony is almost immediately restored, and no reference to this sudden irruption is made in other parts of the poem.

CHAPTER TEN

SOME EXAMPLES ILLUSTRATING THE NEO-CLASSICAL LANDSCAPE CONVENTION IN POETRY

1

Thomas Tickell shared his contemporaries' prepossession in favour of the Thames region. One of his *Epistles, To a Lady, before Marriage*[1] is a deferential invitation to the beautiful Clotilda, who is "by thousands sought", to "flee thy crowd of captives and descend to me" (l.4). The narrator dreams about the surroundings in which, so he hopes, he and his nymph are going to spend their lives together:

> In some small hamlet on the lonely plain,
> Where Thames thro' meadows rolls his mazy train,
> Or where high Windsor, thick with greens array'd,
> Waves his old oaks, and spreads his ample shade,
> Fancy has figur'd out our calm retreat;
> Already round the visionary seat
> Our limes begin to shoot, our flow'rs to spring,
> The brooks to murmur, and the birds to sing.

A bit further on in the poem (ll. 25-34), he gives additional details of the visionary spot:

> 'Midst gardens here my humble pile shall rise,
> With sweets surrounded of ten thousand dyes;

> All savage where th'embroider'd gardens end,
> The haunt of echoes shall my wood ascend;
> And Oh! If Heav'n th'ambitious thought approve,
> A rill shall warble cross the gloomy grove;
> A little rill, o'er pebbly beds convey'd,
> Gush down the steep, and glitter through the glade.
> What cheering scents these bord'ring ranks exhale!
> How loud that heifer lows from yonder vale.

The topographical aspect has been dimmed, the Thames area yielding to the imaginary surroundings. The latter, however, present a structured panorama, with a clear distinction between what is inside the garden, and what is beyond ("bord'ring ranks"). The brook performs two conventional functions, viz. that of "nourishing" the grove and the banks, and that of forming a miniature cascade. Like the scene as a whole, it belongs to both art and nature.

The passage contains a considerable amount of standard diction: lonely plain, mazy train, ample shade. "Fancy" has found a conventional haunt in which the birds are singing, and the brook creates the obligatory play of light when glittering "thro' the glade". Everything is uniformly positive, but also unimaginative. Thus, the poet contents himself with "ten thousand dyes" instead of giving just one significant colour. The creative poet virtually disappears behind the formulae of the convention.

In one of his *Epistles, To Mr. Addison, On his Opera of Rosamond*,[2] Tickell compliments Addison for turning his back on inane Italian operas, "enrich'd with songs, but innocent of thought" (l.2). Addison's "artful song", however, is "soft as Corelli, and as Virgil strong" (ll. 7-8), *musica* and *poesis* forming a felicitous sisterly union. The decoration of the opera, as seen through Tickell's eyes, is a mixture of vision and reality:

> Landscapes how gay, the bow'ry grotto yields,
> Which Thought creates and lavish Fancy builds!
> What art can trace the visionary scenes,
> The flow'ry groves and everlasting greens,
> The babbling sounds that mimic Echo plays,
> The Fairy shade and its eternal maze?

Nature and Art in all their charm combin'd,
And all Elysium to one view confin'd (ll. 17-23).

Allowance must be made for the function of the landscape: it was intended to serve as the background of a fairly artificial genre of musical performance. As Tickell renders it, the scene seems to subject nature entirely to art, for all his joyous outburst about the happy union of the two. The situation is that of a beholder in front of a surveyed, though incomplete, panorama. The scene shows up unmistakable conventional landscape features; the remarkable thing is, however, that even if "lavish Fancy" is claimed to have thought up the view, it remains completely unimaginative, with nothing but standard ingredients and stereotyped qualifiers. The parts, which are not made much of, make up a structured whole. It is noteworthy that several of Tickell's poems pretend that "fancy" has found or devised a scene which turns out to be rather commonplace, also by contemporary standards. That can of course be taken as evidence of the limitation of Tickell's creative power, but perhaps also as an indication that such was the way of describing landscape.

John Hughes' poem *Greenwich Park* mixes topographical and ideal features: the goddess of Beauty, who used to reside in "the Papian isle", has moved her abode to Britain, where she has chosen "a sweeter seat for Love":

And *Greenwich Park* is now her Cyprian grove.
   Not fair *Parnassus* with this hill can vie,
Which swells into the wond'ring Sky,
Commanding all that can transport our Sight,
And varying with each view the fresh Delight.
From hence my Muse prepares to wing her Way,
And wanton, like the *Thames* thro' smiling Meads would stray,
Describe the Groves beneath, the Sylvan Bow'rs,
The River's winding Train, and sweet *Augusta's* Tow'rs.[3]

Hughes has managed to put a good many stock ingredients into that short scene: the "command" attitude from the hilltop, the shifting views of art as well as nature, foreground and background being represented by the groves and London respectively, and the winding Thames (the alexandrine perhaps being intended to suggest the meandering movement). Yet there are some breaches of the genre convention: it does not become clear whether the beholding agent is meant to be the goddess herself or the poet. Secondly, no matter what "my Muse prepares", nothing comes of it, for just as the muse is ready to take off, the poet's attention is distracted by the arrival of five beautiful women, partly historical and partly mythological. Mythology and topography make up a rather ill-matched couple in Hughes' poem, but the interest of the passage is that a view from a hill should be included as a natural ingredient in the description of a "Seat for Love."

That "hilly heights" were suitable *loci* of inspiration is confirmed by another of Hughes' poems, written in memory of Mrs Elizabeth Hughes, who died on 15 November, 1714. Stanza Five illustrates the point:

> Now, Pensive Muse, enlarge thy flight!
> (By turns the pensive Muses love
> The Hilly Heights and Shady Grove)
> Behold where swelling to the sight
> *Balls*, a fair structure, graceful stands.
> And from yon verdant rising Brow
> See Hertford's ancient Town, and Lands
> Where Nature's Hand in slow Meanders leads
> The Lee's clear Stream its Course to flow
> Thro' flow'ry Vales, and moisten'd Meads,
> And far around in beauteous Prospect spreads
> Her Map of Plenty all below.
> 'Twas here---and sacred be the Spot of Earth!
> Eliza' Soul, born first above,
> Descended to an humbler Birth
> And with a Mortal's Frailties strove.
> So, on some Tow'ring Bank that meets the Sky,
> When missive Seraphs downward fly,
> They stop and for a-while alight,
> Put off their Rays celestial-bright,
> Then take some form familiar to our Eye.[4]

The part of the country where the lady was born is celebrated within the framework of a landscape description, and, characteristically, such an account is best given in the form of a view from a hilltop. The convoluted syntax may be intended to intimate the winding course of the river or the wandering movement of the beholder's eyes. The passage contains one unusual departure in that it is not the poet himself who stands on the hilltop: he advises the muse to alight on "yon verdant Brow" because it may give inspiration, and the narrator proceeds to detail what can be seen from that elevated position. The hilltop is elevated in more senses than one, being the place where angels land before assuming a more human frame. That was also the road taken by Elizabeth, and it can be seen as an ingenious exploitation of the landscape convention's intimate connection between mountain and sky. In order to combine the hyperbolical praise of the lady with the requirements of landscape description, the narrator has been forced to add the somewhat pedestrian parenthesis in lines 2-3 of the extract, which, in its over-eager attempt to explain, weakens the description. The landscape is more nature than art – nature leads the river along, and she arranges her "map" in such a way that it makes up a prospect – yet nature is eclipsed by the angelic superstructure of the stanza. Towards the end, not only the lady but also the landscape is lost sight of. An important thing, however, is that landscape descriptions could be incorporated into elegies.

Leonard Welsted, who wrote little landscape poetry proper, shows, in several of his shorter pieces, that he has a feeling for a type of landscape that is more than merely pastoral, yet not quite topographical. His poem *Acon and Lavinia* was printed as an article in *The Free-Thinker* in 1718.[5] Particularly the scene "that blest Lavinia's Leisure" is relevant:

> The Scene, that blest Lavinia's Leisure, smil'd
> With Hills, and Vales, and Woods, a blooming Wilde.
> She shun'd the sultry Ray in Jasmin's Bow'rs;
> She trod on Carpets of sweet-smelling Flow'rs:
> Where'er she turns, luxuriant Landskips rise,
> And still she breathes in Aromatick Skies:

> For, with the Day spontaneous Sweets are born,
> And shed the fragrant Freshness of the Morn.
> Echoes and rude Cascades are heard around,
> While with soft Murmurs, through th'enchanted Ground,
> A winding Rivulet shapes its silver Flow,
> And shows a shining Bed of Sands below:
> Wide-branching Trees are ranged on either Side;
> The branching Shadows tremble in the Tide.

The extract proceeds from a mere enumeration of items to a less nondescript dwelling on them. Though not unequivocally viewed from above, the scene has definite landscape structure and affinities, and the last line makes a truly poetic use of the *topos* "the chequered shade". However, there is no first-person narrator, and the purpose of the description is to show the impact on the landscape of a beautiful woman's passing. The landscapes – the plural makes the word synonymous with "scene" – only come into being thanks to her strolling, which was not an unusual way of paying a compliment to a woman. The purpose of this idealized scene, "th'enchanted Ground", where even the "Wilde" is blooming, is to reflect youthful beauty as described by a passionate lover. Considering the time of writing, the passage is surprisingly stereotyped: thus, virtually all the qualifiers are the expected, and, by 1718, slightly trite ones.

The passages quoted in this section are not remarkable feats of poetic craftsmanship; also, they are intended to do too many things at the same time, and they pile up vaguely positive, but mutually unrelated, features. The landscape is lost sight of because the poet changes horses midstream.

Poets' interest resides in the fact that they include landscapes into slightly unexpected contexts, such as visions and elegies. Also, their panoramas are in the matrix of the Neo-Classical convention. We are allowed to conclude that landscape was felt to have a pervasive symbolic potential, and that the Neo-Classical technique was *the* way of describing a landscape.

2

In the poem *To Mr. Constantine. On his Paintings*, the year of which was given by its author, John Hughes, as 1715, the poet pays tribute to a landscape painter:

        While o'er the Cloth thy happy Pencil strays,
        And the pleas'd Eye its artful Course surveys,
        Behold the magic Pow'r of Shade and Light!
        A new Creation opens to our Sight.
(5)   Here tufted Groves rise boldly to the Sky,
        There spacious Lawns more distant charm the Eye;
        The Crystal Lakes in borrow'd Tinctures shine,
        And misty hills the far Horizon join.
        Lost in the azure Borders of the Day,
(10) Like Sound remote that die in Air away.
        The peopl'd Prospect various Pleasures yields,
        Sheep grace the Hills, and Herds or Swains the Fields;
        Harmonious Order o'er the Whole presides,
        And Nature crowns the Work which Judgment guides.
(15) Nor with less Skill display'd by thee appear
        The diff'rent Products of the fertile Year;
        While Fruits with imitated Ripeness glow
        And sudden Flow'rs beneath thy Pencil blow.
        Such, and so various thy extensive Hand,
(20) Oft in Suspense the pleas'd Spectators stand,
        Doubtful to chuse, and fearing still to err,
        When to thy self they would thy self prefer.
        So when the rival Gods at *Athens* strove
        By wondrous Work their Pow'r Divine to prove,
(25) As *Neptune's* Trident strook the teeming Earth
        Here the proud Horse upstarted to his Birth;
        And there, as *Pallas* bless'd the fruitful Scene,
        The spreading Olive rear'd its Stately Green;
        In dumb Surprise the gazing crowds were lost
(30) Nor knew on which to fix their Wonder most.

The poem peters out with a circumstantial reference to a mythological scene. The intention is undoubtedly to draw a parallel between the spectator's amazement when contemplating Constantine's canvases and ancient man's astonishment at the magic tricks of the gods. However, the poem is interesting on technical grounds: the narrator lets his eye roam over the picture, using the same terminology as he would do when looking at a real landscape. The items are arranged in a prospect with a horizon made up of misty hills, lawns in the middle ground and a grove closer to the beholder, who speaks as if he were standing on a hill.

It is true that no one item is given more attention than any other. Yet Hughes' poem is remarkable for the felicitous succinctness with which it formulates Neo-Classical commonplaces, eg the force of the *clair-obscur* effects (ll. 3-4), the difficulty of telling where the landscape ends and the sky begins (l.8), and the uniformity-amidst-variety idea (ll. 11 & 13). There is much conventional diction in the text (of the type "Crystal Lakes", l. 7), and though the poet is at pains to convey to the reader what impression Constantine's pictures make on him, he offers little more than generalities. For instance, he gives few specific colours, apart from "azure Borders" (l.9), contenting himself with "borrow'd Tinctures" (l.7).

The poem also deserves attention for its treatment of artistic theories. The poet praises the painter for having obtained the desirable blend of natural talent and knowledge of the craft (l. 14) ("nature" may refer both to the actual scene and to the poet's talent, which is controlled by judgment). Even more than that, l.1 contains a discreet allusion to the Horatian *curiosa felicitas*: Constantine is the talented painter whose competence is so considerable that the muse favours him with moments of superhuman perfection. The poet's ideal is life-like reproduction: it is Constantine's imitative technique that strikes the beholder dumb with surprise, and the deceptively realistic fruits and flowers are a distant reminder of the genius of the Greek painter Apelles, and, accordingly, an implied compliment to Constantine.

A modern reader may feel that Hughes does not manage to impart an impression that Constantine's paintings are anything out of the ordinary; the blame may be the painter's as well as the poet's. However, in a contemporary context, the praise was felt to be appropriate.

The poems of Anne, Countess of Winchilsea, were written from 1685 and well into the 18th century (she died in 1720). She devoted many lines to loving and sympathetic sketches of trees; the theme of retreat, which is a recurrent one in her poetry, is invariably associated with high and protecting trees, sometimes "stately woods".

> Fair Tree! For thy delightful Shade
> 'Tis just that some return be made.
> Sure, some Return is due from me
> To thy cool Shadows, and to thee.
> When thou to *Birds* do'st Shadow give,
> Thou Musick do'st from them receive;
> If Travellers beneath thee stay,
> Till Storms have worn themselves away,
> That Time in praising thee they spend,
> And thy protecting Pow'r commend:
> The *Shepherd* here, from Scorching freed
> Tunes to thy dancing Leaves his Reed;
> Whilst his lov'd Nymph, in Thanks, bestows
> Her flow'ry Chaplets on thy Boughs.[6]

Those are the first lines of a short poem, *The Tree*, which ends with a prayer that the tree may be preserved "to future Ages… Untouched by the rash Workman's Hand." Once it "dies", the tree deserves the funeral ceremony of a hero: to be burned, "And some bright Hearth be made thy Urn."

Even if the poem does not describe a complete landscape scene, it illustrates the pervading principle of reciprocity between an item in the scene and those whom it "o'erarches" and protects. The poem looks upon the genus tree rather than a particular specimen, but still it is a far more personal statement than the far-fetched mythological visions of other landscape poems. The last lines of the extract may be a pastoral reminiscence, in the choice of words rather than in actual fact, for the shepherd and his girlfriend are entirely probable in the context of *The Tree*.

The novelty of approach is the personal experience. The poet, feeling that she owes a debt of gratitude to a landscape item, thanks it by celebrating it in a song, which is probably more articulate than the warbling of the birds and the praise of random travellers. The interest of the poem resides in the intimate contact that is established between a human being and a landscape feature. That approach is typical of many Neo-Classical poems.

Together with her husband, Anne lived at the estate at Eastwell, the extensive grounds of which fascinated her. It is on record that Anne loved to take long walks in the Park, whose beauty and loneliness filled her with unspeakable pleasure. Lord Winchilsea subjected the estate to several improvements, and on one of the occasions Anne wrote a poem, *Upon My Lord Winchilsea's Converting the Mount in the Garden to a Terrace, and other Alterations, and Improvements, In his House, Park, and Garden*. From l. 15, the poem runs as follows:

> And as old Rome Refin'd what ere was rude,
> And Civiliz'd as fast as she Subdu'd,
> So lies this Hill, hewn from its rugged Height,
> Now levell'd to a Scene of smooth Delight,
> Where on a Terrace of its Spoyles we walk,
> And of the Task, and the Performer talk;
> From whose unweari'd Genius Men expect
> All that can farther Pollish and Protect;
> To see a sheltering Grove the Prospect bound,
> Just rising from the same prolific Ground,
> Where late itt stood, the Glory of the Seat,
> Repell'd the Winter's Blasts and skreen'd the Somer's Heat.[7]

The poet assures her readers that such intrusions of art are not to be feared – the allusion to Rome stresses the civilizing aspect of the process. The hill has been transformed into a location which yields as magnificent a prospect as a more mountain-like elevation used to do. There is a remarkable view from the newly erected building:

> And now we Breath, and now the eager View
> Through the enlarged Windows takes her Way

Does beauteous Fields and scatter'd Woods survey,
Flies o'er th'extended Land, and sinks but in the Sea.[8]

The poem merits attention, not least on account of its obvious pleasure at the results of the process of landscape gardening and the implicit homage to the designer. Rather than infringing on nature, art enters into a fruitful union with it, and further improvements are forecast. The sheltering grove is a stock ingredient, but here it is put to ingenious uses: it can *prodesse* as well as *delectare*, "Pollish and Protect" being an original formulation of the dyad. Also, the pastoral *topos* of shade is subtly suggested without the word being used, for, in this realistic poem, protection will be needed against the heat of summer as well as the cold of winter.

Hills must have been surrounded with an aura of prestige since the Countess goes to such lengths to justify the levelling of it and to assure the reader that it is a civilizing process. Also, the intention is to plant an artificial grove at the place where nature had originally put one. The poem, which implies at least as much as it states explicitly, is really about nature versus art – without mentioning either of the two terms. It is an instance of Aristotelian *mimesis* applied to landscape gardening: the purpose of art is to make nature look what it was like when "unadorned".

3

There are two main versions of Denham's *Cooper's Hill*, from 1643 and 1655 respectively. Even though the poem is not, from a strictly temporal point of view, a Neo-Classical one, it belongs in this chapter because it is one of the landmarks in the establishment of the Neo-Classical landscape tradition.

There are considerable differences between the two versions. The former of them was composed by a Royalist poet before the outbreak of the Civil War. O Hehir plausibly reads that poem as a warning not to rouse the dormant power of the King.[9] The revision, probably undertaken in the years 1653-54, was made by a defeated Royalist whose King had been executed. This has some bearing on the identity of the victim of the stag hunt, which occurs in both versions. However, it would seem that the really significant thing is the victimization rather than the identity of the scapegoat: violence persists, irrespective of the social system. Technically speaking, the two different stag incidents illustrate a phenomenon which was to become very evident in the later development of the poetical landscape genre, viz. that the frames, which means the convention, are more important than the content: political allusions could be given various references at the poet's discretion.

Undoubtedly, the second version of *Cooper's Hill* is more universal in its scope, and it ends with a wellnigh apocalyptic vision of anarchy. Yet it is remarkable that a declared Royalist like Denham could spend some years after 1653 as the guest of the Earl of Pembroke at Wilton House without being molested. Two activities engaged his attention, viz. the translation of Vergil – actually his theories of translation influenced Dryden – and the drastic recasting of *Cooper's Hill*: less than one third of the original poem remained unchanged, and unchanged lines were occasionally transferred to other contexts.[10]

Cooper's Hill is not far from Egham, the village where Denham spent his childhood. From the hilltop (about 200 feet high), there is a fine view of Windsor, St. Anne's Hill, and the Thames, which winds at the foot of the hill. Thus he lays the groundwork for the sequence prospect/instruction, which was to become one of the cornerstones of Neo-Classical landscape poetry. He puts the idea like this: the poem owes its origin to a strife between his eyes and his thoughts (ll. 11-12) (all references, unless explicitly stated otherwise, are to the 1655 version); both of them attempt to grasp the same data with their specific mode of perception, as object and significance respectively. Therefore, I do not agree with Kitty Scoular when she says: "It is still more an emblem of kingship than a description".[11] Rather, it is the first instance of what was to become a pattern in Neo-Classical landscape poetry: sensation combined with, or leading to, reflections connected with human life in the broadest sense of the term.

Denham's choice of a hill was fortunate: the "picture" from its top contains a number of landscape features, plus some items whose symbolism can be easily exploited: a Royal palace, a church, and the distant view of the capital. The main landmarks occur in both versions of the poem, as does the tripartite division of the *tableau*: the background is given immediately in a prospect-like view of St. Paul's and London, Windsor is in the middle ground, and "a neighb'ring hill" – St. Anne's – is located in the foreground. The Thames serves as the connecting link besides having emblematic functions of its own.

In his reworking of the poem, Denham made some structural and verbal alterations that justify successive poets' and critics' view of it as a landscape poem. For example, the sense of space is more perceptible in the first 25 lines of the later version: the interplay of vertical and horizontal lines is suggested, the poet's eye "contracts the space/That lies between" himself and St. Paul's (ll. 13-14). His imagination is boundless (l. 12), whereas his eye is stopped by the landmarks, which, characteristically, are looked upon in terms of landscape features though they are places of architecture: Windsor is a hill rather than a castle (ll. 42 & 49), and St. Paul's dome is not a church tower, but an aspiring mountain or a descending cloud. That ingenious way of suggesting the distance of the horizon by confessing one's inability to determine the boundary between heaven and earth was destined to become a stock device with the Neo-Classical landscape poets. That is another instance where Denham blazes a new trail for Neo-Classical poets' approaches and attitudes when dealing with landscape.

Thus, the reader is made to follow the poet's alternation between observation and reflection as the poem goes along, that intimate connection between fact and analogy which, ultimately, pointed to a *concordia* between *natura naturata* and man-made civilization. The treatment of the river in the poem is symptomatic. It shows how Denham exploits the associative potential of a landscape item – elegantly and discreetly, because the references are scattered over the whole poem.

The passage from l. 160 to l. 196 contains a eulogy of the Thames. It is one of the poem's themes, and it is emblematic of the principle of *concordia discors*. The often quoted lines "Oh, could I flow like thee..." (ll. 189 et seq.) provide the river with some epithets – deep, yet clear, gentle, yet not dull, strong without rage, and full without overflowing – that can also be qualities that are desirable in a benevolent ruler or a good government; by a small stretch of the imagination, they can also refer to ideal qualities in a human being, among them a poet, and in a poem. The passage is a suitable point of departure for the next lines, which teach us that

> the harmony of things
> As well as that of sounds, from discord springs (ll. 203-204).

Feelings of delight, we are then told, spring "from sev'ral causes". Hence the initial discord (l. 205) is essential, because it is an indispensable prerequisite for the ensuing "form, order, beauty" (l. 206) which governs the universe, both our existence and our attributes: "All that we have, and that we are" (l. 208). It is symptomatic that "form" should be given parity of esteem with two positively loaded words, "order" and "beauty".

The passage shows a very characteristic movement from the concrete scene to a generalizing conclusion, or, to use the landscape poets' terminology, from prospect to instruction. The flow of the river illustrates a universal principle that is applicable to human existence as well. And the river is put to other uses by Denham: it gives twofold wealth to its banks, viz. by fertilizing the soil (ll. 169-70) and by creating a road of commerce and trade (ll. 181 – 88), activities not dissimilar to those ideally required of a king. The river forms a link of reciprocity with the sea (ll. 35-36), to which it is made tributary (ll. 161-65); and, though mountains may frown on it, the gentle stream flows on undisturbedly (ll. 219-20): from an ethical as well as from an aesthetic point of view the poet's solidarity is with the river, which is made explicit in the moral conclusion that follows: winds and storms cannot reach the river in the valley, whereas they beat the "lofty forehead" of the mountain, and that is "the common fate of all that's high or great" (l. 222).

Finally, the river is used in the service of the political and social moral of the poem, which, though more than hinted on the way, is made abundantly clear towards the end. In its normal, sedate course, the river symbolizes the practices and customs characterizing the gently flowing rhythm of a harmonious commonwealth.

But if that peaceful course is interfered with – figuratively speaking if one of the centres of power transgresses the "natural" bounds – the result is flooding, the break-up of system and order, unbridled power leading necessarily to anarchy and disruption. The ideal form of government is a state of balance between the ruler and the ruled.

It will have appeared how Denham paved the way for virtually all the uses that later landscape poets made of the river. Just as, on the concrete level, the river serves as a connecting link between the items that are commented on in *Cooper's Hill*, determining the composition of the landscape scene, so, on the allegorical level, its multifarious functions contribute heavily to clarifying the social and political messages of the poem. And Denham shows a remarkable sureness of grasp because the river and its symbolism are referred to on and off as the poem moves forward, being smoothly and naturally incorporated in the description. That is what justifies the poet's statement that the river is "my theme."

One passage is significantly altered from the first to the second version, viz. ll. 223-28 ("Low at his foot..."). O Hehir calls the emendation "tautological and silly".[12] I think that is a wrong angle, *pace* that learned scholar. The early version placed later in the poem, runs as follows:

> So lookes the Hill upon the streame, betweene
> There lies a spatious, and a fertile Greene (ll. 249-50).

That is changed into the following:

> Low at his foot a spacious plain is placed,
> Between the mountain and the stream embraced
> Which shade and shelter from the hill derives,
> While the kind river wealth and beauty gives
> And in the mixture of all these appears
> Variety, which all the rest endears (ll. 223-28).

The reciprocity theme has been widened to cover more elements of the landscape than before. The crucial thing, however, is that now the items have been placed in a characteristic landscape position:

the plain at the foot of the hill, between the hull and the river, the hill shading and protecting the stream, which serves two basic functions, viz. to create pleasure and to provide fertility. When added up, the ingredients produce "a mixture", and "variety" stands out as one of the glories of the tightly woven panorama. It will be seen that this short scene makes up a replica of the larger landscape to which Denham devotes the rest of *Cooper's Hill.*

Once more, Denham must be credited with originality, for it becomes a Neo-Classical landscape convention that a prospect may contain one or more miniature landscapes. Denham is so fond of this *scene* (he uses the word himself in l. 229) that in the following lines he proceeds to detail what "some bold Greek or British bard" would have read into it (ll. 229 et seq.): stories

> Of fairies, satyrs, and their nymphs, their dames,
> Their feasts, their revels, and their am'rous flames (ll. 231-32).

Those lines, which read like a left-over from a pastoral, and which aptly describe the foreground motif of many a 17th century landscape painting, do not occur in the first version.

Therefore, I tend to disagree with O Hehir when he says that the 1655 version of *Cooper's Hill* was written by a man "whose sense of the actuality of the scene had long since been dulled", and that the final version is "a conceptual poem rather than a visual one".[13] It is true that the later version is considerably gloomier than its predecessor because it ends with a description of the indomitable and ruthless power of the river if challenged, and it does not contain even a hint of a suggestion as to how to remedy chaos. It is also true that the moral message, like the political message, of the 1655 version is repeated with such insistence that only the slow-witted would fail to grasp it. Yet the fact remains that the final version has more of a landscape structure and is a more reliable and detailed picture of the view from Cooper's Hill than the original poem, which means that the poet's "sense of the actuality of the scene" had been anything but dulled. It is imaginable that, for his revision, Denham was inspired by landscape painting to be found at Wilton house, even though, admittedly, his poem contains very few colours.

At least the final version was "visual" enough for numerous poets to follow in Denham's footsteps when describing a landscape scene. For Denham was the founder of the Neo-Classical school of landscape poetry: the poets who came after him imitated his use of the beholder, his principles of structuralization, and his allegorical exploitation of the components. More than that, they took over his trick of introducing a little secluded scene showing in miniature the configurations of the larger landscape, and many of them copied him to the extent of naming their poems after some hill even if what they described was not the hill itself but the view they could have from its top.

It is perfectly understandable that Dr. Johnson should praise Denham for his description of landscape in *Cooper's Hill*, for landscape forms the axis on which everything in the poem turns, the political and moral speculations arising out of the contemplation of an actually existing panorama. Take landscape away, and the structure of the poem disintegrates.

Cooper's Hill is one of the few pieces of literature that was universally acclaimed during the period that is analysed in these pages. It should be added, though, that different writers and critics do not appreciate it for identical reasons, but they all agree that Denham's poem has got "something", and several of them have got a clear conception of the novelty of Denham's achievement.

Joshua Poole excerpted lines from the poem for his *English Parnassus*, and purple passages were culled from it, with the same didactic intention as Poole's, by Bysshe in his *Art of English Poetry* from 1705. The significant point is that what Bysshe selects are passages concerned with landscape, eg "Hunting" (the hunting scene of *Cooper's Hill*),[14] "Mountains",[15] and "Rivers" (the homage paid to the Thames).[16] Gildon quotes the same selections in his *Complete Art of Poetry* from 1718, the only difference being that his excerpts are shorter.

None of those writers comment on the passages they have selected, but it should be remembered that the books of Poole, Bysshe, and Gildon were intended to be primarily didactic: the purpose of those *artes poeticae* was to teach budding writers (and schoolchildren) the art of composing a description successfully, and since the passages excerpted are mainly about landscape,

Poole and the others must have felt that Denham was worth imitating on that point.

The prestige enjoyed by *Cooper's Hill* is also proved by the fact that, in 1676, it was translated into Latin hexameters by the Rev. Moses Pengry.[17] And Oldham's *Two Pastorals out of the Greek Bion* contains the following couplet:

> And *He* whose Song rais'd Cooper's Hill so high,
> And made its Glory with Parnassus vie.[18]

The reference reveals familiarity with at least the opening lines of Denham's poem in which Cooper's Hill, on which the poet is standing, is by the poetic process itself made into a Parnassus. The value of the tribute is enhanced by the fact that Oldham does not mention Denham by name but takes it for granted that his poem is able to speak for itself. Besides, the author of *Cooper's Hill* figures in very august company: in the context, Oldham pays homage to a few select masters of poetry who are dead at the time of writing; among the others mentioned are Chaucer, Milton, and Cowley.

Tickell refers deferentially to "Great Denham's Genius",[19] and proves indirectly the high repute in which *Cooper's Hill* was held:

> When youthful Harrison, with tuneful Skill,
> Makes Woodstock Park scarce yield to Cooper's Hill.[20]

Equally interesting are critics' attempts, begun soon after the publication of the poem, to range it into a suitable "kind". The difference of the affiliations suggested is evidence that, at the time of publication, the poem was recognized to be unorthodox. Already in the 1650s, Herrick published his poem *To Mr. Denham on his Prospective Poem*, the title of which indicates that Herrick considered the prospect element of *Cooper's Hill* its distinctive feature. On that point, he was indirectly contradicted by Dryden, who, towards the end of 1663, affiliated Denham's poem to the noblest of genres, which is, of course, no little compliment:

> The sweetness of Mr. Waller's lyrick poetry, was afterwards followed in the epick by Sir John Denham, in his Cooper's-Hill;

a poem which your Lordship knows, for the majesty of the style, is, and ever will be, the exact standard of good writing.[21]

Yet, as the 17th century draws towards its close and the theory of kinds was slowly being undermined, poets and critics increasingly admire Denham's poem without necessarily considering it in terms of a genre piece, but for its own qualities – for its descriptions as well as for its moral. Lady Winchilsea, contemplating the beauties of the park at Eastwell, feels that

> a pleasing wonder through my fancy roves…
> Like mighty Denham's, then, methinks my hand
> Might bid the Landskip in strong numbers stand,
> Fix all its charms, with a Poetick skill
> And raise its Fame above his *Cooper's Hill*.[22]

There are evident similarities between *Cooper's Hill* and Pope's *Windsor Forest,* but in some *Observations*, from 1717, Dennis pounces on the dissimilarities, at the same time making his preferences crystal clear:

> Denham presents no object to his Reader, but what is truly in the Compass of his Subject. Whereas Half of the Poem of *Windsor Forest* has nothing in it, that is peculiar to Windsor Forest. The Objects that are presented to the Reader in this latter Poem, are for the most part trivial and trifling, as Hunting, Fishing, Setting, Shooting, and a thousand common Landskips. Whereas of a thousand Objects that *Cooper's-Hill* presents to the View, *Sir John Denham* chooses only the most Instructive, the most Noble, and the most Magnificent.

Dennis instances St. Paul's and Runnymead, and he goes on to deplore the utter lack of design in Pope's poem. *Cooper's Hill*, on the other hand, has "an Admirable Design" and "a Beautiful Disposition of Parts". Besides, it presents us with a great and most useful Instruction, viz. that we should beware of a furious ill-grounded Zeal, or of a dangerous Hypocrisy, that Apes it.[23]

Dennis' dislike of Pope is easily accounted for, and it cannot be called entirely unwarranted. Perhaps his compliments to Denham rather spring from a wish to denigrate Pope, to whom he does not even refer by name. For example, hunting seems to be "trivial and trifling" when it is included by Pope, whereas Denham, who also includes a hunting scene, is praised for dealing only with what his subject requires. However, it is not only that there is more pertinence in Dennis' words about *Cooper's Hill* than in his strictures on *Windsor Forest*, it is also that Dennis' comments give us a possible clue to the high repute in which Denham's poems continued to be held.

Dennis has obviously understood what Denham was doing in *Cooper's Hill*: he has an eye for the competent design of it, and for the moral it teaches. But, equally interestingly, he pays tribute to Denham for keeping to his subject and, as appears from the last sentence of the first quotation, for making a conscious selection of landscape items so as to present to his reader those that were useful, which means, in this case, noble and instructive. And that, of course, is the technique adopted by the Neo-Classical poets, making landscape items the necessary but not sufficient content of the landscape poem. Therefore it is not difficult to see the justification of Dr. Johnson's statement to the effect that "*Cooper's Hill* is the work that confers upon him (sc. Denham) the rank and dignity of an original author",[24] "original", of course, being the crucial word of the encomium.

Most of Denham's other work is translations from the Classics, political pieces, often with a strong partisan bias, and a few elegies. However, in his *Art of English Poetry,* Bysshe ascribes a twelve-line text to Denham, which he quotes in his list of purple passages under the entry "Brook". I have not been able to find a possible larger context for the lines in Denham's *oeuvre:*

See gentle Brooks, how quietly they glide,
Kissing the rugged Banks on either Side:

> While in their crystal Streams at once they show
> And with them feed the Flow'rs which they bestow:
> Tho' rudely thronged by a too near Embrace
> In gentle Murmurs they keep on their Race
> To the lov'd Sea; for streams have their Desires,
> Cool as they are, they feel Love's powerful Fires:
> And with such Passion that if any Force
> Stop or molest them in their am'rous Course,
> They swell, break down with Rage, and ravage o'er
> The Banks they kiss'd, and Flow'rs they fed before.[25]

Internal evidence points to Denham, or at least a very skilful imitation of him. One idea of the "Brook" passage is similar to the final image of *Cooper's Hill*, viz. the prophecy that if the progress of the river is hampered, it will "swell", and "ravage" the banks. However, the tone of this image, as of the whole text, is radically different from that of *Cooper's Hill*. The *"Brook"* is an erotic poem, its "story" being that the brook rejects one importunate suitor because it is strongly attached by another who is more kindred. The amorous note is struck already in l. 2 ("kissing the rugged Banks..."), and is consistently upheld in the rest of the poem.

Though built with the same material as *Cooper's Hill*, the *"Brook"* is a far less gloomy poem, and it lacks the social analogy of *Cooper's Hill*. Whoever the author may be, he plays on the erotic motif with considerable elegance; to see what a lucky touch he has we need only think of the many pretendedly erotic but fairly mechanical comparisons between the features of a landscape and a woman's body with which Neo-Classical writers would try to divert their readers. Love governs the treatment of the landscape theme in the *"Brook"*, for which reason its author had to drop the idea of the cyclical movement of the water, which is suggested in *Cooper's Hill*, and which is a recurrent *topos* with many of Denham's successors. The author of the *"Brook"* writes with his tongue in his cheek, indeed the last five lines are a disrespectful pastiche of Denham's monumental ending of *Cooper's Hill*.

4

One of the longest pieces of Tickell's *Miscellanies* is *Oxford. A Poem*, which was dedicated to Lord Lonsdale in 1707. The poem is interesting because it shows the strength and flexibility of the Neo-Classical landscape convention. In the descriptive passages, Oxford is treated in terms of a landscape: there are no street scenes, and, on the whole, the seat of learning is made more rural than is warranted by topography. The writer deduces several lessons from his descriptions, two outstanding ones being reflections on the past and present history of the celebrated town and its university, and a comparison with Lonsdale's "rural seat", Lowther. Here are lines 23-42:

> Where shall I first the beauteous scene disclose,
> And all the gay variety expose?
> For wheree'er I turn my wondering eyes
> Aspiring tow'rs and verdant groves arise,
> Immortal greens the smiling plains array,
> And mazy rivers murmur all the way.
> O! might your eye behold each sparkling dome
> And freshly o'er the beauteous prospect roam,
> Less ravish'd your own Lowther you'd survey,
> Tho' pomp and state the costly seat display,
> Where art so nicely has adorned the place
> That Nature's aid might seem a useless grace,
> Yet Nature's smiles with such various charms impart
> That vain and needless are the strokes of Art.
> In equal state our rising structures shine,
> Fram'd by such rules and form'd by such design
> The here at once surpris'd and pleas'd we view
> Old Athens lost and conquer'd in the new;
> More sweet our shades, more fit our bright abodes
> For warbling Muses and inspiring gods.[26]

The first four lines of the extract paint the rich variety presenting itself to the beholder's eyes when taking a bird's eye view of Oxford. The concomitant sense of bafflement – for once the beholder's eyes are "wondering" and not "wandering" – is a recurrent motif in landscape poetry. However, the scene has little structure and as yet gives the reader little chance of identification. Only later in the extract is the locality indicated ("dome" and "Old Athens", for example).

It is noteworthy that Oxford is claimed to be preferable to Lowther because it is more of a landscape. Equally interesting, the comparison is established in terms of the contrast art/nature: the "pomp and state" of Lonsdale's "costly seat" is contrasted with the "sweet...shades" and "bright abodes" of Oxford. Like the opening landscape scene, the lines juxtaposing the two localities are fairly vague. Thus, there are no concrete details about the architecture or garden planning at Lowther. Oxford is claimed to be more "natural" than Lowther, which seems to be too "nicely adorned" by art. Somehow, the "rising structures" of Oxford must be "natural" as well.

It is evidence of the powerfulness of the mould of the convention that such a fairly traditional landscape can be found attractive, and that the contrast between Oxford and Lowther is announced in such rigid terms. What appeals to Tickell is the blossoming of the arts and learning that he finds at Oxford.

The conception of Oxford as a landscape is pursued in later sections of Tickell's poem:

> Loth to depart I leave th'inviting scene,
> Yet scarce forbear to view it o'er again;
> But still new objects give a new delight,
> And various prospects bless the wand'ring sight (ll. 171-74).

And

> Here colleges in sweet confusion rise,
> There temples seem to reach their native skies;
> Spires, tow'rs, and groves compose the various show,
> And mingling prospects charm the doubting view (ll. 189-92).

Throughout, the vocabulary and the mode of perception are clearly indebted to the landscape tradition, and landscape items are combined with man-made architecture. The prepossession of the river is another landscape feature:

> In vain the groves demand my longer stay,
> The gentle Isis wafts my Muse away;
> With ease the river guides her wand'ring stream,
> And hastens to mingle with uxorious Thame (ll. 325-28).

The adjective "uxorious" was cited by Poole in his *English Parnassus* as a possible epithet for rivers,[27] and it became part of the stock diction of landscape poetry, perhaps because the pathetic fallacy could smoothly be worked into the pattern of the Great Design. Tickell's poem characterizes "Thame" as a husband dotingly fond of his wife, the Isis. The two streams enter into a marriage-like union and become one water.

Tickell's *Oxford* is remarkable for the resources that an ingenious use of the tradition has permitted the poet to draw on. To the *topos* of the shifting views has been added the unwillingness to leave the scene; to the view from the hilltop has been added what amounts to a declaration of love to the panorama; to the familiar groves as landmarks have been added temples where divine lore is taught. The poem to some extent sacrifices topography for the benefit of an account of what the place meant to Tickell. It is worth noting that he found it natural to couch his delight in the idiom familiar from landscape descriptions.

5

According to Jean Hagstrum, Pope's "texture" (is) "to an extent before unrealized, woven of pictorial images".[28] Pope's landscapes – and there are many of them in his *oeuvre* – are delicately poised between nature *per se* and dressed-up nature. And even if, to a superficial glance, many of his landscapes may seem to be merely incidental, they are generally arranged in a way that proves his familiarity with pictorial procedure. He compared Calypso's bower in the Fifth Book of the *Odyssee* with "an admirable rural landskip", and he is the first great English landscapist in verse "to compose his picture within the frame, and paint it in the colour of nature".[29] Yet his fondness for colour does not make him blind to the requirements of design: he exploits space with an almost Poussin-like virtuosity.

He has a rare talent of fitting his landscapes to the genre in which they occur: those of his pastorals are polished and stereotyped; that of the final section of *The Dunciad* is a bleak mixture of black and brown, and that of *Eloisa to Abelard* is a projection of the mood of the protagonists:

> The darksome pines that o'er you rocks reclin'd,
> Wave high, and murmur to the hollow wind,
> The grots that echo to the tinkling rills,
> The dying gales that pant upon the trees,
> The lakes that quiver to the curling breeze... (ll. 155.60).

The scene is that of a landscape poem ("yon rocks"), and the items are the familiar ones (grots, trees, breeze), but the impression is a negation of the optimism and reverence for nature found in conventional landscape poems. It is a recognizable panorama, but the comments on it have been given a slight twist by a subtle use of qualifiers: darksome pines, quivering lakes, and tinkling rills might be standard characterizations, and dying gales even a positive sign that calm was approaching. However, grottoes were not usually echoing because they were anything but empty, being filled with all manner of artificial knick-knacks, and curling movement of the water boded no good. By means of those discreet pointers, supported, of course, by the story that is told in the poem, the ominous undertone of the other seemingly noncommittal qualifiers is brought to the fore, and the scene appears as if seen by the despairing lovers. And yet, in spite of the sorrow, the landscape is tailored to the familiar pattern, and it achieves its effect because Pope played on the response he knew he could presuppose in his readers.

Both the 1717 and the 1735 edition of Pope's *Works* include some shorter occasional pieces having as their subject items of *natura naturata*. Here is one about a favourite theme of Pope's, the river, which he found serviceable on several levels:

Hail, sacred spring, whose fruitful stream
Fattens the flocks, and cloaths the plain;
The melancholy poet's theme,
And solace of the thirsty swain.

Thou fly'st, with eager haste,
Behind thy self thou still dost stay;
Thy stream, like his, is never past,
And yet is ever on the way.

While mankind boasts superior sight,
With eyes erect the heav'ns to see;
The starry eyes of heav'n delight
To gaze upon themselves in thee.

A second sun thou dost present,
And bring new heav'ns before our eyes;
We view a milder firmament,
And pleas'd, look downward to the skies.

Thy streams were once th'imperial test
Of untaught nature's humble pride,
When by thy glass the nymphs were drest,
In flow'rs, the honours of thy side.

Of thee they drank, till blushing fruit
Was ravish't from the tender vine;
And man, like thee, was impollute,
Till mischief learn'd to mix with wine.[30]

The poem is from *Verses in Imitation of Cowley. By a Youth of Thirteen*. Norman Ault feels confident that *The River* is actually an early achievement and was composed not later than 1710.[31] These stanzas, perhaps written by a boy in his teens, are profounder than many a grown-up middling poet's performance.

The apostrophe of Stanza One enumerates various qualities of the river – any river, it seems, – giving not only a justification for celebrating it but also, as the rest of the poem testifies, an indirect criticism of the fairly limited uses to which poets conventionally put the river. For the strength of Pope's poem is the, literally speaking, cosmic deductions he makes when looking at, or thinking of, a river: presumptuous man has learned to scan the sky with complex instruments, but the sky itself does not consider it beneath its dignity to find a true reflection of itself in the limpid waters of the river. That is an ingenious exploitation of the traditional Neo-Classical mirror image, for usually the river just reflects the trees and hills on its banks. So the poem soon moves far away from the conventional utility/fertility approach of Stanza One. The paradox of the river, flowing and yet staying, which fascinated other poets than Pope, is extended so as to apply to man's relationship to life and the world at large. There may be a warning in the poem against making detours when simple, obvious, and, at the same time, impressive, solutions are close at hand: we can discover the greatness of the universe by just looking into a river instead of using complicated telescopes, etc.

The idea of the river as a symbol of humility and a means of taking the great ones down a peg, is pursued in the reflections on the past: common people mirrored themselves in the river and saw their fine faces, and young maids found flowers by its side instead of dressing up in gaudy clothes. Pope's intention in the poem is to contrast art and nature, sophistication and simplicity, his preference being with the latter alternative of the two pairs. The last stanza is a skilful summing up, illustrating the art versus nature theme with the observations on wine, and at the same time pointing back to the innocent nourishment of the river mentioned in the first stanza. Thus the poem is successfully rounded off.

Like Denham's *Cooper's Hill* and Dyer's *Grongar Hill*, Pope's *Windsor Forest* is recognizably topographical without being obtrusively or exclusively so: all three poems blend loco-descriptive and meditative strains, and, besides the locality, points of content and general structure are similar in Denham's and Pope's poems: the function of the Thames, the hunting-scene, and the allusions to history and religion. There is little doubt that, like many of his contemporaries, Pope looked upon *Cooper's Hill* as a prototype.

Around the year 1700, Pope moved with his parents from London to the village of Binfield in the district known as Windsor Forest. Audra and Williams emphasize the importance of understanding the etymological meaning of the word forest if one wants to grasp the associations surrounding the area: originally, a forest was a legal rather than a topographical term, referring to the land outside (*foris*) the common law. In such land, certain areas were reserved for the King's recreation, containing not only woods, but also lawns, fruitful pastures, and green retreats.[32]

After the conventional invocation of the Muse and the reference to Granville as the "commander" of the song, *Windsor Forest* gives a summary account of the whole landscape in terms of reconciled opposites (ll. 11-16). Items are juxtaposed (woodland and plain), and contrasted (hills and vales), elements are opposed (earth and water seem to fight against each other), and the whole panorama is an epitome of the world, "harmoniously confus'd". The resulting state is not chaos but "Order and Variety" – *concordia discors*.

That is a brilliant setting of the scene, outlining the background for the later elaboration of selected aspects of it. Denham's opening in *Cooper's Hill* is not nearly so tightly woven, indeed, compared with Pope's wide-ranging but not overburdened account encompassed within six lines, Denham seems to take a long time to get into his stride.

The following lines are an amplification of the bold strokes of the introduction: there are groves, lawns, glades, trees, and hills, all standard features, and all behaving in the standard fashion: the trees "arise", the glades are "opening", and the plains "extend". Only in ll. 33-35 does the narrator say in so many words that he finds himself on a hill, a "more humble" mountain than "high Olympus", it is true, but still an elevated position that enables the poet to celebrate the landscape in a song. A fair sprinkling of "here"s and "there"s (ll. 17, 21, 23, and 24) give the impression that the beholder is moving his head, and the sense of space is conveyed by the "blueish Hills" of l. 24 – the colour recommended by painters for the hills of the distant horizon – and the plains that "extend" (l. 23). There is a breeze blowing, for the groves are "waving" (l. 17), and – a more unique and precise observation and an original twist of a stock expression – the corn forms a "waving prospect", which creates a *clair-obscur* effect analogous to the "chequer'd Scene" (again an imperceptible, but elegant change of the conventional formulation "chequer'd shade"), where the light is now admitted, now excluded (l. 18). The play of light is consistently referred to by its effects: "opening glades" (l. 21), the thin trees shunning each other's shadows (l. 22), the full light on the plain (l. 23), and the hills partly hidden in the clouds (l. 24). The heath (l. 25) is a kow-tow to topography, but, with his characteristic elegance, Pope incorporates that unusual ingredient smoothly not only into the picture, but also into the *concordia discors* atmosphere of the landscape: although "wild", the heath is not all "sable waste" (l. 28): it is set off with "tufted Trees and springing Corn" (l. 27),

And 'midst the Desart fruitful Fields arise (l. 26).

The forbidding barrenness of the heath is toned down, and Pope makes it a valued member of the landscape features.

It will have appeared that Pope's description of the landscape has an unmistakable touch of the grace beyond the reach of art, and in his treatment of colour he scores his triumph: instead of stating that the "hues" of the scene are pleasant, he thinks up words that suitably describe the desired nuance, the poet emulating the painter's use of his palette: "russet Plains" (l. 23), "blueish Hills" (l. 24), "purple Dyes" (l. 25), "sable Waste" (l. 28), "Blushing Flora paints th'enamel'd Ground of the panorama" (l. 38), and, of course, the passage describing the colours of the different fish (ll. 141-46). Indeed, so skilful is Pope's handling of colours that even the conventional "verdant" (l. 28) tends to become a precise observation because it is used as a generic term to indicate the indomitable luxuriance "'midst the Desart" (l. 26). Characteristically, the "non-landscape" of the past (ll. 43 et seq.) is virtually devoid of colour:

A dreary Desart and a gloomy Waste (l. 44),

a scene whose uniformity was barren because it was not based on variety, one without changes of light, and showing no sign of cultivation.

The past which Pope outlines in ll. 40 et seq. is far from being a Golden Age, and the landscape of these lines is an extension of the disposition and attitude of the rulers of that time. That is the *Penshurst* motif again, but of course Pope was not content merely to parrot a Neo-Classical commonplace. For one thing, Pope intimates that nature is always benevolent and that it is the sovereign's duty to see to it that his subjects can enjoy nature's bounty to the full. Secondly, the lines about the misuse of nature and the concomitant cultural regression throw the opening landscape description into relief: Queen Anne's reign is a period of serene harmony, accordingly the landscape shows up a perfect *concordia*. For peaceful development is a key theme of *Windsor Forest:* the 1713 version was occasioned by the Peace of Utrecht, and the balance of tensions displayed in the first fifty lines of the poem was intended to serve as a model for good government.

Rivers play a prominent part in the poem: the Thames runs below Windsor Forest, and the stag-hunt is associated with one of the tributaries of the "great Father of the British Floods", the Lodona. In lines 337-48, the Thames is compared to a king to whose throne all the tributaries pay allegiance, the implication of course being that in God's design it is natural, even necessary, to have a peaceful arrangement of allegiances and supremacies. The hierarchic structure is universally acknowledged, and the resulting *cliens/patronus* relationship safeguards social equilibrium. That is another of the poem's subdued assertions of a social parallel. And in ll. 219-34, there is a long apostrophe to the Thames, which is exalted to the positions of the ruler of the landscape, surveying the woods and the other beauties "on thy Banks". The idea is that of a benevolent monarch presiding over his well-ordered state, but the unmistakable martial allusions dropped on several occasions, eg

And future navies on thy Shores appear (l. 222)

and

Bear *Britain's* Thunder, and her *Cross* display
To the bright Regions of the rising Day (ll. 387-88)

leave us in no doubt that we have to do with a ruler both in name and fact.

Quite naturally, the main interest centres on the part of the Thames running past Windsor and its immediate neighbourhood, not only because of its

> sequester'd Scenes,
> The bow'ry Mazes and the surrounding Greens (ll. 261-62),

but also because that region has been consecrated by what Cowley and "Majestic Denham sung" (l. 271). And the apotheosis of the locality and the tribute to Pope's great predecessors, whom, it is implied, Pope feels unworthy to emulate, are ingeniously intertwined with an invitation to Granville, the man to whom the poem is addressed:

> Make Windsor Hills in lofty Numbers rise
> And lift her Turrets nearer to the Skies (ll. 287-88).

The river Lodona is exploited for another familiar *topos*, that of the mirror image:

> Oft in her Glass the musing Shepherd spies
> The headlong Mountains and the downward Skies,
> The watry Landskip of the pendant Woods,
> And absent Trees that tremble in the Floods;
> In the clear azure Gleam the Flocks are seen,
> And floating Forests paint the Waves with Green.
> Thro' the fair Scene rowl along the ling'ring Streams,
> Then foaming pour along, and rush into the Thames (ll. 211-19).

Once more, we must admire the way that Pope uses a convention and at the same time rises above it. In the crystal surface of the water – and, exceptionally, "rowl" does not spell confusion – the configurations are distinctly reflected, even such as are at a distance. The river assembles the items, just as a Claude glass would do. And the "Scene" is a "watry" landscape, seen, not from a hill, yet somehow from above, by the shepherd on the bank. The motif is arranged and rounded off as if for a painting. The reciprocity idea is hinted at: the water reflects the scene, and, seen in the limpid surface of the water, the mountains must look "headlong" and the "Skies" felt to have a "downward" movement. In their turn, the landscape objects "paint the Waves with Green".

The composition of *Windsor Forest* and the complimentary reference to Denham are evidence that Pope intended to make landscape the basic theme of the poem. The scene contains both English and Arcadian ingredients, and it is organized around the natural harmonizing of dissimilar items: woods (whose constituent parts are in discord), hills, valley, plains, earth, and water. The alternate tides of the river are further proof of ever present and ubiquitous opposites that are ultimately reconciled: the "slow rowl" proves that, on a higher level, the outcome is calm and balance, and the idea of harmony is extended to characterize the relationship between a monarch's rule and the mode of his "landscape".

Dennis is obviously unfair when he sees *Windsor Forest* as a poem dealing mainly with hunting and shooting, and it is difficult to agree with his objection that local colour is missing. He is deplorably wrong when he says that the poem lacks design, and the criticism of the "thousand common Landskips" is patently absurd. *Windsor Forest* is, in the pithy phrasing of Jeffrey Spencer, "a metaphor of the theme order in variety".[33] It is also, mainly owing to Pope's masterly use of colour and his original treatment of conventional landscape features, the finest illustration we have of the early 18th century conception of the Horatian maxim *ut pictura poesis* within landscape literature.

6

John Dyer's poem *Grongar Hill* is remarkable right from the beginning: it opens with a short prelude where the poet is still at the foot of the hill, deliberating with himself whether to use *pictura* or *poesis* as the medium in which to celebrate ir. Dyer was also known to his contemporaries as a painter, though it is not known whether he ever tried his hand at Grongar Hill. That beginning makes the poem more of a personal testimony than is usual with the landscape genre, and that tone is perceptible on and off in the moralizing as the poem goes along.

Before going into detail with his description, Dyer takes a bird's-eye-view of the landscape as seen from the top of the hill: thanks to the transparency of the air, he is given an undimmed view of it. True to the role of a conventional beholder, he begins by taking a prospect: "old castles on the cliff" (l. 49), "the spires" (l. 51), and "the mountain-heads" (l. 54). Next, looking downwards, he becomes cognizant of what is between himself and the horizon: various sorts of trees, "a long and level lawn" (l. 66) and "Towy's Flood" (l. 69). The time motif is appropriately introduced in connection with the "ancient towers" crowning the "brow" of the hill; they are now "the raven's bleak abode"; yet, "time has seen...this broken pile complete, big with vanity of state" (ll. 84-87). From then on, the poem shuttles regularly between observation and reflection, the latter consisting of general moral maxims as well as personal considerations.

Thus, the rivers, which are introduced immediately after the towers (ll. 93-102), are used to inculcate a moral lesson: their various journeys to the deep is "like human life to endless sleep" (l. 97). This part of the poem ends with a recognition that "Nature's verdure" is arranged so as to instruct and delight: "to instruct our wandering thought" (l. 100) and to "disperse our cares away" (l. 102).

The following sections of the poem have a more stanzaic structure, each division containing an observation plus a reflection, often of a personal kind. When looking at the distant "mountain's southern side", for example, the poet comes to think that "distant dangers" always seem negligible, and that we are apt to "mistake the future's face" (ll. 120-21). And he hopes that he may always be able to "content me with an humble shade" (l. 131), for he is perfectly comfortable "as on the mountain-turf I lie" (l. 138). Thus, gradually, we are approaching the theme of the poem, *bene qui latuit vixit*: "Quiet" and "Pleasure" are "close allied" (l. 154) in rural retreat.

Grongar Hill contains a good many points of technical and conceptual relevance that deserve closer scrutiny. Thus, in the second line of the poem, the Muse of Painting is said to be resting on a hill on a "purple evening", which may be an allusion to peaceful sunset pictures. At the same time, it is symptomatic that evening is seen in terms of colours and not, for example, in terms of stillness. However, the poet's account of what he sees from the hilltop takes place in mid-day, "while Phoebus riding high/Gives lustre to the land and sky" (ll. 11-12): the brilliance of the light is referred to, not the discomfort of the heat. Dyer's approach is the opposite of that of his landscape colleagues, who would chiefly be preoccupied with the pastoral reminiscence, shade. In both instances, Dyer's painter's eye makes him deviate from conventional associations surrounding evening and mid-day. And in l. 9, he begs the Muse of Painting to grant him "thy various hues". The characterization of the trees later in the poem (ll. 57 et seq.) shows that his prayer was heard: the gloomy pine, the blue poplar, the yellow beach, and the sable yew are specimens seen by a man who has a well-developed eye for nuance.

However, the Muse of Painting can give him little assistance when he is resting at the foot of the hill. That landscape is not as interesting as a prospect, and, characteristically, it does not lead to any reflections. The place at the foot of the hill is purely pastoral with its "mossy cells" and "silent shade" (ll. 15 & 17); the items are nondescript, unstructured and devoid of independence. The *stylus humilis* of a pastoral is matched by the humble physical position of the protagonist.

The ascent of the hill (ll. 27 et seq.) is the first turning-point of the poem: there is a change from past reminiscence to present action, from passive contemplation to active movement, and from generalizations to concrete sensation. The reader is made to feel that the poet makes a leap out of convention into reality.

The description of the ascent is supremely successful in at least three respects. First, vertical movement is expressed in terms of horizontal extension: the mounting is not described directly, but conveyed by the poet's watching of the ever-widening horizon. The repetitions of "still it widens" give an impression of vertiginous height and speed, which latter feature is emphasized by the "vistas shooting beams of day" (l. 30). Secondly, the ascent yields a sense of greater perspective and an awareness of colour, which means that approaches known from other landscape poems are intimated even before the poet reaches the hilltop. In spite of his breathless speed, he becomes cognizant of the *chiaroscuro* under the trees on the slopes, the "chequer'd sides" (l. 27), and he takes the time to draw the first moral parallel to the configurations of the panorama: it is the unhappy fate of "all height" (l. 35) sooner or later to have to "withdraw their summits from the skies" – a realization that is particularly pertinent to someone who is working his way upwards in hilly country. The climber is beginning to acquire a sense of proportion and perspective, thanks to his comparatively elevated position, and he finds it natural to transfer it to the human scene.

Thirdly, already during the poet's climbing of the mountain, the items of the surrounding world are recognized as having independent existence, indeed as being autonomous agents. There are no verbs of perception (like "see" or "hear"). The landscape is the object of the beholder's vision, but it is also its own subject, so to speak. The beholder is an observing agent, but what he perceives is a landscape which has assumed its form independently, without his mediation. The movement seems to be just as much from the objects towards his eyes as *vice versa*. The objects are furnished with an inherent dynamism as if to suggest conscious reactions, sometimes even friendly moves, on their part: the mountain "withdraws" from the sky, the spires "rush" (l. 51), the trees "ride", and the rivers not only "run" (l. 93) – which is perhaps less unusual – but they also "go/A various journey into the deep" (ll. 96-97). Even more surprisingly, the vista, too, is an agent: the prospect "spreads" and "adds a thousand woods" (l. 38), it "widens" (l. 39), and "sinks the newly-risen hill" (l. 40). The initiative rests entirely with phenomena outside the narrator, and the grammatical construction implies equality and, simultaneously, reciprocity between the beholder and his surroundings.

Throughout, the poem is characterized by a subtle blend of respect for, and transgression of, the Neo-Classical landscape tradition. The poet makes it clear that what he sees from the hilltop is a landscape – the word occurs several times in the poem. Yet the domination aspect is absent, for the items are stubbornly themselves. Instead, the beholder "reads…the face of nature" (ll. 45) as if he were looking at a portrait. The panorama consists of, among other things, a lawn, a hill, and a river, and a contrast is established between the lawn, which represents a variegated spectrum in the sunshine (uniformity amidst variety), and the dark hill, which is away from the beams of Apollo. The reader is continuously and discreetly reminded of the contrast between vertical and horizontal: "the fountain's fall, the river's flow" (l. 105), and "the woody valley" versus "the windy summit". However, the oppositions are more than merely directional: "the pleasant seat" and "the ruined tower" are juxtaposed (l. 109), as are "the naked rock" and "the shady bower" (l. 110). Thus Dyer gives us to understand that *discordia* is operative on many levels: size, comfort, utility, and degree of civilization, and since the whole picture breathes harmony; the range of *concordia* must be all-embracing.

Dyer does nothing by halves, and yet he does not seem to press his point. Another example occurs at l. 123, when he comments on the specious attraction of "yon summits"; inevitably, the account contains a moral warning, yet, for all the familiarity of the lesson, it is remarkable how aptly Dyer manages to characterize the nastiness of the summits in one line (126) without overburdening it, by simultaneously referring to a bunch of the qualities that were most obnoxious to landscape poets: "barren", ie not amenable to vegetation and cultivation, "brown", ie showing the negation of colourful variety, and "rough", ie difficult to climb and uncomfortable to recline on.

Like all landscape poets, Dyer was enamoured of trees, and the host of trees he catches sight of from the hilltop prompts the first value judgement of the poem: "beautiful" (l. 58). It is in line with Dyer's descriptive technique that the qualifiers of the trees are partly conventional: "slender fir" (l. 61), "sturdy oak" (l. 61), partly original, testifying to a talent of rendering in words a precise visual experience: "poplar blue" (l. 59), "yellow beech" (l. 60). The trees are not only such as create an atmosphere (pine and yew), which means that they are part and parcel of the connotative inventory of the scene, but also such as it would actually be possible to see on the slopes (beech and fir). We see the same compliance with the requirements of verisimilitude in the reference to the animals inhabiting the "dark hill" (ll. 77-83): they are neither dragons nor vampires, but ravens, toads, and adders. They are not allowed to make their appearance and are intended to induce a mood of weirdness in order to facilitate the reader's grasp of the moral parallel. But the point is that they are not improbable in the context.

Dyer's exceptional ability to blend tradition and originality also becomes manifest in the discreetly pastoral strain that he adopts towards the end of *Grongar Hill* (ll. 139 et seq.). After "reading" the landscape, he reclines and begins to take notice of sounds and smells: the gentle breeze (l. 139), the murmur of the river (l. 141), the shepherd's pipe (l. 142), the warbling of the birds (l. 144), and the fragrance of the flowers borne on the wind (l. 140). Thus, by the very structure of his poem, Dyer shows that the other senses are secondary to sight. And the pastoral heritage, which is only motivated by tradition, is introduced at a time when the poet has begun to talk about sounds, which means that he does not have to see the shepherd or devote too much attention to him. Moreover, the description of sounds and smells are run-of-the-mill formulations – the more striking when compared with the original visual observations – such as "the wanton Zephyr" and the "murmuring waters", spiced with newly formed observations, such as the comparison of Zephyr to a bird who "perfumes his wings" (l. 140) in the valley, after which it soars above the mountain tops.

Time and again, Dyer delights his readers with his perspicacity: the "proud castles" are "towering" not towards but "in" the skies (l. 50), just as the "windy summit" rushes not towards but "on" the sky (l. 108). The lawn (l. 63) is as colourful and gay as "the opening dawn"; the *tertium comparationis* of this Dylan Thomas-like formulation is the intensity and freshness of the colours, a circumstance that is likely to appeal to a painter's eye. For of course what distinguished Dyer from the common herd of Neo-Classical landscapists in verse is the felicitous union of the painter's eye and the poet's pen: only an observer familiar with pictorial technique would have been able to compare the church spires to "ascending fires" (l. 52) or would have seen that the (probably horizontal) meadows in the middle ground are "streaks" (l. 118). Also, a painter would naturally observe how the growths on the mountain sides are "gilded" by the last rays of the setting sun (l. 120). But again, Dyer's mastery becomes particularly impressive when he surpasses convention by suggesting it; for instance, it is a moral commonplace for landscape poets to assert that worldly power and influence are short-lived, and we meet the thought in *Grongar Hill* too. However, to put the idea across, Dyer says that worldly power is like "a sunbeam on a winter's day" (l. 90), an unusual phrasing, yet entirely compatible with the atmosphere of the poem, in which Dyer, the painter, has shown great sensibility to the influence of "Apollo's beams" on the colours and freshness of the scene. Consequently, the nadir must be "a winter's day", when the sun is at best low and when the outlines of the landscape can be blurred by fog or even snow.

Dyer's precise and straightforward use of colours throughout the poem becomes the more striking when we consider that he renders height, length, width, and distances metaphorically. Earlier we saw how the idea of ascent was conveyed by the increased horizontal extension of the view. By the same token, he imparts an impression of the height of the "ancient towers" (l. 71) by imagining a downward glance from them: the view is vertiginous. And later in the poem (l. 119) he does not state in so many words that the stream in the distance looks narrow; he says "methinks it could be crossed in a step".

That is consonant with Dyer's treatment of time in *Grongar Hill*. Once more, the description of the ascent of the hill early in the poem is a prototype, for time is not indicated by precise physical measurements but is considered in terms of the activity that is going on, ie it is the Bergsonian *durée*. On the large scale, the passing of time is shown by the ruins that are the remains of former glory. Actually, the poet can sense the passing of time by witnessing the decay going on before his eyes: "huge heaps are crumbling" (l. 85). The moral conclusion is obvious: time, the great leveller "level lays the lofty brow" (l. 85). But the different time rhythms of the beholder's personal experience are also conveyed by his activities. For example, at l. 103 there is another turning-point in the poem: the beholder rouses himself from his reverie and looks afresh at his surroundings. The conventional approach would be to use the cliché of the wandering eye, or to assure the reader that a host of items were crowding on the poet's sight. However, Dyer proceeds differently: the swift movement of his head is indicated by the breathless enumeration, in the following lines, of all the features that meet his eye. The inventory is made abrupt by the repetition of the definite article and the addition of a succinct qualification, and by the fact that sometimes two items are packed into one line. Accordingly, the "ever new" of l. 103 is perfectly justified. Significantly, the word time is not used, either in the preceding interval of passive reflection or in the present scene of hasty looking around; yet the contrast between the two durations becomes abundantly clear. We may compare the technique with the one used at l. 118, where the poet intimates that he is turning his head by giving us the "content" of the movement: the meadows "cross my eye".

The human parallel is never lost sight of. The ivy supports the decrepit walls and prevents them from falling. The use of the personal pronoun ("her", l. 74) and the metaphor "arms" in the same line, hint discreetly at some kind of human, perhaps loving, partnership, the walls shielding the ivy from the winds, whose influence is perceptible in many passages of the poem. Thus, the mutual dependence and support which obtain between pairs of larger items (river and hill) also manifest themselves on a more modest scale: the landscape as a whole shows evidence of a close co-operation. Also, the walls fall down owing to their advanced age: they are "hoary" and "mouldered" (l. 83), two qualifiers that illustrate the pervasive correspondence between animate and inanimate, in spite of the physical separation of the two worlds.

In the moralizing passage, the conventional attitudes and the personal testimony may, at the beginning, come to seem at odds with each other. Dyer repeatedly stresses the moral familiar from Neo-Classical landscape poems that life should not be centred on external trappings and that human-built edifices invariably end up as monuments of man's foolish presumption: castles become ruins, whereas mountains persist. It is true that Dyer tackles the problem more elegantly than most of his colleagues, for he makes the items and incidents of the poem convince us by their mere presence instead of raising schoolmasterly forefingers. But there is no warrant in the poem for the statement (l. 84) that "time lifts the low". However, the concluding moral (ll. 120 et seq.) has a public as well as a private aspect: "still we tread the same old way" (l. 127) and "the present is still a cloudy day" (l. 128) are traditional expressions of the conception of the world as a vale of tears. That is made even gloomier when seen in the light of the section that precedes, for there we are informed that there is little good in store for us from the future: dangers are lying ahead, and we can delude ourselves with hope only for a limited span of days.

However, Dyer's own problem is a different one, as appears from the more personal tone of the next passage: "may I with myself agree" (l. 120) may indicate that he is aware of a potential conflict within himself between two sides of his temperament, the conflict being liable to be resolved by a kind of spiritual *concordia*. He realizes that "passions" (inside him) and "wishes" (pointing beyond him) (l. 132), which are, characteristically "rolling", may present dangers to his mental equilibrium.

At the very end of the poem, Dyer ingeniously connects the public moral and the private one by implying that if everyone would live up to the ideals of Quiet and Peace – his own favourites – pleasure and harmony would be bound to ensue. The whereabouts of Peace are neither "the lofty door" (l. 145) nor the "marble floor" (l. 149), places that may be subsumed under the designation "the domes of Care" (l. 151). Quiet, which is one of the conditions of inward peace, does not step on marble floors, but moves in rural retirement, or amidst grass and flowers (l. 152) and meadows and mountains (l. 153). If we remember the localities celebrated by the poet as the poem goes along, we realize that he has found the quiet he so ardently desires – for a time, at least. This quiet is accompanied with pleasure (l. 154), and the poem rings out with Quiet as the agent, hearing the singing of the thrush as the only sound in the perfect stillness of the groves of Grongar Hill (ll. 156-58). Again, a varied uniformity.

Grongar Hill balances between reality and imagination, but the reality is that of a recognizable English landscape rather than a strictly topographical account of the view from the top of Grongar Hill. Owing to its effortless command of descriptive technique, the poem represents the Neo-Classical tradition of landscape poetry at its zenith, showing features in their full bloom which we have found in embryo in earlier poets, and bringing tendencies and conventions to an elegant climax. Technically speaking, we have come a long way from Denham's *Cooper's Hill*.

Dyer's poem *The Country Walk* appeared in 1726, in Savage's *Miscellany* together with five other poems by Dyer, among them the first version of *Grongar Hill* in the form of a Pindaric ode. It is testimony of the powerfulness of the Neo-Classical landscape convention that the title, *The Country Walk*, heads a poem which is to some extent structured as a conventional Neo-Classical landscape poem. Besides, Grongar Hill features as one of the landscape features. It is true that there are more animals in it than in a genuine landscape poem, and there is a long excursus on the fate of the poet, during which reflection (ll. 41-82) the narrator is lying down. Yet the narrator only partly keeps his promise of the early lines:

I am resolved, this charming day
In the open field to stray (ll. 5-6),

and no attempt is made to shape a coherent picture of the items he sees before ascending the hill. There are "shady vales and mountains bright" (l. 20), "thousand flaming flowers" in the fields (l. 24), and a "rivulet, gliding smoothly by" (l. 30). However, the scarcity of colours in this part of the poem is striking.

"Looking at landscape" was inextricably bound up with the beholder's elevated position. However, the ascent of *The Country Walk* is described with considerably less elegance than in *Grongar Hill*:

Up Grongar Hill I labour now...(l. 100),

and the account is as cumbersome as the climbing seems to have been though the hill is the same in both cases. Significantly, it is only after the ascent has been achieved that the poem reaches some degree of unity, and Dyer expresses himself with remarkable succinctness the moment he is on safe ground within the tradition: he "descries" nature's "magazines" that lie before him (ll. 104-05), and he leaves it to the syntax to intimate the taking in of the objects at a glance, accompanied by swift turnings of his head:

> Temples!- and towns! – and towers! – and woods!
> And hills! – and vales! – and fields! – and floods! (ll. 106-7).

And when the sun is setting, Dyer's painter's eye does not desert him:

> And yonder hill remoter grows,
> Or dusky clouds do interpose (ll. 142-43).

However, the scene Dyer surveys in *The Country Walk* not only includes more human beings, it also has fewer landscape details than is customary. Also, it must be admitted, it has a good many commonplace formulations of the type "some flood/That sweetly murmurs in the wood" (ll. 47-48), and they are not thrown into relief by such elegancies as we meet in *Grongar Hill*. The landscape is sometimes pedantically topographical (the view from Grongar Hill), sometimes slightly idealized. Strange to say, the prospect is not identical with the one we know from *Grongar Hill*, for it is as if the narrator of *The Country Walk* is at pains to include as many details from "nature's magazines" as possible: the gardens, the terraces, and the lakes – such particularities are entirely absent from *Grongar Hill*.

The significant fact about *The Country Walk* is the peculiarities of the reflections sparked off in the poem. The speculations about the poet's lot are made before the ascent, which is in itself unusual because they do not grow organically out of observations of the landmarks of the scene, and they have a pronouncedly personal undertone. Also, *The Country Walk* is a more restless poem than *Grongar Hill*, which may sound paradoxical in view of the fact that the poet lies on his back during one fourth of the poem. But "the poet's busy brain" (l. 52) works the more intensely when he disregards the charms of the countryside. And throughout the poem he takes great care to keep the reader informed of the least movement he makes. His enumeration of those details, and of others, enhances the atmosphere of restlessness.

The Country Walk is deficient in structure, both as a piece of poetry and as a landscape poem. On the other hand, it shows the scope of the landscape genre because Dyer uses it to turn the projection-of-a-mood convention upside down: he acknowledges the charm of the day he has chosen to sally forth (l.5), and the "face of Nature" does not leave him cold. But the beauty and harmony of *res* only contribute to casting his own sadness into relief. There is an undertone of despair in his comment on the gentle flow of the brook:

> A rivulet, gliding smoothly by;
> Which shows with what an easy tide
> The moments of the happy glide (ll. 30-32).

This contrasts sharply with the poet's ceaseless roving in the landscape without finding peace or genuine pleasure anywhere. The climbing of the hill is not the response to an alluring fascination, rather it is a manifestation of his restless melancholy:

> Up Grongar Hill I labour now
> And reach at last its bushy brow (ll. 100-01),

which differs considerably from the eagerness with which he climbs the same hill in *Grongar Hill*:

> About his chequer'd sides I wind…(ll. 27 et seq.).

Nature is happy in *The Country Walk*, and the human beings who appear in the poem as her sons and kinsmen are also serene and satisfied – at least Dyer thinks so. But personally he pines for "Clio far away" (l. 67), and he feels that the day would be "bless'd" if only Clio were with him (ll. 154-56). Whether Clio is the conventional pastoral pseudonym for his Beloved, or whether the reference is actually to the Muse of History, remains obscure. It is a fact that, already in his youth, Dyer found it immensely difficult to work persistently, and he made successive attempts, over a period of years, to finish *The Ruins of Rome*. Incidentally, the opening lines of *The Ruins of Rome* speak in disparaging terms about the Grongar Hill poems:

> Enough of Grongar, and the shady dales
> Of winding Towy, Marlin's fabled haunt,
> I sung inglorious. Now the love of arts,
> And what in metal or in stone remains
> Of proud Antiquity, through various realms
> And various languages and ages famed
> Bears me remote...[34]

The Country Walk is a kind of companion piece to *Grongar Hill*, a more topographical and also a more personally tinged variant of the theme of the latter poem. It belongs to the landscape genre, but it distinguishes itself from other, more orthodox, specimens of the "kind" in several important respects, not least the fact that the beholder longs for the company of another person to such an extent that he is impatient with the scene that spreads before his eyes.

CHAPTER ELEVEN

THE CRUMBLING OF THE CANON

1

During the period under consideration in this book, the achievements of science and philosophy were beginning to have considerable implications for aesthetics. Many of the opinion-forming people – including authors and critics – had one or more branches of science as their hobby, which meant that they would familiarize themselves with the findings, and perhaps also the methods, of science. This had two significant corollaries, viz. a change in the attitude to Antiquity and a change in the conception of imitation

Those Neo-Classicists who really familiarized themselves with Horace's *Ars poetica* found to their dismay that the work was far from being a model of clarity and precision. But also Aristotle and Homer were obviously in a disadvantageous position when matched with philosophers and scientists like Descartes, Locke and Newton, who took their starting-point in what was given and who could point to immediately comprehensible and palpable results of their thinking. The empirical approach of the "modern" thinkers encouraged people's interest in, and preoccupation with, what was given and present, with their immediate surroundings. At first glance, that tendency could not but prove beneficial to the development of the landscape genre. But it was a double-edged sword, for it inevitably reduced the significance of the thinkers of the distant past, and of their assumptions and findings.

The writing had been on the wall for a long time. Cowley's *Proposition for the Advancement of Experimental Philosophy*, published in 1661, advocates the foundation of an academy to promote the cause of "experimental philosophy". In the Preface, he performs a veritable egg dance when expatiating on the teaching to be given in such an institution: on the one hand, we should certainly study the works of the Ancients carefully, but on the other, we should not hesitate to improve on their conclusions wherever possible:

> This therefore being laid down as a certain foundation, that we must not content our selves with that Inheritance of Knowledge which is left to us by the labour and bounty of our Ancestors, but seek to improve those very grounds, and adde to them new and greater Purchases; it remains to be considered by what means we are most likely to attain the ends of this virtuous Covetousness.[1]

And those "means" are worth looking at a little more closely. It is not "the solitary and active Contemplation of Nature, by the most ingenious Persons living, in their own private Studies"[2] that will lead us to our goal. Rather, we must be instructed by "sensible objects" (by which Cowley means objects liable to be perceived by the senses), for if we do not choose such guides, both our "Reasoning Faculty" and our "Fancy" will dream and produce

> nothing but either deformed Monsters, or at best pretty Mermaids. 'Tis like Painting by Memory and Imagination, which can never produce a Picture to the Life.[3]

Cowley's ideal, then, is imitation rather than *mimesis,* and his statements were to prove seminal: the scientific attitude that arose in the 17th century puts the emphasis on things rather than on words, on "sensible Objects" rather than on airy speculation.

Literary criticism was more conservative than either philosophy or science. Until the end of the 17th century, the Ancients remained what Hazard calls "des dieux protecteurs",[4] and though their authority was considerably impaired during the first decades of the 18th century, most writers and critics were hesitant to discard them altogether. Other critics were more intransigent. That appears clearly from the interesting stock-taking which Blackmore undertakes in his *Essay upon Epic Poetry* from 1716. His principal object is to attack the Neo-Classical rules for epic poetry (to which his own epics did not conform very strictly!), and at one point in the essay he gives vent to his impatience at the fact that Aristotle's yoke has been thrown off within philosophy only:

> They had as great Reason to have proceeded to the Examination of his Rules in the Art of Poetry, & to have made Enquiry if those Rules were settled on better Foundations. But it is not the Authority of the greatest Masters, but solid and convincing Evidence that must engage our Belief and make us subscribe to any Maxims in any Art or Science whatsoever.[5]

The thought is no less interesting than the choice of words: by borrowing terms from science, Blackmore indicates the desirability of applying scientific criteria within the field of art as well. It is true that he does not specify in what the "solid and convincing Evidence" consists, but it is made abundantly clear that it is something that differs radically from submissive acceptance of the rules inherited from the Ancients.

It is a well-known fact that portraiture was one of the most popular Neo-Classical genres of painting. Owing to its possibilities of making the models "heroic", it had evident affinities with high-ranking literary genres like tragedy and epic poetry. But there was more to it than that. In *Creation*, Blackmore extols the talent of the portrait painter in the following words:

> Behold the strong emotions of the mind
> Exerted in the eyes, and in the face design'd.
> Such is the artist's wondrous power, that we
> Even pictur'd souls and colour'd passions see,
> Where without words (peculiar eloquence)
> The busy figures speak their various sense.
> What living face does more distress or woe,
> More finish'd shame, confusion, horror, know,
> Than what the masters of the pencil show?[6]

The artist's products equal the "living face" in regard to expressiveness, indeed surpasses it in that the portrait's emotions are more "finish'd" or perfect. That is of course an instance of the conventional tribute paid by poets to painters who were praised for having transcended the limitations imposed by their medium. But the principle of imitation is also involved: in one of the lines preceding the above quotation, Blackmore says that the painter's "strokes affect with Nature's self to vie", and the "Nature" which is imitated is "Reality". So it is not a matter of *mimesis*, which endeavoured to avoid objectionable details, and the point is that the procedure adopted by portrait painters would very often work against the imitative principles according to which the artist would stamp his material with a replica of the universal form: portraiture sets limits to the use of the Idea as the standard of imitation. That was bound to have consequences for landscape description.

Cowley, who was profoundly interested in science and therefore an interesting forerunner of theories that did not win full recognition until several decades after his death in 1667, has this to say about mimetic theory in one of his late odes, *To the Royal Society:*

> Who to the life an exact piece would make,
> Must not from others work a Copy take;
> No, not from Rubens or Vandike;
> Much less content himself to make it like
> Th'Idæas and the Images which lie
> In his own Fancy or his Memory.
> No, he before his sight must place
> The natural and living face;
> The real object must command
> Each Judgement of his Eye, and Motion of his Mind.[7]

Since the ode is a tribute to The Royal Society, it is not surprising to find praise of the method which that august institution quickly became known to adopt: disinterested observation of the individual phenomenon, irrespective of the observer's "own Fancy or Memory", and scorning to take a copy from "others Work". The remarkable thing is that this approach should be held to be appropriate to the art of portrait painting as well, and, probably, a few decades later, to art as a whole. Conflicting statements on the subject of imitation complicated the critical discussion from the 1660s and onwards.

2

Dryden prefaced his translation – or rather paraphrase – of Dufresnoy's *De arte graphica* (1695) with an essay which he called *A Parallel between Poetry and Painting*. He confesses that the writing of it took him no more than "twelve mornings",[8] and he even adds the disclaimer that some readers may be surprised to learn that he spent so much time on it (p. 352). Little or no revision was made, and the work ends abruptly "without finishing the discourse" (p. 352). Dryden is well aware that something has been left unsaid, but pleads that it is of "too nice a consideration" for an essay (p. 352). He admits that he has only drawn half a portrait – the metaphor taken from one of the most distinguished genres of painting – "to the knees…the rest is left over to the imagination" (p.352). But he does not sketch the lines along which the imagination might profitably work, although he does not exclude the possibility – continuing his use of pictorial metaphors – that a better artist may finish the work "in the invention, design, and colouring" (p. 307). Finally, along with many deprecatory remarks on the last page of the essay, we also find the admission that "this *Parallel* is probably not very good" (p. 352).

It is indeed an unsystematic, inconsistent, and self-contradictory piece of writing – and for that very reason of considerable interest. It is surely symptomatic that Dryden should have prefaced a translation of a theoretical work on painting with an essay on the parallel of painting and poetry, for the emphasis of the original is not on the juxtaposition.

Dryden's essay is a torso, but it touches on all the points with which criticism was grappling in those years: idea, imitation, art versus nature, *prodesse/delectare*, rules, the hierarchy of genres, the stages of the genesis of a work of art, colour versus design, and the rivalry for priority between the Sister Arts. All those issues are postulated by Dryden to be relevant to *poesis* as well as to *pictura,* hence the title of the essay. But, more than that, the *Parallel* is a work reflecting a period of transition. What it actually boils down to is a marshalling of the pros and cons of the Neo-Classical tenets. On all the points referred to above, we witness a clash between orthodox and unorthodox ideas, and Dryden quotes profusely from both camps without definitely committing himself to either. The reader cannot help agreeing with Dryden when he sighs that "I have not engaged myself to any perfect method" (p. 307). As a faithful Neo-Classicist, he seeks support in the works of some predecessors, but he makes a somewhat random selection of sources, and the "various parts" are not smoothly integrated so as to make up "a perfect whole". *Discors* cannot be said to lead to *concordia,* which was in itself a liability.

Very early in the essay, Dryden gives a quotation running to several pages from the Italian critic Bellori's *Idea del Pittore, dello scultore & del'architetto* from 1664. Bellori, who was still alive when Dryden wrote the *Parallel,* was one of the great popularizers of the aesthetic theories of the Renaissance, and he had written a biography of the painter Poussin.

Dryden appropriates, rather uncritically, Bellori's version of the concept of Idea: ideas are "those first forms which derive from God's contemplation of His own excellencies" (p. 307), and poets and painters form in their minds a model of the superior beauties. Bellori believes that the Idea is a processed aggregate of sense impressions (a theory which has obvious implications for Lockean epistemology), and the Idea becomes "the original of those arts" (Bellori was concerned with painting and sculpture). The Idea is "that perfect and excellent example of the mind" (p. 298); later in the essay (p. 304) it is made clear that by "example" Dryden means "prototype" or "exemplar" (he uses this latter word). Since the beauties of a picture are derived from the idea of beauty lodged in the artist's mind, "nature" should be corrected to "what she ought to be, and what she was created" (p. 307), and somehow the idea "descends" and sets the standard for the artist's hand (p. 298). Neither Bellori nor Dryden seem to be aware that, in this theory, the artist to some extent imitates something inside himself. Dryden did realize that such ideality is "of little use in portraits"

(p. 307), but he does not suggest a different ideal of imitation. And he does not argue with Bellori but contents himself with saying, "I must needs say, there is something in the matter" (p. 304).

Quite logically, Dryden immediately afterwards draws on Philostratus' proem to *Figures*. The gist of Dryden's quotation is that painters should imitate "from the life". Philostratus stresses the desirability of pictures rendering the models' actual feelings and passions "to make the dumb as it were to speak" (p. 305). In Philostratus' theories, which are exclusively concerned with portraiture, there is room for neither ideas nor introspection, and Dryden quotes him with the same approval as that found in the passages he borrowed from Bellori. It is impossible to reconcile the two theories, and Dryden makes no attempt to bridge the gap. He is aware of the two-facedness of the concept of imitation, and he seems prepared to recognize two types, one valid for portraiture, the other applying to other genres, eg landscape description.

One maxim crops up repeatedly, and with little variation, in the *Parallel*, viz. "To imitate nature well in whatever subject is the perfection of both arts" (p. 322). However, "imitation", as used in the *Parellel* remains ambiguous. At one moment, it is asserted that life-like imitation gives pleasure, for "truth is the object of our understanding" (p. 324). But a few lines further down, the talk is about "not only imitation of nature, but of the best nature" (p. 325), ie a *la belle nature* approach. The thought is immediately followed up: poetry and painting "present us with images more perfect than the life of any individual" (p. 325). And yet again, the aim to be pursued in portraiture is "likeness" (p. 308), which means that portraits may have to be provided with "warts and moles" (p. 309), and only the artist's judgement decides how far to go in the way of heightening, for it is "the just images of nature which are the adequate pleasures of the mind" (p. 317). On the other hand, imitation in the sense of copying is rendered impossible by the recommendation that neither *pictura* nor *poesis* should include irrelevant matter, things "not proper or convenient to the subject", for everything "must be of use to carry on the main design" (p. 327).

Of course it is a truism to state that "as they (sc. *pictura* and *poesis*) are arts, they must have rules" (p. 318). More interestingly,

Dryden proceeds to draw a parallel with the method of Hippocrates within medicine, who managed to "arrive at that which is hitherto unknown, by that which is already known" (p. 319). The implication is that the rules of art are derived from practice, a procedure followed by Aristotle in his *Poetics*. However, in the same passage we find the prevalent Neo-Classical line of argumentation that rules are deduced from nature because she is always the same and "can never be contrary to herself" (p. 319). The task assigned by Dryden to rules is that of teaching us to see "when nature was imitated, and how nearly" (p. 322), for it can happen to any man that his judgement is misled by "depraved appetites and ignorance of the arts" (p. 322). Rules serve a didactic purpose, then; Dryden compares them to "a door to conduct you into a house" (p. 326). So rules are also aesthetic guides for the recipient of the work of art; how far they are helpful to the creative artist, remains obscure. In the early parts of the *Parallel,* when he leans heavily on Bellori, Dryden seems to be perfectly willing to let the artist obey the idea in his mind and transpose it into concrete form without any assistance from rules. At least, rules are not referred to once in that context. And towards the end of the essay, Dryden attacks rules indirectly by saying that the artist's own estimation was at least as important as, if not superior to, any extraneous rule. Correctness ought not to be an end *per se*: too much care often "takes away the spirit", and even if a work has few flaws, it may have an equally small number of beauties, and the recipient is left with "a dull correctness" (p. 351).

And in a detailed appreciation of Vergil's metaphors later in the *Parallel,* Dryden says that the *curiosa felicitas* – he uses the Horatian phrase – can be achieved by poet and painter alike, but in that situation rules are of no avail: "these hits of words a true poet often finds" (p. 349). The "hits" seem to present themselves spontaneously, so to speak, and the artist's judgement enables him to estimate their value and usefulness for his purpose: both painter and poet will know "when the colouring and expression are perfect, and then to think their work is truly finished" (p. 351). Words and colours are on the same level, it appears, and *je ne sais quoi* is the ultimate arbiter.

The delicate problem of *prodesse* versus *delectare* and the desired proportion of each in a work of art, is dealt with in several passages in the *Parallel* and, as in the case of other catchwords of contemporary aesthetics, Dryden does not commit himself to any unambiguous preference.

Dufresnoy had seen a parallel between painting and poetry in the following terms: painting was to please the eye, and poetry the mind. Dryden echoes him: "the chief design of poetry is to instruct" (p. 311) and painting is to please the eye. However, in the same passage he deplores the predilection of both poets and painters to please, and later he talks in disparaging terms about the merely entertaining elements of the two arts (p. 318), but when he recapitulates the paragraph in which that criticism occurs, he puts it like this: "one main end of poetry and painting is to please" (p. 318).

Similarities in the process leading to the creation of a work of art are commented on at some length. Dryden is obviously exhilarated by the realization that there exist ultimate authorities within the various branches of the two arts: Le Bossu for epic poetry, Dacier for tragedy, and Dufresnoy for painting. Dryden quotes profusely, disregarding the fundamental differences between the systems of Le Bossu and Dufresnoy: the former makes the didactic element the foundation stone of the whole edifice: a poet will start with a moral, which "is the groundwork of his instruction" (p. 310), after which he proceeds to "invent" the fable that accords with the moral. Dufresnoy's conception differs radically from that of Le Bossu in that he leaves out the moral aspect altogether, and Dryden seems to agree as heartily with him as with Le Bossu.

The structure of the *Parallel* confirms its author's confession that it was written in haste: there is no division into chapters, and the composition throughout is pretty rambling, the result being that the various parts are dealt with in a rather haphazard fashion. Ideas tumble over each other at breakneck speed; they are taken up for no obvious reason, dropped again, to be resumed a few pages later, and a line of thinking is started before a previous one has been brought to anything like a satisfactory conclusion. There are innumerable digressions, and more than one passage must have been committed to paper on a sudden impulse. For instance, the reader is mildly surprised to find, more than half-way through the essay, the following statement: "Perhaps the comparison between painting and poetry is altogether not so just as it might have been" (pp. 332-33). It is characteristic of the composition of the essay that this train of thought is immediately abandoned, and Dryden goes on to illustrate the parallel by juxtaposing the main figure of a picture and the hero of a tragedy (p. 333).

Dryden does not quote any contemporary English critic, and no critical problem is thoroughly or independently analysed. The greater part of the essay is made up of quotations and second-hand knowledge, and Dryden has no qualms about citing irreconcilable statements. This is no doubt partly due to hasty work, but there is more to it than that. The essay is actually a *tour d'horizon* of the problems facing criticism of art in the last decade of the 17th century. Dryden does not propound any fresh theories – the *Parallel* does not show him as an original critic – and yet he does not stand up as a staunch defender of the *status quo*. The content of the essay tells us more about the fluctuations of Neo-Classical critical theory than about the parallel between the Sister Arts. In its hesitant attitude towards, and discreet questioning of, some of the basic tenets of the Neo-Classical canon, it is a superb reflection of the aesthetic climate of the 1690s.

The *Parallel* is not a piece of sustained criticism, and it is the work of a man with a literary bias. That is proved by the framework of the essay and, equally importantly, by the exemplifications and digressions. To Dryden, as to many a contemporary *connoisseur*, the parallel consists in the fact that the problems which literary theory was engaged in, are assumed to be problems for pictorial theory as well. The starting-point is virtually always *poesis* and the headings under which literary criticism was wont to subsume its discussions are taken to be not only immediately applicable to, but the only ones imaginable within, the Sister Art. The parallel is pursued with relentless consistency, and painting is consequently placed in a strait-jacket where it is obviously sometimes pretty uncomfortable. It is emphatically a case of *ut poesis pictura*.

3

The Neo-Classical body of doctrines was liable to be undermined by tendencies inherent in the edifice right from the start. Even the most ardent spokesmen for the canon had to concede that there were flaws and imperfections. The incapacity of the rules to account for certain striking and commonly recognized beauties in a work of art was only one instance. Another was the element of subjectivity that was allowed to play an important part, also in the early stages of the establishment of the canon. A critic like Dennis, who was neither a rebel nor a revolutionary, promoted passion to be the prime agent in creator and recipient alike, and he did not at all see that position as being incompatible with the "rational" canon. It was only Pope, who disliked Dennis for personal reasons, who suggested that he was transgressing the bounds of decorum.

Earlier it was pointed out that Neo-Classicism admitted purely subjective and undefined concepts like grace, genius and *je ne sais quoi* as part and parcel of their canon. The Neo-Classicists were agreed that what is reasonable is that which explains and can be explained. Yet Boileau was able to speak enthusiastically about "ces sortes de Beauté...qu'il faut sentir et qui ne se prouvent point",[9] and in *Entretiens d'Ariste et d'Eugène* (1671) le père Bouhours extolled *je ne sais quoi* for its very irrationality: "incompréhensible et inexplicable...et si on le découvrait, il cesserait d'être ce qu'il est".[10]

The fact is that no really rational argumentation was ever attempted in order to support or define the categories of the canon. And, after all, what had Horace himself done? If his ramshackle poem *Ars poetica* was to be taken as an example of unity, clarity, and simplicity, where did that leave unity, clarity, and simplicity? He might be preaching one thing, but he was definitely practising another. So perhaps the *Ars poetica* was doubtful warrant for the Neo-Classical set of doctrines? If pursued, that thought might lead to the conclusion that arguments derived on the basis of ancient sources were not as strong as was desirable. Pope expressed the dilemma with his usual elegance:

> Horace still charms with graceful Negligence,
> And without Method talks us into Sense.[11]

Thus reason, combined with the considerable weight of personal preferences, came to undermine a structure that was praised for its rationality. Besides, the Reason and the Nature that Neo-Classicism worshipped were made vague by the extensive areas they were supposed to cover. The Neo-Classicists soon realized that they were actually best suited to characterize their antipodes, such as the absence of, or the deviation from, possible or conventional behaviour, or grotesque aberrations from reason. It was a far more complicated task to make a precise and balanced use of the two terms to, for example, assess the qualities of a work of art.

On the whole, the spirit of the rules was not one to promote simplicity and ease, but rather one that endeavoured to create difficulties in order to have the pleasure of resolving them. In the words of E.H. Gombrich,

> the sins to be avoided multiplied till the artist's freedom was confined to an ever narrowing space; all he dared to do in the end was insipid repetitions of safe solutions.[12]

To put it differently: a good many of the prescriptions were negative, which might of course satisfy the age's concern with the *difficulté vaincue*, but which certainly also caused them to be felt more and more as shackles. No critic tried to place the canon on a truly empirical foundation by walking in the footsteps of Aristotle and establishing a body of doctrines on the basis of analyses of the structure and content of contemporary or near-contemporary writing. Unfortunately there were no major works in recent English literature that could be held up as models truly worth imitating for their observance of the rules. It is also remarkable that there was no comprehensive English work of criticism which did for English literature what Boileau had done for French with the *Art poétique*, viz. legislate for poetics in general. Many late 17th century publications bore the title of *Ars poetica*, but the content was idiosyncratic advice supplemented with quotations of successful formulations worthy of imitation. Critics seemed to shy away from methodological treatment of eg lyrical poetry.

The canon in its entirety was rarely explicitly formulated, which might tempt critics to add to it or subtract from it according to their own preferences or aversions. For it is a striking fact that the body of rules was a restraint upon poets rather than critics. Sheer subjectivity within criticism was legitimate, and it was the critics' idiosyncracies that decided if and how far the poets had observed the rules.

A further complication was that if a writer adhered too unswervingly to one rule, he might be liable to transgress another: succinctness was part of decorum, but too compact formulations might lead to obscurity; attempts at elevation of style were admissible, but far-fetched grandeur was tantamount to bombast. The inevitable inference was that even an ostensibly rational system left some loopholes for the display of individual preferences: the ultimate responsibility rested with the poet.

Even the most favoured genre, the epic, caused some worries. For one thing, the concept of the hero was undergoing a change, and the tendency started well before the turn of the century. Secondly, some epic writers – especially, of course, the inferior ones – took their didactic responsibilities immensely seriously, initiating their readers not only in politics, but also in complex problems of battle strategies, abstruse scientific deliberations, or muddled accumulations of details. Thirdly, what was undeniably most popular with the readers was the supernatural or even mysterious element, which was, of course, suspicious on ideological grounds.

Drama was the field where the impact of the rules could be tested immediately. Already before the year 1700, Restoration dramatists, who played havoc with any rules inherited from the Ancients, unashamedly confessed that the box-office counted for more than finicky theoretical considerations. Besides, the classical canon had completely ignored comedy, which was a very popular genre in the last decade of the 17th century. In 1702, George Farquhar published *A Discourse Upon Comedy*, in which he said that the rules for English comedy do not lie

> in the Compass of *Aristotle*, or his followers, but in the Pit and Galleries…We have nothing to do with the models of *Menander* or *Plautus*, but must consult Shakespear, Jonson, Fletcher, and others,

who have kept the English stage alive "by Methods different from the Ancients".[13] Farquhar adds that it is a far more serious offence for a dramatist to connive at vice than to disobey the unities.[14] And if it was demonstrable that a play pleased the audience in spite of the fact that it flouted the rules – so much the worse for the rules.

More and more, critics tended to agree with the statement put forward by Sir William Temple as early as in 1692 in *Miscellanies, the Second Part:*

> The truth is, there is something in the Genius of Poetry, too Libertine to be confined to so many rules: and whoever goes about to subject it to such Constraints loses both its Spirit and Grace, which are very native, and never learned, even of the best Masters.[15]

"Spirit" and "Grace" are essential to poetry in Sir William's opinion, and they carry more weight than the "Constraints" of the rules. When even the master poets find it difficult to learn the secrets of grace and spirit, how much worse does the mediocre hack fare who suffers from the delusion that all he need to know is the rules. The conclusion, which Temple does not explicate, is that rules are expendable.

That the orthodox Neo-Classical canon tended to disintegrate soon after 1710 did not mean, of course, that gradually literature became a chaos of wildly incongruous elements. What happened was rather that the word "rule" was given novel content and came to refer to one or more of the structuring principles of a given art, for instance "those natural Rules of *Proportion* and *Truth*", of which Shaftesbury speaks so enthusiastically in his essay *Sensus Communis*.[16] And Dennis' symptomatic jump from "the Rules" to "Rules" in a passage from 1701 (*The Advancement and Reformation of Modern Poetry*) is another straw in the wind: we must be on our guard against chaos

> at a time when the Rules are neglected by some and slighted by others ... Rules are necessary, even in the inferior Arts, as in Painting and Musick.[17]

The remarkable thing is that, by and large, the old terminology lived on without anyone seeming to care that the content was no longer what it used to be. Few critics seem to have been aware of the extent to which they lived under a new dispensation. What early 18th century critics had to say about the landscape poem is shaped by pictorial theory and practice, but also by the matrix of the pastoral and eclogue theories, which had, in their turn, been established on the basis of deductions made from the works of Theocritus and Vergil.

4

One crucial point about the change that was becoming perceptible as early as the 1690s was that the concept of decorum was reinterpreted. Thus, *The Guardian* could say in 1713:

> Under natural pleasures I comprehend those which are universally suited, as well to the rational as the sensual part of our nature.[18]

It is true that the same passage issues a warning against "excesses of any kind" since "they are hardly to be esteemed pleasures, much less natural pleasures". Obviously, the Neo-Classical fear of the non-rational comes out clearly in those words, but it is significant that sensual and rational aspects are awarded parity of esteem. Of course, Neo-Classical fundamentalists like Rapin and Boileau had recognized the power of genius and the attractions of grace, but those imponderables were seen in terms of an ingenious superstructure of their rigid systems – grace, for example, being that which went beyond the rules – and to a smaller extent as concepts worth isolating for any intrinsic interest that they might possess.

No new canon of precepts was devised to replace the one that was becoming outdated, and, paradoxically, the cult of Homer reached unprecedented heights after the gradual collapse of the system that was assumed to be based not least on his poetry. "Feelings" gradually took precedence over rules. "Le sentiment", said Dubos, teaches us far more about the quality of a work of art than do all the critical treatises that endeavour to explain it. Indeed, the role of reason, in the process of evaluation, is reduced to accounting for the decisions of the feelings.[19] Thus, prescriptions deriving from the Ancients were supplanted by others that were no more exact or permanent, such as the instincts of the writers and the taste of the receiving public.

The idea of using a physiological faculty as the standard of evaluation is met with as early as in Quintilian, who talks about "quod sensitur latente judicis, velut palato".[20] The metaphorical sense is carried on in the European languages about the middle of the 17th century: taste, goût, gusto, and Geschmack are used to designate a certain susceptibility to artistic performances. The fact that the idea of taste considered a sense organ the source of appreciation and evaluation was to prove both an asset and a liability. On the one hand, treatments of taste were required to make at least a show of scientific approach and accuracy if they were to be taken at all seriously by an age that busied itself with empirical facts. That is why some critics played for safety by making taste coincide with the requirements of reason. Thus, taste tried to answer the sceptic's charge that reasoning about the arts was no proper reasoning at all, but merely a disguised form of irrational response. On the other hand, it was abundantly clear that taste – like genius, grace and *je ne sais quoi* – was inextricably interwoven with most unscientific emotions and responses. And the difficulty was accentuated where taste was concerned. For whereas genius was acknowledged to be unlearnable and a prerogative reserved for a minority, a good many critics worked on the assumption that taste was a talent that could be imparted to mankind at large.

The implication of the deference shown to taste was that it was possible to judge art by other than purely schematic criteria. The first occurrence of the word in its aesthetic sense in the Neo-Classical age is in some remarks which Dryden's brother-in-law, Sir Robert Howard, wrote in 1668, in the preface to his tragedy, *The Great Favourite*:

> ... for in the difference of *Tragedy* and *Comedy* and of *Fars* it self, there can be no determination but by the Taste.[21]

Howard proceeds to give an account of the operations of taste, in which he says that taste manifests itself as "a like or a dislike" – it is akin to belief. And that, of course, is a decisive statement. René Bray may be right when he says that originally good taste was nothing but "le bon sens dans sa formation critique".[22] It is also true that individual taste was in an awkward position in the early stages of uncompromising Neo-Classicism, which elevated Universal and Permanent Reason to an almost metaphysical level. Yet the fact remains that the moment taste came to be acknowledged to be a general human faculty, it was difficult to deny any individual reader the right to state his own preference without being looked askance at. And as it turned out, not all readers, when exercising their taste, were able to see the beauty of works that were written according to the canon. The dilemma, which was never solved by Neo-Classicism, was the following one: how is it possible to reconcile the fact that sense organs are largely identical in all human beings (apart, of course, from pathological aberrations) with the empirical observation that taste is differently developed in different people? The fondness of the age for generalizations and its assumption that human nature is everywhere the same, tended to expect taste to be more or less identical in mankind at large. On the other hand, that position was made increasingly untenable owing to the growing preoccupation with history and the belief in changes due to climatic and geographic conditions, and also owing to the empirical fact that even experienced critics did not see eye to eye over the achievements of a poet – so tastes *were* different.

Needless to say, also earlier ages had been able to state their likes and dislikes where works of art were concerned. And it is remarkable how even the lawgivers of the canon, Rapin, Le Bossu, and others do not avoid an element of subjectivity or "taste", even if they rarely use the latter word. Value judgements like "agreeable" and "beau" rub shoulders with modifiers like "un peu trop" and "autant que possible" in their critical pronouncements. However, Neo-Classical critics – French as well as English ones – would open their works of criticism with what sounded like categorical imperatives, and that would distract attention somewhat from the ensuing modifications.

Taste enjoyed such popularity because it enabled the reader of a book or the beholder of a picture to couch his response in a technical jargon that seemed to be an elaboration and a serviceable supplement of the existing critical vocabulary. The criticism deriving from, and determined by, the Neo-Classical canon centred on the stages of the genesis of the work of art and, to a greater extent, on the accordance of the finished product with the rules. This tended to lead criticism into binary oppositions and ensuing simplification: what conformed to the canon was good, what did not, bad. However, such assessments said little or nothing about the impact of the work on the recipient, and the concept of taste provided the critic as well as the intelligent layman with a powerful tool that permitted somewhat more varied and personal verdicts.

Taste was a welcome addition to the fold. It is characteristic that critics endeavoured to establish commonly acceptable standards for what taste could be justly claimed to be, and it is also characteristic that they had widely divergent opinions about what ingredients went into it. In one of the *Spectator* essays (No. 409), Addison defines taste as

> that Faculty of the Soul, which discerns the Beauties of an
> Author with Pleasure, and the Imperfections with Dislike.

Others held that taste was the privilege of an educated minority and read more into it than a more or less instinctive talent for recognizing the beauties and defects of a work of art. To such critics, it also comprised a knack of elegant expression and, more generally, good breeding and a good-natured disposition. To Shaftesbury, for example, taste is associated with relish and choice, and he sees the perfect human being as a judicious blend of taste and morals.

The stern intransigence of the 1680s came gradually to be replaced by a willingness to admit new ventures within aesthetics and to tackle them with less prejudice.

5

> Il n'ya rien de correct dans le dessein, rien de juste dans l'ordonnance, rien de droit dans la pensée, rien de beau dans les sentiments, rien de touchant dans les affections, rien d'heureux dans l'expression, ni rien d'achevé dans les autres parties de l'éloquence que par cet art merveilleux des bienséances.[23]

That declaration of content for the *bienséance* is given by Rapin. It is noticeable how many subjective and non-rational terms the French critic finds it necessary to resort to in order to pin down the constituent parts of the *summum bonum* of the Neo-Classical canon; also, that the *bienséances* – the plural implies an aggregate of aspects – is an art. The tenor of the passage is favourable to the recognition of individual taste and to the virtue of pleasing the reader.

In the last quarter of the 17th century, pedantry increasingly came to be looked upon as bad taste, for which reason emphasis in the arts was placed at least as much on the *delectare* as on the *prodesse* of the Horatian dyad. But of course even the most uncompromising Neo-Classical poet did not deliberately set out to bore his readers. Thus Dacier maintained that "les règles et ce qui plaît ne peuvent être deux choses opposées ".[24] Much Neo-Classical literature was didactic, and the pleasure it aimed at arousing was strongly tinged with ethical or religious considerations. For example, Granville shows us the universal applicability of the Horatian pair in his short poem *To Mira*, the tone of which can be surmised from the following couplet:

> Plants, Fruits, and Flowers the fertile Fields produce,
> Not for vain Ornament, but wholesome Use.[25]

The tendency to make the delight element more of a central point manifests itself in either of two ways: poets realize that instruction can be made more palatable if the pill is sugared, and the idea of delight is given a broader content. "For a poet, that he may be sure to instruct, is obliged to give all the delight that he can", wrote Dennis in 1696, in the *Remarks on Prince Arthur*,[26] and in his *Parallel,* Dryden's loyalties were split between pleasing and instructing.

The pleasure element is the cornerstone of J.-B. Dubos' *Réflexions critiques sur la Poésie et sur la Peinture* from 1719: one does not read a poem to be taught, but to be given a sense of pleasure, he said. If we want to be taught, we turn to philosophers or historians, but we do not open a book of poetry out of a desire to learn. The ancient triptych of *prodesse, delectare* and *movere* is reduced by Dubos to two requirements, for "plaire" and "toucher" are used as quasi-synonyms, the "toucher" element of "plaire" being stressed throughout. Actually, the talent of moving a recipient in a pleasurable way becomes *the* criterion of a great artist:

> C'est à l'invention des idées et des images propres à nous émouvoir qu'on distingue le grand Artisan du simple Manoeuvre.[27]

Dubos' work is from a period when whole-hogging zealotry had gone out of Neo-Classicism, and the actual shift of emphasis is not as pronounced as Dubos' enthusiasm seems to indicate. But the tendency had been under way for nearly two decades. It is a well-known fact that Dennis saw it as the prime function of a literary work to appeal to the reader's passion. And Granville wrote in 1701:

> Ladies and Beaux to please is all our Task,
> But the sharp Critic will Instruction ask,[28]

a statement that is as critical of the empty-headed beaux as of the pedantic critics (apart, of course, from having a tinge of male chauvinism), and which illustrates the creative writer's dilemma. But what Granville's couplet also shows is that it was no longer sufficient to write according to the rules. And by about 1710 it was, to all intents and purposes, impossible to get an audience for a work of art that was exclusively didactic. Thus, whereas the word "instruct" hardly ever appears alone in the theoretical declarations of purpose after about 1710, the word "delight" and its synonyms increasingly do. It would be rash to conclude, however, that the didactic element is discarded altogether. But the *utile* aspect is combined with, or made ancillary to, less austere requirements.

Hutcheson's *Inquiry into the Original of our Ideas of Beauty and Virtue* from 1725 clinches the contest: *delectare* has won the day. The book chiefly discusses the various ways in which an artist can afford pleasure to his public, and in the preface to the second edition, which came out in the following year, a sign of the popularity of the work, he examines the "various Pleasures which Human Nature is capable of receiving", and he will not rest content with the current watered-out reflections on "Sensible and Rational Pleasures".[29] He is at pains to distance himself from Locke's exclusive concentration on the rational parts of the human mind.

He repeats the standard Neo-Classical definition of beauty as "some kind of *Uniformity* or *Unity* of Proportion among the Parts, and of each part to the Whole".[30] However, beauty is incompatible with over-punctilious pedantry since absolute regularity does not necessarily yield maximum pleasure. Fortunately, it will often happen that

> strict Regularity in laying out of Gardens in *Parterres, Vistas, parallel Walks*, is often neglected, to obtain an Imitation of Nature even in some of its Wildness.
> And we are more pleased with this *Imitation*, especially when the Scene is large and spacious, than with the more confin'd Exactness of regular Works.[31]

According to Hutcheson, who is typical of the decade in which his *Inquiry* was published, regularity is less pleasurable than a modicum of wildness because nature was claimed to abhor straight lines. In his book, which contains many examples from *natura naturata*, Hutcheson endeavours to put his message across by bringing rational analysis to bear on irrational factors, which of course shows his ultimate confidence in the power of reason. His book ends with a series of eulogies on the excellent arrangement of the world and the exquisite rationality of the Supreme Being. At the same time, he recognizes sources of pleasure that had been eschewed by most writers and critics in the heyday of Neo-Classicism. For example he says that "a *tempestuous Sea*, a *craggy Precipice*, a *dark, shady Valley*" may tend to excite horror at first, but when "Experience or Reason has removed the fear" such scenes "may become the occasions of Pleasure".[32] Both the examples and the words Hutcheson uses to characterize the response – horror and pleasure – clearly belong within the realm of the sublime.

6

Sublimity had gradually acquired positive connotations but was vaguely, if at all, defined. Neo-Classicism knew and accepted that type of concepts: genius and judgement are cases in point. Yet, sublimity was a thing apart in the thinking of the age: it could be an attribute to an object in *natura naturata* as well as to an idea in Scripture; it was applicable to a recipient's reaction as well as to a verbal formulation. Thus, unlike genius, sublimity was at the same time something inside a person and outside him, but sublime feelings were never aroused by promptings from another human being. What sublimity did, then, was, on the one hand, to underline the *movere* aspect in the individual, on the other to reinforce that correspondence between the ego and *res* which engrossed the Neo-Classicists. And they were not slow to recognize a similarity between disproportionate objects and the transcendence of stylistic conventions that was required to describe them.

The unfinished critical treatise *Peri Hupsous* has mistakenly been ascribed to the Greek philosopher Longinus (210-71). The work was written at some time in the first century A.D.[33] by an unknown author, who is generally referred to as Pseudo-Longinus. The structure of the work puzzles a modern reader, as do many of its author's statements and *obiter dicta*. Fogginess abounds, and contradictions are not difficult to find. Yet the author, who will for practical reasons be called Longinus in the following pages, said something that was bound to have reverberations in an age that was genuinely preoccupied with the question of quality in art. He had no doubt that art does have rules, but he refuses to grant them absolute validity. He only recognizes such rules as are inherent in a given art, which is at best a vague indication, but which made it a legitimate pursuit to take an interest in, and perhaps admire, "irregular" works. Longinus also invites critics to reflect upon the question of which is preferable, grandeur attended by some flaws of execution, or a modest success of impeccable correctness. His own answer was a tolerant one: geniuses cannot be expected to be faultless, and he admits that he does not like a style that never rises above modest eloquence, never stumbles, and never requires correction.[34] This view of "the sublime genius that sometimes errs", as Dryden puts it,[35] is echoed by many of the lesser lights of the Neo-Classical period, who, hiding behind Longinus, indirectly confessed their inability to live up to the august stipulations of the canon, or, simply, to produce a decent work of art.

Longinus' book is primarily about stylistic figures and their supposed effect, which is also reflected in the title of John Hall's translation from 1652, *Peri Hupsous, or Dionysius Longinus of the Height of Eloquence rendred out of the originall by J.H.Esq.* Longinus devotes many pages to an enumeration of instances of various types of verbal sublimity. The key word itself is, in the process, watered down to such an extent that it becomes synonymous with what is good in literature.

Neo-Classical infatuation with Longinus began with Boileau's French version of *Peri Hupsous*, which was published in 1674, ie the same year as his *Art poétique*. That Boileau should have published those two works in the same year is a telling coincidence. Boileau was no expert in Greek, and his *Traité du Sublime* is more of a paraphrase than a meticulous and faithful rendering of the original, which was considered a perfectly legitimate procedure in those days. And he plays fair with his readers from the outset: they should not expect "de trouver ici une version timide et scrupuleuse des paroles de Longin".[36] He is anxious to give not just a translation of Longinus, but "de donner au public un traité du Sublime, qui pût être utile",[37] a phrasing that suggests that Boileau worked out his *Traité* with a didactic purpose.

In one of the first pages of his treatise, Longinus calls sublimity "a kind of eminence or excellence of discourse", and in the same passage he refers to the "wonder and astonishment" aroused in the reader.[38] Boileau follows suit: starting from style – "le Sublime est en effet ce qui forme l'excellence et la souveraine perfection du discours"[39] – he soon proceeds to deal with its effect on the reader:

> (Le Sublime) ne persuade pas proprement, mais il revit, il transporte, et produit en nous une certain admiration mêlée d'étonnement et de surprise, qui est toute autre chose que de plaire seulement ou de persuader.[40]

It will be seen how *delectare* (plaire) and *prodesse* (persuader) are insufficient in themselves and have been made subservient to an intensified kind of *movere* (transporter).

In his *Traité*, Boileau elaborates on an aspect which was to prove seminal, viz. the postulation of a correspondence between sublime ideas and sublime style, in the sender as well as in the receiver of the message. Thus sublimity becomes not only a set of stylistic devices but also a way of inventing, thinking, feeling, and responding, and it came to be used as an attribute of items of *natura naturata* that evoked sublime ideas.

An early exemplification of Boileau's suggestions is John Dennis' account of his crossing of the Alps, which appears in a letter dated at Turin, October 25, 1688:

> As soon as we had conquered half of it (sc. Mount Aigrebellette), the unusual heighth (sic) in which we found ourselves, the impending Rock that hung over us, the dreadful Depth of the Precipice, and the Torrent that roared at the bottom, gave us a view that was altogether new and amazing...A Mountain's craggy Clifts, which we half discern'd, thro' the misty Gloom of the Clouds that surrounded them, sometimes gave us a horrid Prospect... In the mean time we walk'd upon the very brink, in a litteral sense, of Destruction; one Stumble, and both Life and Carcass had been at once destroy'd. The sense of all this produc'd different motions in me, viz. a delightful Horrour, a terrible Joy, and at the same time, that I was terribly pleas'd, I trembl'd.

(About the Savoy Mountains): There craggy Rocks look'd horrid to the eye, and Hills appear'd on every side of so stupendous an Heighth that the Company was divided at a distance, whether they would believe them to be sunny Clouds, or the Snowy tops of Mountains. Here appears a Hill with its top quite hid in black Clouds and beyond that Hill, & above those Clouds some higher Mountain show'd its hoary Head...The uncouth Rocks that were above us, Rocks that were void of all form, but what they had receiv'd from Ruins; the frightful view of the Precipices, and the foaming Waters that threw themselves headlong down them, made all such a Consort up for the Eye, as that sort of Musick does for the Ear, in which Horrour can be joyn'd with Harmony.[41]

The matrix of the scene is that of a contemplated landscape with mountains, water, clouds, and prospects, the sum total of which makes up a harmony comparable with that found in music. Incidentally, the beholder's doubt as to whether the landmarks in the distance are sunny clouds hanging low or snowy tops of mountains came to be a conventional *topos* in Neo-Classical landscape descriptions. The insistence of the observer's feelings at the moment of sensation is unusual for the late 1680s. In the same letter Dennis assures his correspondent that his reaction to conventional landscape scenes is "consistent with reason", but the sublime Alpine massif obviously transports him. The feelings, it will be seen, are contradictory, but still the outcome is pleasure, in the same way as the opposing elements of the scene co-operate to produce harmony. In actual fact the formulation "delightful horror" came to be a nutshell characterization of a recipient's response to sublime landscape scenes and descriptions of them.

What few references there are to Longinus in England before 1674 consider him a rhetorician. Thus Cowley's *A Proposition for the Advancement of Experimental Philosophy* from 1661 suggests that an academy should be established for the promotion of philosophy, and he recommends some authors for the curriculum: "for the Morals and Rhetoric *Aristotle* may Suffice, or *Hermogenes* and *Longinus* for the latter".[42]

However, after the publication of Boileau's *Traité* in 1674, a new dimension is added without the old one being entirely discarded. Boileau was one of the architects of the classical canon, and his words carried more weight than Hall's translation had done even if some of the Frenchman's statements seem fairly heretical from an orthodox point of view.

Longinus became popular almost overnight in England, and towards the end of 1674, or in the early part of 1675, Dryden asserts that Longinus "was undoubtedly, after Aristotle, the greatest critic among the Greeks".[43] In the same years, Dryden uses the word sublime about the subject as well as the wording of a literary composition. He does not define the word, but it seems to have vaguely positive connotations; also, sublime style is remote from literalness:

> All reasonable men will conclude it necessary, that sublimest subjects ought to be adorned with the sublimest, and consequently often, with the most figurative expressions.[44]

However, loftiness was liable to degenerate into pompousness. In *Soliloquy: or Advice to an Author,* Shaftesbury is none too enthusiastic about sublimity, which, to him, is tantamount to a pursuit of the sensational:

> In Poetry and study'd Prose, the *astonishing* Part, or what commonly passes for Sublime, is form'd by the variety of Figures, the multiplicity of Metaphors, and by quitting as much as possible the natural and easy way of Expression, for that which is most unlike to Humanity, or ordinary Use.[45]

Undoubtedly, Shaftesbury has got a point there: in several of its manifestations, the sublime style is poles apart from what is felt to be "ordinary" use of the language. Shaftesbury is even convinced that the intended horror effect is an appeal to primitive instincts in man:

> *Astonishment* is of all other Passions the earliest rais'd in raw and unexperienced Mankind.[46]

However, the aristocratic *connoisseur* was fighting a losing battle. Many critics from the second decade of the 18th century were prepared to throw didacticism and restraint to the winds. "For a painter should not please only, but should delight, should transport, should surprise," exclaimed Jonathan Richardson,[47] and he carries the note of inane panegyric to exaggerated lengths:

> By the sublime in general I mean the most excellent of what is excellent, as the excellent is the best of what is good.[48]

And Leonard Welsted claimed that "the Sublime and Pathetic" were not only possessed of their own "inherent brightness", but they also bore "a natural affinity…to the secret springs of the soul",[49] a statement that suggests a deep-seated concord between human nature and sublimity.

Sublimity is of relevance for the subject of this book for several reasons. For one thing, it is associated by French criticism with "noble taste" – Roger de Piles says that "le grand goût, le sublime, et le merveilleux ne sont que la même chose"[50] – which makes it an offshoot of the uncanonical tendencies that were a prerequisite for the emergence of the landscape poem. Secondly, all critics agreed that sublimity was to be found, and was a *desideratum*, in both painting and poetry. Thirdly, and perhaps most significantly, sublimity came to be naturally associated in England not merely with stylistic effects, but also with items of landscape like mountains, rivers and prospects.

Longinus' tenets gained widespread support in the early years of the 18th century because of its insistence that the great poet is a good man, his stressing of the emotional element in the reader or the spectator (Dennis is a faithful disciple of Longinus in this respect), and his belief that feeling is at least on a par with, if not superior to, reason where critical judgement was concerned. He also gave support to the conviction that natural objects might give pleasure in spite of, or perhaps on account of, irregularities of form. A form-obsessed age was intrigued by a critic who preached defiance to the limits of form: the imprecise and the grandiose made an impact by its very clash with the Neo-Classical *esprit géométrique*. Thus one of the favourite concepts of Neo-Classicism, viz. limitation, was no longer looked upon as a *sine qua non*. One feature common to all things sublime in nature and art is large size, and what distinguishes the experience of anything sublime is that the soul, or the imagination, is filled to overflowing. Addison felt satisfied that

> God has made our soul naturally delight in the apprehension of what is great or unlimited.[51]

More generally, sublimity was a catalyst in the gradual but perceptible process of change that the idea of decorum was undergoing around the turn of the century. The ultimate result of the shift was that art was no longer looked upon as the fulfilment of a set of more or less arbitrary norms, but as a prompter of subjective experiences.

The sublime feeling was a compound one. Mixed emotions were not treated favourably in the early part of the Neo-Classical period, which also frowned on mixed genres, maintaining that the "kinds" ought to work with basic and fairly manageable problems in an acknowledged system of presentation in order to provoke predictable and decorous responses in the readers.

But, more than being a compound, sublimity was often made up of contrary feelings, which, ultimately, made it an illustration of the principle of *concordia discors*. Sublimity achieves its pleasure-conferring effect owing to a mental *concordia* between glaringly discordant feelings, "delightful horror", to use Dennis' formulation.

The cult of sublimity was instrumental in directing the attention of readers and writers towards details in the surrounding scenery that were liable to promote a thrill of pleasure. In the "full-grown" landscape poem, there are frequent hints of sublimity, such as woody mountains with deep shades, grottoes, ruins of abbeys, and inaccessible craggy cliffs.

7

A fundamentally new approach to the triangle artist, artefact, and recipient is perceptible in aesthetics between 1700 and 1725.

Shortly after the turn of the century it was becoming permissible, even desirable, to discuss art in terms that were different from the code language of orthodox Neo-Classicism. The unities, for example, had been applicable to works of art only, unusable to anything in "reality"; invention was a talent in the poet and the critic, not in mankind at large; *bienséance* was a characteristic of a work of art and not a universal moral guide. Art was held in fairly watertight compartments and hence was susceptible of treatment in a terminology specially devised for art and meaningful for little else than the artist or the artefact. In cases where the system was acknowledged to be insufficient, a vocabulary was used that was naturally vague (*je ne sais quoi*), but whose reference rarely pointed beyond a pretty narrow artistic context.

With the decline of the Neo-Classical canon, however, a change sets in. The words and concepts used to deal with art in the widest sense of the term were frequently some that had a wider range of application, and, no less importantly, criticism began to occupy itself increasingly with the aesthetics of reception. Taste was an ingredient of the artist's creative talent, but it was also an acquired and well-developed impressionability and responsiveness where artistic achievement was concerned, and, besides, the word was used to describe the way a person conducted himself and arranged his life. Sublimity was found in natural objects, in works of art, in man's reactions, and in verbalizations of his attitudes. Orthodox Neo-Classicists were satisfied that their body of doctrines had its foundation in nature. The remarkable thing is that nobody ever suggested that terms like taste or sublimity were "against nature", even if they implied a radical break-away from the old pattern.

The scope of critical terms was extended: criteria that had been the exclusive prerogative of the poet or the *connoisseur* were gradually supplemented by others that were believed to be obtainable by, indeed were the rightful property of, a larger circle. The discussions of the possible universality of taste are illustrative.

The significance of that "opening up" should not be overlooked. After 1700, a stretch of common ground was slowly established between things aesthetic and "the world without Verona walls". Art became more of a social factor, one among several amenities of life, rather than a sum of uninspired observances of "laws" that were often felt to be trammels. Aesthetics contributed to the setting up of more comprehensive ideals that defied boorishness and endeavoured to heighten standards. That had also been the original object of the Neo-Classical canon, but its norms were gradually felt to be outmoded.

The sympathetic benevolence and mildly optimistic didacticism that pervades the articles in the host of periodicals that saw the light of day in the first decades of the 18th century (eg *Spectator*) is a straw in the wind.

Leonard Welsted's words in *A Dissertation concerning the Perfection of the English Language, the State of poetry, &C*, from 1724, summarize the new position succinctly: the rules are no more

> than a sett of very obvious thoughts and observations, which every man of good sense naturally knows without being taught, and which never made a good poet, or mended a bad one... Those observations or rules were primarily formed upon, and designed to serve only as comments to, the works of certain great Authors, who composed those works without any such help.[52]

The latter part of the quotation presents an aspect of the problem of rules that was also debated by the early Neo-Classicists, viz. how did the great originators of the rules manage without codified prescriptions? However, far from being embarrassed by such a question, many critics saw the position as the ultimate proof that rules were derived from nature – an attitude that is seemingly supported by Welsted in the former half of the quotation. However, the point he is making is that the rules are self-evident, and that they have little to offer in the way of help to a faltering author. Neo-Classicists had maintained that the rules were permanent and universal; Welsted's assertion is that they are time-bound and, by inference, transitory, for they were devised for the nonce. But he was treading on dangerous ground: for if the rules were no longer believed to be universal and permanent, what then about reason, whose very universality and permanence were held to be reflected in the rules? None of the later Neo-Classicists faced this issue squarely. Instead, they solved this problem as they solved others where terminology was concerned: they preserved the word, in this case reason, but imperceptibly changed its content.

Welsted goes on to say that it is a well-known fact that "the secret, the soul of good writing, is not to be come at through such mechanical Laws" as the rules.[53] However, no prominent Neo-Classical critics had maintained that, witness their recognition of factors like genius and *je ne sais quoi*. Actually, Welsted echoes the traditional Neo-Classical view of the genius as the poet who can write a masterpiece without obeying any rules.

Welsted ends his slightly impatient comment in the following manner:

> I am not to be understood as if I would throw the talent of writing in verse into a lawless mystery, and make of it a wild, ungoverned province, where reason has nothing to do. It is certain, everything depends on reason and must be guided by it; but it is as certain, that reason operates differently, when it has different things for its object. Poetical reason is not the same as mathematical reason.[54]

That is more than the conventional Neo-Classical fear of chaos as the only alternative if the strong hold of reason is weakened. The originality of the statement resides in the fact that Welsted realizes that reason is not an unqualified Absolute, but diversified into types. At the same time, Welsted's words show the characteristic unwillingness to jettison reason even where poetry was concerned, or, no less typically, to drop a term (sc. reason) even if its content had been changed. The last sentence of the quotation is a succinct presentation of a problem which has occupied literary discussion since Welsted's time.

8

There is one area in which the changes detailed in the previous section had a perceptible effect, viz. the attitude to descriptions. As has already been pointed out, Neo-Classicists were critical of mere verbal showing off on the part of the poet. However, their criticism was not directed against words as such, but rather against their misuse. Thus the situation was analogous to what happened within the Sister Art, where colours would sometimes fall into disrepute because they were suspected of muddling and defiling the beauty of the design so that the didactic element was glossed over or forfeited. Although words were conventionally held to be the literary counterparts of the colours of painting, no Neo-Classical author or literary critic seriously maintained that words *per se* were an inferior part of the finished product, a vulgar polish that marred the perfection of the *dispositio*. On the contrary: the very length of such epic poems as were written in the four decades from 1680 to 1720 made some kind of variation or relief for the reader almost indispensable. And episodic digressions where the writer used his mastery of words to appeal to his reader's imagination, and which sexed up the protracted moralizing of the main plot, became immensely popular. The *delectare* criterion was probably also what caused Aristotle to give priority to tragedy over epic poetry: reasonably speedy movement gives greater pleasure than endless tortoise-like progress.

Addison is one of the writers who is clearly aware of the power of words to influence readers:

> Words, when well chosen, have so great a force in them, that a description often gives us more lively ideas than the sight of the things themselves,

he says in *Spectator* No. 416. He goes on to say that "beautiful descriptions and images are the spirit and life of poetry". On the face of it, that statement might be taken to refer just as well to stylistic subtleties, but that is disproved by the passage as a whole. Addison compares the seeing of an object "in reality" with the reading about it in a book: when we see an object, "we have only so much of it painted on the imagination as comes in at the eye," whereas in descriptions "the poet gives us as free a view of it as he pleases", revealing to us "parts" that we did not observe of our own accord, or which "lay out of sight when we first beheld it."

John Hughes wrote a short essay, published in 1715, *On Descriptions in Poetry,* which contains a brief theoretical introduction on the subject of description:

> They are form'd of Ideas from the Senses, which is sometimes call'd *Imaging*, and are thus, in a manner, like Pictures, made Objects of the Sight; whereas moral Thoughts and Discourses, consisting of Ideas abstracted from Sense, operate slower, and with less Vivacity.[55]

The argumentation is obviously indebted to Locke's epistemology, and an interesting angle is suggested: descriptions – of concrete objects, we must assume – can be contemplated like pictures, a line which was pursued by Dubos and eagerly embraced by Neo-Classical theorists in England as well. Abstracts, it seems, produce less vivid imprints on the reader's mind; but Hughes has no doubt that it is their capacity to evoke pictures that makes descriptions popular with readers.

The second part of Hughes' essay *On Descriptions* adduces examples of the way in which the *topos* "morning" has been described by lyric and dramatic writers, such as Shakespeare, Vergil (translated by Dryden), Tasso (translated by Fairfax), Spenser, Milton, and Otway. The collection itself as well as the conclusions Hughes draws on the basis of the excerpts are worthy of notice. In the first place, Hughes recognizes individual variation and does not set up a superior or absolute standard according to which his examples are to be assessed. Secondly, his remarks on the aspect of imitation are a tribute to the poet's descriptive power. On the one hand, he is convinced that the surrounding world presents itself in largely the same form to all observers, for there is "a general Similitude in all true Descriptions of the same objects drawn by several Hands",[56] but on the other the Degree of Likeness, and the different Manners of expressing it by those several Artists, make a very distinguishable and entertaining Variety.[57]

The whole thought is reminiscent of the distinction between permanent and variable features in the art of portraiture. Only, here it is fitted into one of the favourite patterns of the age: the artist's idiosyncracies may make for some *discordia,* but the latter will be "heightened" by the major *concordia* arising from the fact that the object before the artist's eyes and what they see in their imagination is the same.

The importance of Hughes' theoretical considerations is not weakened by the fact that his aim is not primarily aesthetic. He has a patriotic axe to grind, as appears from the sentence with which he winds up his samples of "morning" passages: English poets have described morning

with at least as much Elegance of Fancy as many others have done, and with more Variety.[58]

In an essay from *The Guardian* (Friday June 19, 1713), the writer not only distances himself from descriptions as mere ornament but also invokes the aid of the Sister Art to give a name to the felicitous literary description, viz. painting in poetry, and he is pleased to say that he has got beyond the childish stage when he was charmed by "points and turns of wit". At the present moment

I can take a manly and rational satisfaction in that which is called painting in poetry. Whether it be, that in these copyings of nature, the object is placed in such lights and circumstances as strike the fancy agreeably; or whether we are surprised to find objects, that are absent, placed before our eyes; or whether it be our admiration of the author's art and dexterity; or whether we amuse ourselves with comparing the picture and the original; or rather (which is most probable) because all these reasons concur to affect us, we are wonderfully charmed with these drawings after the life, this magic that raises apparitions in the fancy.

The pictorial terminology leaps to the eye: "lights", "placed", "picture" and "original" are words that a painter would also use. The objects are "copied", but still the author's talent – the manual skill implementing the lofty inspiration – is a significant factor. The "paintings" refer to the written descriptions (perhaps in metaphorical language) of scenes that you would find in a picture, as well as the "apparitions" conjured up in the recipient's imagination. The recipient's response is taken into consideration and "rational satisfaction" does not exclude being "wonderfully charmed": the writer wants to make it clear that he is writing under the auspices of reason, and that being charmed is not against reason. The quotation is relevant for the attitude it reveals: literature, or some parts of it, could become, or at least be compared to, a picture – another instance of *ut pictura poesis*.

CHAPTER TWELVE

THE LANDSCAPES OF JAMES THOMSON'S SEASONS

1

The first book of James Thomson's *Seasons* was *Summer*, published in 1727. Apart from two pastoral narrative scenes, *Summer* sets forth the progress of a summer day with such activities as hay-making, sheep-shearing, and bathing. Lines 52-66 contain a genuine landscape scene:

>   Young day pours in apace
> And opens all the lawny prospect wide.
> The dripping rock the mountain's misty top
> (55) Swell on the sight and brighten with the dawn.
> Blue through the dusk the smoking currents shine;
> And from the bladed field the fearful hare
> Limps awkward; while along the forest glade
> The wild deer trip, and often turning gaze
> (60) At early passenger. Music awakes
> The native voice of undissembled joy;
> And thick around the woodland hymns arise.
> Roused by the cock, the soon-clad shepherd leaves
> His mossy cottage, where with peace he dwells,
> (65) And from the crowded fold in order drives
> His flock to taste the verdure of the morn.[1]

The stage is set for a familiar Neo-Classical scene: a beholder who keeps consistently in the background, sallies forth on a summer morning. The "lawny prospect" (l. 53) might indicate a position from where he is able to survey a considerable area, but perhaps he just looks across a flat lawn. The landscape is not made into a picture, and the localities remain imprecise. There are reminiscences of sublimity in the misty mountain top that "swell(s) on the sight" (ll. 54-55), and the shepherd of ll. 63 et seq. is a mixture of convention and realism, and words like "flock", "mossy" and "peace" – standard pastoral ingredients – complete the impression of a mixture of different traditions of description.

The "smoking currents" of l. 56, which is a pithy verbal reproduction of a light effect, are signs of work or other kinds of activity. Apart from this allusion to civilization, the rest of the passage is nature, and in a more "unadorned" version than we know from orthodox Neo-Classical landscape descriptions. For instance, Thomson's predecessors were not interested in the awakening of the animals, for small-scale time was no concern of theirs. On the whole, the excerpt from *Summer* is characterized by its microcosmic approach, and the macrocosmic inference, which remains implicit, is that the sounds of the waking birds are a thrilled and ingenious homage to the holiness of nature ("hymns", l. 62). The narrator seems to understand the pleasure felt by the animals, but he is very careful not to obtrude his own presence on the scene.

The lines have intimations of movement and action in them, thus being more dynamic than the mainly static Neo-Classical *tableaux*. The landscape is no more than a sketched background (prospect, rock, mountain), and the scene as such is not focused on. It is a series of personal observations of specific details which co-operate to create a mood of unreflecting delight at the awakening of nature and its inhabitants.

The following passage describes a different time of day:

(1380)
>   Now the soft hour
> Of waking comes for him who lonely loves
> To seek the distant hills, and there converse
> With nature, there to harmonize his heart,
> And in pathetic song to breathe around
> The harmony to others.[2]

The lonely wanderer is probably not a particular person, yet he is less general than the anonymous Neo-Classical beholder, who felt and acted as the representative of mankind. The emphasis in Thomson's lines is on the longing to get to the hills: his wanderer – and the narrator understands him and enters into his situation – wants to reach out to the items of *natura naturata*, to "converse with nature" (ll. 1381-82). The Neo-Classical beholder *has* found a point of vantage from which he can survey the scene; he would soliloquize, intermittently appealing to the reader or to an unidentified bystander, and he would *contemplate* nature and make some deductions on the basis of his observations, but he would not enter into a communion with it: to him man and nature were two distinct worlds. The Neo-Classical poet would get his heart "harmonized" by looking at, and pondering on, the Great Design that was perceptible behind the objects spread before his eyes. But those objects did not add up to become some kind of mysterious entity. In a sense he might be said to "breathe around the harmony to others", but his song can hardly be called "pathetic". The approach of Thomson's lines is poles apart form the Neo-Classical one.

A few lines further on in *Summer*, the narrator invites Amanda to join him: "Which way, Amanda shall we bend our course?" (l. 1401),

(1406)   ... or ascend
       While radiant Summer opens all its pride,
       Thy hill, delightful Shene? Here let us sweep
       The boundless landscape; now the raptured eye,
(1410) Exulting swift, to huge Augusta send,
       Now to her sister hills that skirt her plain
       To lofty Harrow now, and now to where
       Majestic Windsor lifts his princely brow.
       In lovely contrast to this glorious view
(1415) Calmly magnificent, then will we turn
       To where the silver Thames first rural grows.
       There let the feasted eye unwearied stray;
       Luxurious, there, rove through the pendent woods
       That, nodding, hang o'er Harrington's retreat;

(1420) And, steeping thence to Ham's embowering walks,
Beneath whose shades, in spotless peace retired,
With her the pleasing partner of her heart,
The worthy Queensbury yet laments his Gay,
And polished Cornbury woos the willing muse,
(1425) Slow let us trace the matchless vale of Thames;
Fair-winding up to where the muses haunt
In Twit'nam's bowers, and for their Pope implore
The healing god, to royal Hampton's pile
To Clermont's terraced height, and Easter's groves
(1430) Where in the sweetest solitude, embraced
By the soft windings of the silent Mole
From courts and senates Pelham finds repose.
Enchanting vale! Beyond whate'er the muse
Has of Achais or Hesperis sung!
(1435) O vale of bliss! O softly-smelling hills!
On which the power of cultivation lies,
And joys to see the wonders of his toil.
Heavens! what a godly prospect spreads around,
Of hills, and dales, and woods, and lawns, and spires,
(1440) And glittering towns, and gilded streams, till all
The stretching landscape into smoke decays!
Happy Britannia! Where the Queen of Arts,
Inspiring vigour, Liberty, abroad
Walks unconfined even to thy farthest cots,
(1445) And scatters plenty with unsparing hand.[3]

The lady, Amanda, is almost immediately lost sight of, and apart from the "us" of l. 1408, the poet might just as well have been alone. Down to l. 1416, the stage direction is the familiar Neo-Classical one: landscape, hill, shifting views, distant town, castle, and river. Indeed, the locality is the Thames region so beloved by the Neo-Classicists. Variety is ensured by the contrast between the "calmly magnificent" flow of the river (l. 1415) and the beholder's rapid *tour d'horizon*.

However, the Neo-Classical basis has been provided with a novel and more enthusiastic superstructure: "delightful Shene" (l. 1408), the idea of "sweeping" the scene with "the raptured eye/

Exulting swift" (ll. 1409-10), the straying of the "unwearied" eye (l. 1417), and the prospect, which is claimed to be "boundless" (l. 1409) (even though the eye is stopped again and again!) – all this is characterized as a feast (l. 1417). Such unfeigned and almost ecstatic pleasure is virtually unknown with Thomson's Neo-Classical predecessors.

At l. 1417, the point of the poem where the reader has been taught by orthodox landscape poetry to expect a more detailed account of the landscape or one of the historical or mythological "foreground incidents", Thomson makes idiosyncratic use of the tradition, of which, however, the reader is constantly but discreetly reminded. The drama of the stag hunt has been replaced by an enumeration of the names of a number of deserving men, who are supposed to be so familiar to the reader that their respective merits are passed over in silence. The common denominator of all the persons alluded to is rural habitation, and "the silver Thames" – a Neo-Classical echo – preserves its well-known function as a connector – this time, however, of the outstanding personalities. The Thames valley may be "matchless" (l. 1425) and "enchanting" (l. 1433) owing to its intrinsic beauty which was what the Neo-Classicists thought, but also because it joins in association, and inspires Thomson to refer to, all those eminent men.

Thomson avoids social or moral analogues (apart, perhaps, from the snob value of the names mentioned), but preserves verisimilitude, for the long excursus is sprinkled with landscape items like shade, height, groves, and soft windings: a harmony is postulated to exist between the "vale of bliss" (l. 1434) and the "spotless peace" (l. 1421) (a felicitous formulation) of the many celebrities. Strange to say, the landscape scene is almost devoid of colours, and it is almost "pure nature": the famous men use nature as a haven, and a reference is made to some architectural achievements on their part. Apart from the praise of cultivation (ll. 1436-37), the only suggestion of nature having been cautiously tampered with is the "embowering walks" of l. 1420, where the implication probably is that art has helped nature on the way and produced a result that is beautifully "natural". The Neo-Classicists did not know the word bower. It is true that they made their trees "o'rerarch", but the emphasis was only partly on the creation of shady walks as a refuge for human retirement; rather, the role of the trees was to be a fellow player in the scene.

After the long digression about famous men associated with the Thames region, the landscape again imposes itself on the narrator's senses, and the whole prospect is recapitulated (ll. 1438-41). Some of the terminology is familiar from Thomson's predecessors: "spreads" (l. 1438), "gilded streams" (l. 1440), and "stretching landscape" (l. 1441). But distance is successfully and originally conveyed by the introduction of one of Thomson's favourite devices to signify drifting movement and altered light, viz. smoke (l. 1441). The passage rings out on an optimistic note of patriotism, which was also hinted at in Pope's *Windsor Forest*. But, most commonly, the Neo-Classical landscape descriptions come to a quiet end after the poet has expressed his concern for mankind at large.

Thomson uses the beloved Thames valley for purposes that are not identical with, yet not entirely at odds with, what his predecessors read into it: he pays an indirect tribute to the region by making it the home of men of high repute, and he is inspired by the Thames valley to a patriotic outburst celebrating the freedom and prosperity of England.

2

Spring appeared in 1728; in that section of *The Seasons*, Thomson outlines the influence of that season on the whole gamut of creation, from inanimate objects to man. In l. 101, the poet saunters into the country:

>   Now from the town
> Buried in smoke and sleep and noisome damps
> Oft let me wander o'er the dewy fields
> Where freshness breathes, and dash the trembling drops
> (105) From the bent bush, as through the verdant maze
> Of sweet briar-hedges I pursue my walk;
> Or taste the smell of dairy; or ascend
> Some eminence, Augusta, in thy plains,

	And see the country, far-diffused around,
(110)	One boundless blush, one white-empurpled shower
	Of mingled blossom; where the raptured eye
	Hurries from joy to joy, and, hid beneath
	The fair profusion, yellow Autumn spies.
	If, brushed from the Russian wilds, a cutting gale
(115)	Rise not, and scatter from his humid wings
	The clammy mildew; or, dry-blowing, breathe
	Untimely frost – before whose baleful blast
	The full-blown Spring through all her foliage shrinks,
	Joyless and dead, a wide-dejected waste.[4]

Characteristically, Thomson provides the town with the same attributes as poets had done for nearly a century: it is an unhealthy place full of smoke. On the other hand, there is no indication that he intends to settle permanently in rural surroundings. We are made familiar with the details of the first-person narrator's route, a technique analogous to that employed by Dyer in *The Country Walk*. The narrator's walk takes him into a kind of nature which is geared to human inclinations: the maze is, after all, no more than "sweet briar-hedges" (l. 106), and he skirts a place where nature's products are processed; that prompts an ingenious telescoping of two senses into one phrase, "taste the smell" (l. 107). Neo-Classical poets, apart from Dyer, had no synaesthesia although they were intensely preoccupied with the kinship of the arts, but Thomson seems to have taken little interest in that sisterhood.

The ascent is only one of several possible pastimes. The vista's lack of structure is expressed pithily in one, almost Homeric, epithet: "far-diffused" (l. 109), which is elaborated in the following line's "one boundless blush..." The beholder's eye hurries across the boundless scene, and his attention is arrested by the profusion of flowers, and not the landmarks of the standard landscape picture. Thomson, who makes a modest use of colour words in his landscapes, has one astonishing new formation in his very original account of his visual apprehension of the luxuriance of the flowers, viz. "white-empurpled" (l. 110).

The whole account achieves its effect by being a palimpsest, so to speak, on a well-known prototype: the contemplation of the objects of the landscape has been replaced by an enraptured awareness of the multitude of spring flowers, and the time motif is appropriately integrated by the beholder letting spring be the herald of autumn. The hypothesis as to what may befall the beautiful flowers is a placid echo of the stag hunt or other dramatic incidents introduced by Thomson's predecessors. The precise pictures of the activities of the two kinds of wind emphasize the precariousness and the vulnerability of the tender buds and blossoms, but Thomson does not seem to be interested in any human parallels. As always, he fairly soon loses sight of the landscape to concentrate on something else, in this case climatic circumstances, such as the influence of various kinds of weather on nature.

In a later passage, a prospect inspired Thomson to some reflections on language:

>
> Behold yon breathing prospect bids the muse
> Throw all her beauty forth. But who can paint
> Like Nature? Can imagination boast
> (470) Amid its gay creation, hues like hers?
> Or can it mix them with that matchless skill
> And lose them in each other, as appears
> In every bud that blows. If fancy then
> Unequal fails beneath the pleasing task
> (475) Ah, what shall language do? Ah, where find words
> Tinged with so many colours and whose power,
> To life approaching, may perfume my lays
> With that fine oil, those aromatic gales
> That inexhaustive flow continual round?[5]

It is uncertain to whom the speaker addresses his question, and where he is standing; but the distant prospect gives inspiration, indeed it orders the muse to do her best. The Neo-Classicists would generally ignore the element of life implied in Thomson's "breathing" (l. 467), but actually the extract expresses the poet's resignation before the task of "painting" the beauties of the scene. The rhetorical questions cause the narrator to lose sight of the concrete details of the prospect in his attempt to contrast nature's mastery as a painter with the deficiencies of both imagination and language.

It is noticeable that although "hues" seem to be a basic characteristic of the contemplated panorama, no specific colour is given. Thomson does not try to render the individual or mixed colours in exact terms, and in a way it can be said that the muse disobeys the duty imposed on her in the opening lines, or rather, she uses a detour in an attempt to reach the goal. Thomson's purpose seems to be to characterize the powerlessness of imagination (l. 467) and, consequently, of language (ll. 473-75). The Neo-Classical idea of words as the dress of thought is discernible behind the perfume image of l. 477: words are the beautifiers (*pace* Polonius) of his song. Neo-Classicists put that relationship more simply, and Thomson's peculiar interrelationship of the senses, using a smell image to characterize the power of words, is totally unknown to them. The idea that language should be as powerful as life is another instance of Thomson's transcending of the Neo-Classical pattern: they worked securely within their tradition and were satisfied that their stock diction gave a reliable picture of *res*. The Neo-Classicists would never evade the pleasurable task of celebrating a prospect, and the problem as posed in this extract, as well as the attitude and its verbal expression, were simply beyond their ken. Thomson's angle of approach is well known within the ecphrastic tradition, and it anticipates the impotence many Romanticists feel vis-à-vis the power of language.

There is another landscape description in lines 516-34 of *Spring*:

>   At length the finished garden to the view
>   Its vistas opens and all its alleys green.
>   Snatched through the verdant maze, the hurried eye
>   Distracted wanders; now the bowery walk
> (520) Of covert close, where scarce a speck of day
>   Falls on the lengthened gloom, protracted sweeps;
>   Now meets the bending sky, the river now
>   Dimpling along, the breezy ruffled lake
>   The forest darkening round, the glittering spire,
> (525) The ethereal mountain, and the distant main.
>   But why so far exclusive? when at hand,
>   Along these blushing borders bright with dew

>   And in yon mingled wilderness of flowers,
>   Fair-handed spring unbosoms every grace –
> (530)   Throws out the snow-drop and the crocus first
>   The daisy, primrose, violet darkly blue,
>   And polyanthus of unnumbered dyes;
>   The yellow wall-flower, stained with iron brown,
>   And lavish stock, that scents the garden round...[6]

The narrator finds himself in a garden, but his wandering eye is tempted beyond it and "meets" the more distant landscape. However, after briefly summarizing what he sees there, he concentrates once more on the beauties of what is near at hand, viz. the flowers of the garden.

The prelude is the familiar one: a beholder allowing his eye to roam hastily, taking in so many details that he is on the point of becoming confused. The run-on lines confer an atmosphere of breathlessness on the description and, of course, form a sharp contrast to the orthodox Neo-Classical technique in which one item of information coincided with one line. The garden is "finished" (l. 516), but art has been applied very prudently: there are valleys (l. 517) and walks (l. 519), and perhaps the vistas of l. 517 have been carefully designed. The garden is not rigidly separated from the adjacent landscape, "the verdant maze" of l. 518 probably being the confused luxuriance of the flora of the garden rather than being a hedge.

The passage is remarkable for its light effects rather than for its colour terms: "green" (l. 517), "verdant" (l. 518), "darkly blue" (l. 531), "unnumbered dyes" (l. 532) "yellow" (l. 533), and "iron brown" (l. 533) are nothing out of the ordinary. But "bowery walk" (l. 519), "speck of day" (l. 520), "bending sky" (l. 522), "the river...dimpling along"(ll. 522-23) (which is also rhythmically functional), "forest darkening" and "glittering spire" (l. 524), and the "blushing borders" (l. 527) all show Thomson as an expert when it comes to finding striking verbal equivalents for the changing nuances of light. So his despair earlier (ll. 473-5) at his power of finding verbal equivalents for the sense impressions that met his eye must have been a conventional *licentia poetica*.

Thomson shows his originality in other ways as well: The

"bowery walk" is a favourite item of his; here, it is the horizontal contrast to the vertical "bending sky" (l. 522), the contrast also being one of *clair/obscur*. His eye "meets the bending sky" (l. 522); the Neo-Classicists would never use such a precise qualifier about the sky, which to them was rather the place where the clouds were sailing. Also, it will be seen how Thomson is at least as interested in darkness as in light: the "covert close" of l. 520 and the "lengthened gloom" of l. 521.

The Neo-Classical tradition becomes perceptible the moment his eye moves beyond the garden: though the objects are the usual ones, no attempt is made to particularize the account, or to give it topographical verisimilitude. Yet the qualifiers are far from being the standard ones: the "breezy...lake" (l. 523), and the "ethereal mountain" (l. 525). However, after those elegant intimations of what he could do within the compass of very few lines, Thomson turns away from the larger vista to feast his eye on the smaller slice of *natura naturata* which is near at hand. And here, he is fascinated by the ingredients (ll. 530 et seq.) rather than by the structure, although some spatiality is suggested ("these", l. 527), "yon", (l. 528).

He has chosen his favourite time, viz. morning, and the flowers are genuine spring flowers. Spring, which is personified, shows its lavishness, and the "grace" of the small flowers is implicitly, and favourably, contrasted with the impressiveness of the landscape outside the garden. The "wilderness" (l. 528) is modified by the fact that it is made up of flowers, and the whole passage reads as an enthusiastic tribute to Spring and Nature, who manifest their magnificence even in the smallest of flowers.

3

Autumn, published in 1730, is mainly devoted to vivid pictures of shooting and hunting, the reaping of the fruits of the earth, and the mirth of the country after the harvest has been gathered. Here is a scene from "this glad season":

> In this glad season while his sweetest beams
> The Sun sheds equal o'er the meekened day,

                Oh, lose me in the green delightful walks
(655)   Dodington, thy seat, serene and plain;
            Where simple nature reigns; and every view
            Diffusive spreads the pure Dorsetian downs
            In boundless prospect – yonder shagged with wood,
            Here rich with harvest, and there with flocks!
(660)   Meantime the grandeur of thy lofty dome
            Far-splendid seizes on the ravished eye.
            New columns swell, and still the fresh Spring finds
            New plants to quicken, and new groves to green.
(665)   Full of thy genius all, the Muses' seat!
            Where, in the secret bower and winding walk,
            For virtuous Young and thee they twine the bay.
            Here wandering oft, fired with the restless thirst
            Of thy applause, I solitary court
(670)   Thy inspiring breeze, and meditate the book
            Of Nature, ever open, aiming thence
            Warm from the heart to learn a moral song...[7]

The Neo-Classicists would often open their accounts with a reference to the position of the sun in the sky, but they would not refer to a specific season, and they would not want to eliminate the difference between subject and object as Thomson does when he begs to be "lost" in the walks. The Neo-Classical approach was rather that which is suggested in l. 661: an item which has its independent existence forces itself upon the sight of the beholder. The "view" and "downs" of ll. 656 & 657 are Neo-Classical reminiscences; but Thomson is fond of a "boundless prospect", which the Neo-Classicists were not. The scene of the extract is a mixture of "simple nature" (l. 656) and art: Dodington has arranged walks (l. 654), and he has erected a "lofty dome" (l. 660). The references to harvest and flocks are not only true pictures of autumn and its activities, but also discreet suggestions of the richness of Dodington's seat. For, of course, in spite of the narrator's assurance that his surroundings are "genuine" nature, what he describes is the extensive estate of Dodington, and his purpose is not to give a pedantically correct account of it but to convey an impression of the successful co-operation between nature and Dodington's planning – the idea we know from Ben Jonson's *Penshurst*. Dodington dominates the estate, also intellectually speaking, and ll. 662-64 ingeniously connect the activities of Dame Nature and Dodington: both of them cause things to grow, columns to swell. As the passage goes along, it more and more assumes the form of a tribute to Dodington's charisma, perhaps because the narrator/poet hopes that Dodington will become his patron. At least the mere presence in Dodington's neighbourhood is claimed to stimulate the poet's inspiration, indeed, the very winds are able to set him aglow. Dodington's rural seat furnishes an excellent opportunity to read the book of nature, which is always open, and the poet's heart is warm, which means that an essential condition for the Muse to exercise her beneficent influence has been fulfilled.

The lines describe a ritual which is less mechanical than that of Thomson's predecessors among the Neo-Classical poets. His landscape is made subservient to something else to an extent which is unknown in most of the Neo-Classicist poets. The passage is an elaborate compliment to the owner of the estate, perhaps also a request for more than spiritual assistance.

4

The seasons and their changing manifestations are the centres of interest to James Thomson's long poem. He registers the landscape features that we know from the Neo-Classical tradition, but they do not seem to have the intrinsic value that they had to his predecessors. Rather they function as the backdrop for that which really absorbs his interest. Thomson's approach in making his landscapes dependent on a season is alien to the Neo-Classical convention. That puts some restraints on Thomson's accounts, which obey a verisimilitude that is different in kind from the Neo-Classical attempts at topographical approximation. Thomson has to take into account changes of climate and time of the day, which were completely ignored by his predecessors, whose "sightings" are taken in clear sunlight and, unlike Thomson's, never in the early morning when the dew is still fresh on the ground, or after a shower when leaves and flowers are dripping wet.

The contrast in *The Seasons* is not so much one of art versus nature – art actually makes a very unobtrusive appearance in his scenes – as one of large landscape versus small garden. The garden – which is anything but the neatly planned and symmetrical French arrangement – fascinates him far more than it did those poets that went before him. But his landscape descriptions bear some resemblance to those of the Neo-Classicists in that they are interspersed with small interludes, eg the eagerly watchful spider on the catch (*Summer*, ll. 267-80), the return of the shepherds in the evening (*Summer*, ll. 1664-81), or even a stag hunt (*Autumn*, ll. 425-57).

However, there are noticeable differences: the fact that his landscapes are far from always unambiguously seen from above, and his repeated wish to touch diverse landscape objects or to move towards them, means that the Neo-Classical idea of the appropriate distance – one of their basic tenets, deriving from Horace's *si propius stes* – is abandoned. Moreover, his syntax is not as mechanically end-stopped as eg that of Denham and Pope. Run-on lines are used effectively by him, not only to convey the course of a river, but also to impart an impression of the breathless haste with which he takes in the objects of the scene. Thomson writes in blank verse, and it would be an exaggeration to call him an elegant versifier.

Thomson's command of colour is sophisticated. Some of his colours are admittedly traditional, "red", "blue" and "brown" alternating with the watered-out "verdant" and the indiscriminate "unnumbered dyes". However, he reveals a considerable talent of going beyond the poetic diction-like possibilities of the Neo-Classicists, and he manages to impart to his reader the colour of a scene or an item by describing the effect of the wind, the clouds, or the sun on it: in *Summer*, for instance he lets "the smoking currents" shine through the faint morning light. Actually, his dependence on a specific season is turned to account by Thomson, who has an expert eye for the subtle interplay between varying intensities of light and the flowers, bushes and trees of spring, summer, and autumn.

Like the Neo-Classical poets, Thomson is a moralist, but his moral is often implicit: the sheer pleasure of looking at even the most insignificant and everyday flowers testifies to a warm affection for nature, which went against Neo-Classical decorum. Thomson has none of the middle-of-the-road maxims that permeate the landscape scenes of those who went before him: to him, a mountain is an impressive, perhaps even "ethereal" structure entirely devoid of social overtones. However, in other contexts than strictly landscape ones, he does embark on political speculation of a very matter-of-fact kind. In *Summer*, for example, he imagines the "wonders of the torrid zone" (ll. 633 et seq.), but soon realizes that those countries (ie "Afric" and others) have not got

> Kind equal rule, the government of laws,
> And all-protecting freedom which alone
> Sustains the name and dignity of man.

Later in the same book, there is an enamoured praise of contemporary England (ll. 1147 et seq.), which can rejoice at a rich soil and "a merciful clime", glowing meadows and shining villas, and cities full of the sons of art and trade. Immediately afterwards follows a paean of British poets and scientists, old ones as well as modern ones. Thomson's delight at English scenery naturally leads to outbursts of affectionate patriotism. His conclusions are more precise and in a literal sense more down to earth than those of the Neo-Classicists, whose overall concern was a mixture of wonder and awe at the Great Design. Actually it was only Pope, among the Neo-Classicists, who got on to talking in some depth about politics, past and present, in some passages of *Windsor Forest*.

However, from a literary point of view the really significant difference between the works of the orthodox Neo-Classicists and Thomson's *Seasons* is in the attitude to *natura naturata*. There is a shift of emphasis and a dissolution of the Neo-Classical convention. In important respects, Thomson's approach heralds that of the Romanticists' cult of Nature: his "song" is, in his own words, pathetic, ie emotionally tinged; he is fond of "bowers"; he wants to "meditate" on the book of nature – an anticipation of the Romantic predilection for "reading books in brooks"; he "converses" with nature and makes frequent use of that Romantic favourite figure, the wanderer; he conceives of nature as a mysterious power, and he would like to enter into a kind of communion with it. He could feel the animals' delight, as Wordsworth could in *Written in Early Spring*, and he feels inclined to converse with nature, as Wordsworth did in *Tintern Abbey*.

CONCLUSION

1

Horace formulated the maxim *ut pictura poesis*, but did not elaborate on it. With their respect for the Ancients, it was natural for the Neo-Classicists to adopt and develop the idea, and they implemented it in one genre, viz. the landscape poem.

But, more generally, much of the Neo-Classical speculation and theorizing on art and the relationship between the arts ultimately derives form Classical Antiquity and the Renaissance. Cicero, for example, gives the following definition of proportion, a concept which is central to Neo-Classicism: "apta composition membrorum".[1] According to Cicero, proportion is mathematical by nature, but originates in music. However, the principle can be smoothly transferred to other arts: it is possible for an artist, eg a sculptor, to acquire a sense of proportion by imitating the most harmonious and beautiful "natural bodies"[2] – art can with advantage imitate nature. In *Tusculanae disputations*, Cicero makes proportion an indispensable ingredient of beauty: a suitable structure of the parts with sweetness of colours added.[3] Cicero's definition was originally aimed at painting, but since both the Renaissance and Neo-Classicism equated colours with words, Cicero's statement could without difficulty be applied to literature as well.

In Cicero's theoretical reflections, we find anticipations of many discussions that preoccupied Neo-Classical poets and critics: the appropriate (Cicero, as we saw, uses the word *apta*) distribution of parts and wholes, the often reiterated assertion that art should imitate nature, and, last but not least, the intimation that there is a common denominator valid for all the arts, which makes parallels and comparisons natural and informative.

2

In many respects, Neo-Classicism follows in the footsteps of the Renaissance, both in its conception of the essence and function of art and in the categories and terminology used to discuss theoretical issues within the arts.

Both ages are partial to the idea that art is a reconciliation of opposites, a state of equilibrium between ethics and aesthetics. If it is presupposed that a spectator's contemplation of a picture should yield pleasure to the eye as well as to the mind, the juxtaposition between painting and poetry immediately suggests itself, as it did to both the Renaissance and Neo-Classicism. Moreover, to both ages, the ideal work of art was not only one that, technically speaking, respected the principle of *concordia discors*. The idea of balance went further in that the ideal work of art represented a state of equilibrium between the artist's native talents and the rules to which he submits himself, between the forward push of inspiration aided by genius and the restraining and salutary pull of reason and judgement. Though realizing their desirability and fascination, neither age ventured a definition of genius, judgement or *je ne sais quoi*, none of which was found to be incompatible with reason, indeed they were acclaimed as prerequisites for the production of a genuine masterpiece.

In order to be able to discuss theoretical issues with some degree of precision, the Neo-Classicists needed a terminology as well as a conceptual frame and some principles of categorization. Renaissance thinking and its mediation through near-contemporary French thinkers proved immediately serviceable. Bellori and Junius, both painters and art theorists, served as important connecting links between the Renaissance and Neo-Classicism. The theories of those critics were carried to fruition towards the end of the 17th century. The influence of Bellori on Dryden's *Parallel* is obvious, and Francesco Junius' *De pictura veterum* appeared in

1637, his own English version of it, *The Painting of the Ancients*, following in 1638. The author was the friend of Rubens, van Dyck, and Inigo Jones.

Junius' book is especially interesting for its discussion of colours, but it also touches on some of the points that were taken up by the Neo-Classicists: poetry and painting have several points in common (the difference of medium is, as was the case with the Neo-Classicists, virtually passed over in silence): they have the same purpose, viz. the imitation of nature, and in order to achieve that end they use identical means, viz. imagination, sensuous illusion, emotion, and the glorification of men and gods.[4] Junius also points out that Greek used the same verb (*graphein*) to designate the act of painting and writing; and, interestingly, he uses the formulation *perlegere oculis* ("read with the eyes") about a beholder's contemplation of a picture.[5]

Inversely, the triad for literature, viz. invention, disposition, and elocution, established in his *Ars poetica* from 1527 by the Italian humanist and poet Marco Vida, is used by Ludovice Dolce in *Dialogo della pittura* (1557), when he describes the principles of good painting: he talks about invention, design, and colour. However, Dolce adds a fourth requirement, viz. that the work of art should stir the recipient emotionally,[6] ie the *movere* aspect that was ultimately instrumental in causing the collapse of the Neo-Classical canon. By the same token, Vida's tripartite system was adapted by the 17th century pictorial theorist Dufresnoy, and it forms the basis on which Neo-Classical discussions of literary creation and execution are anchored.

However, Neo-Classicism did not adopt Renaissance literary ideals lock, stock, and barrel. For one thing, the Renaissance knows no counterpart of the Neo-Classical landscape poem, which means that it has no literary genre purporting to imitate the art of painting. In a more general way, Neo-Classicism was more imbued with *l'esprit géométrique* than was the Renaissance. The Neo-Classicists were virtually obsessed with rules and classifications: they decomposed the creative process into discrete stages, and they evaluated artists by assigning them places in subjectively established hierarchies.

3

Landscape poets were susceptible to influence from painting because a picture was a useful support for clarifying the mimetic quality of poetry, which reflects the world indirectly, by means of words, and there was no inherited literary convention to guide a writer who sought to give a detailed but non-chaotic overview of an outdoor scene. The age was sensitive to pictures and the picture-creating faculty of the human mind: it was an asset for a verbal account to prompt pictures in a recipient's mind.

Neo-Classical landscape poets learned from landscape painters how a segment of the surrounding countryside could be isolated and made a *locus poeticus*. They also learned how to exploit the horizontal and vertical lines in the field of vision, and to turn spatial depth and dimension to account.

Landscape descriptions were not unknown in other genres, eg the great epic poems, but there they were mostly stereotyped backdrops for the action of the poem. In the Neo-Classical poems, landscapes exist in their own right, they are carefully, but cautiously "heightened", clearly framed and, more often than not, abundantly coloured. In one respect, then, Horace's statement came true (in a sense he did not initiate himself): literature acquired some of the characteristics of a picture. And since painting primarily appealed to the eye, poetry, too, makes sight the Queen of Senses. Smells and sounds do occur, but they are always subordinated to the impressions received by the eye.

The Neo-Classical beholder institutionalized the technique of the "wandering eye", which, combined with the swift glances in the direction of the horizon, intimates the depth and breadth of the contemplated panorama. The movement of the poet's eye is horizontal, vertical, and meandering, and the parallel with a person looking at a picture is obvious. The situation of the beholder is not unlike that found in the beloved Romantic *topos*, the halted wanderer. His attention is captured by something in the surrounding world which causes him to stop. An interaction is established between the beholder and that which is beheld: reception is invariably followed by reflection and interpretation.

Aesthetic ideals were involved, too: *poesis* learned from *pictura* (and might have learned from *musica*) that a beautiful object is not a mere random juxtaposition of felicitous strokes, but a coherent ensemble of parts that are interdependent, hence necessarily connected. Minor faults have to be admitted, indeed welcomed in order to set the harmony of the whole into relief. The good *dispositio* – in poetry as well as in painting – is one that adapts all the elements to its overall subject, at the same time preserving the greatest possible harmony inside the whole.

The landscape poets' imitation of their pictorial colleagues went so far that they would adopt features from painting that might sometimes seem out of place in their seemingly topographical accounts. It was not unusual for painters to arrange what Friedländer calls a "*Begebnisbühne*" in the foreground of their pictures.[7] Some poets also force an open space into the foreground of their scene, and imagine a pastoral, mythological, or historical interlude being performed there. The stag-hunt is a popular ingredient even in poems that purport to describe an English panorama. The inspiration may have come from a great pictorial landscapist like Claude Lorrain: there is a famous painting by him from 1672 called *The Stag Hunt* (Brussels). Besides introducing a change in the purely descriptive mode, such incidents – and both human beings and other animals than stags will sometimes invade the scene – have decidedly moral or symbolic overtones, eg the great one being pursued and brought to death by the smaller ones, or a tyrant suffering his well-deserved overthrow. It is remarkable that, once the hunt is over, harmony and serenity is almost immediately restored. The sudden irruption remains a parenthesis since no reference is made to it in other passages of the poem. Such scenes bear some resemblance to the "inset stories" we know from 18th and 19th century novels. An analogous breach of reality is the suspiciously large number of grottoes found in the Thames valley if the poets are to be believed.

Of course either of the two arts had what was felt to be shortcomings vis-à-vis the other. The grievance against painting is its irremediable stasis. Poets are always anxious to distance themselves from the still-life tendency of many landscape pictures, whose masses of trees have an almost architectonic and consequently rigid and motionless structure. In *The Wonders of the Rock* from

1681, Charles Cotton deplores the limitations of pictorial representation compared to the achievements of nature herself:

> The *Groves*, whose curled *Brows* shade ev'ry Lake
> Do ev'rywhere such waving Landskips make,
> As Painters baffled Art is far above,
> Who *Waves* and *Leaves* could never yet make move.[8]

One point where poetry is seriously at a disadvantage is of course the conveying of the artistic impression: painting had colours whereas poetry was forced to use words, ie the impression had to be mediated via another medium. More generally, the poet had to place objects that were absent before the reader's eyes. Another drawback was that, unlike the painter, the poet was unable to combine and render the whole scene in one comprehensive view. The beholder of a picture can take in many items at a glance, but the written account does not permit any such total apprehension. On the contrary, landscape poems progress at a sedate, enumerating pace, each line adding a new feature to the vista.

4

The Neo-Classical landscape poems describe a civilized, domesticated slice of *natura naturata*. The poems are not patriotic paeans, yet the scene is unmistakably English.

The change of seasons, the great cycle of nature, and the passing of time have been suspended. The season of the poems is unspecified summer. Snow, ice, fog, thunderstorms and lightning are ingredients in the sublime types of description, but in the orthodox Neo-Classical poems it never even rains. By the same token, the time of day is vaguely afternoonish: it is not the freshness of the morning or the fascination of the sunset that tempt the poet to sally forth.

The landscape scene is not characterized by human or any other activity. Fertility is frequently mentioned, but that, too, is a latent phenomenon whose usual consequence, viz. harvest, never occurs.

The poems read like a snapshot, not a succession of situations. Apart from the incident that is sometimes claimed to have taken place in the foreground but never occurs in the "now" of the poems, the poems are purely descriptive, never narrative, and they are not set in a narrative context. Even pretendedly topographical poems are never tourist guides, and the panoramas are always more or less discreetly "arranged". The "story" that the poems tell is the gradual revelation to the beholder's eye of more and more landscape features and, implicitly, their symbolic overtones. The poem is over when the scene before the poet's eye is "full", ie when the items that allow him to deduce a moral have been registered. By and large, the items are given equal weight, for they are not in the poem for any inherent value that they may possess, but as players in a great symphony. And the instruments of the orchestra show little variation.

The Neo-Classicists were not linguistically oriented in the sense of investigating the nature and status of the connection between visual fact and verbal formulation. They do not seem to be aware of any difficulty of rendering a spatial art in a linear medium. They will often allow the visual to rub shoulders with the verbal without any mediation as when a visual phenomenon is just stated verbally without being made the object, grammatical or otherwise, of a beholder's activities.

They tackled the issue pragmatically: the word was the dress of the thought. They adhered to Cato the Elder's advice to orators: rem tene, et verba sequentur: they "held" the matter, and the words followed, often in terms of programmed responses to what lay beneath their feet.

The synthesis that is created by the form and the content is strengthened both by the syntax and the vocabulary of the poems. They were cast in a mould that allowed few variations. Since the beholder enumerates the ingredients rather than evaluates them, a frequently occurring syntactical pattern is parataxis. Lines may either be written in blank verse or form heroic couplets. It must be admitted that not a few Neo-Classical poets are miserable versifiers.

The items of the landscape are, to a large extent, standard ones because they are there for a moral purpose, and so is the vocabulary used to designate them. A poetic diction evolved, reminiscent of that of the pastorals. The few human beings in the poems are *swains, nymphs,* and *wanderers,* or *herds* tending their *flocks.* The streams are *brooks* or *rivulets* (sometimes also rivers), and they *meander* through the objects of the panorama, some of which are *mossy banks,* hiding *grottoes,* and the water *glitters* to the beholder's eyes. The items are presented as an *array,* where *hills* are balanced by *vales,* and *glades* are protected by the *shade* offered by the *overarching trees.* The elements of the vegetable kingdom are often subsumed under the term *verdure,* and whereas trees and bushes are hardly ever individualized, their *dyes* and *hues* are often given in considerable detail – as if the description was of a painting.

The Neo-Classicists were fond of general terms so the poets could take it for granted that also the recipients, for whose favour all Neo-Classical poets catered, would find general terms "natural" and satisfactory. They had a fondness for one type of adjective-noun constellation: a qualifier whose content applies to the whole group rather than an individual specimen precedes the generic noun (*the silver stream*). The objects of the landscape are almost invariably provided with a qualifier. Here, too, a standard type of expression became the rule, indeed in many cases the adjective preceding the noun reads like a Homeric *epitheton ornans*: *silvery stream, meandering/soft-gliding rivulet,* (the brook's) *winding train, gloomy/shady/flowery/ sheltering/verdant grove, bowery grotto, sylvan bower, smiling meads, crystal lake, hilly heights, simple/chequered shade, lonely plain* and *calm retreat.*

As will be seen, the adjectives tend to be routinely descriptive rather than evaluative. Actually, the orthodox Neo-Classical landscape poems contain very few value judgements where the ingredients of the panorama are concerned. The items are on the same level and are supposed to speak for themselves, and poets describe the characteristics you would notice in a picture.

The poets use a wide spectrum of colour adjectives: a flower can be *verdant, gaudy, vermilion, purple, silver* and *freckled.* However, also in this case the true poet shows his mastery in the way he transgresses the convention by suggesting vestiges of conformity to it: in *Windsor Forest,* Pope describes the "various Race" of fish supplied by "our plenteous Streams":

The bright-eyed Perch with Fins of Tyrian Dye.
The silver eel in slimy Volumes roll'd:
The yellow Carp with Scales bedropt with Gold,
Swift Trouts, diversify'd with Crimson Stains...[9]

5

The stereotyped content and the code-like language made the matrix of the Neo-Classical landscape poem something of a Procrustes' bed. However, at the same time, it is a convenient frame which gave poets the support and security of a "kind", and also left room for a modicum of independence, witness Pope's elegance and Dyer's sophistication. James Thomson developed the description of the scenery further in his *Seasons*. He broke the mould by making the four seasons the "protagonists" of his poem, reducing landscape to an ancillary role, and he abandoned the moralizing aspect altogether. And the genre proved eminently compatible with the age's idea of originality: to the Neo-Classicists, originality referred to the elegance with which a poet could imitate or emulate his contemporaries and predecessors, the faithfulness with which they could put new wine on old bottles without reducing themselves to mere copyists. Admittedly, some poets leaned heavily on the convention without contributing very much of their own making – and the results were as could be expected.

To a modern reader, the weaknesses of the genre are not difficult to catch sight of: its repetitive terms, its cautious morality and its almost programmed responses are potentially deadening. But the poems were more than literary exercises. They were carriers of messages that some opinion-forming circles of the period, including men of letters, considered urgent in a world that was beginning to change – problems concerned with power, ambition, worldly possessions, human dignity, ethics, and the attitude to nature. The landscape poem is the mediator of an understanding that the age considered essential.

Landscape features show a nature-given variety. But, in accordance with the maxim put forward by Katherine Philips, "order...

is nothing else but harmony, where different parts are brought to agree",[10] poets would strive to plan their description so as to avoid making it a confused heap of details. That might be done, for instance, by assigning a role to, and stressing the co-operation of, the individual features

> And all the Rivers and the Forests nigh
> Both Food and Game and Exercise supply,

wrote Cowley in his translation of Vergil's Georgic *O fortunatus nimium*.[11] The quotation illustrates both the *concordia discors* and the *prodesse et delectare* maxims.

The Neo-Classical landscape poem became an explicit writing out of the attitudes shared by many people around the turn of the 18th century, eg a pronounced desire to understand and explain the world – and thus perhaps control it: One of the ways of making the world comprehensible was to let an observant person try to view it in terms of a structured whole. Landscape came to mean not only picture, but also arrangement, modest variation and manageability, which means that it came to be regarded in much the same light as an object in science. To use Richard Pearce's phrasing, Descartes "imposed a frame upon the clutter and continuity of history from the perspective of an ideal, solitary, and detached observer".[12]

Neo-Classicism was an age of scientific and philosophic discovery, and trying to understand things by looking at them – or into the human mind – engaged people's feelings as well as their intellects. Landscape poetry owed its popularity to the fact that it was both an optical phenomenon and an interpretation of reality. Landscapes are more than "mere ornament", for they not only describe, they also express. Ascent of the hill facilitates the poet's grasp of the scene and his understanding of the great design: *si monumentum requiris, circumspice*.

The items of the landscape scene are both objects and symbols, and the poems are metaphorical as well as quasi-realistic. Since the purpose is to show the beauty of the Great Design by the intermediary of *natura naturata*, the description is bound to be more than a kaleidoscopic inventory.

The genre is not original in that it exploits hitherto unnoticed aspects of a landscape. On the contrary, the items of the Neo-Classical landscape poem are extremely common ones and have been used in descriptions since the days of Theocritus. So what the Neo-Classicists demonstrate is the idiosyncratic use of a convention rather than newness. However, the Neo-Classicists did not mind repetition, and the age was partial to unexceptionable truths: the blessings of the "middle state" seem to consist in the fact that it is neither swaggeringly high nor despicably low. And no Neo-Classical poet ever suggests any really workable idea to remedy the plight of those who were really low. The poems are not penetrated with social indignation, and the poets' attitude was that those who were "low" had that position because that was the way things were, and the existence of the high and mighty and the abject and lowly was a necessary variety element to obtain social balance.

6

The Neo-Classical beholder has only a limited similarity with the Romantic seer facing "nature". The Neo-Classicist does not indulge in vague reverie; his is a purposeful observation, not passive receptivity; he seeks the hilltop to gain solitude and food for meditation, but his *locus inspirationis* was far more restricted than that of his Romantic counterpart. It would be an exaggeration to say that his only feeling is that of standing amidst a host of symbols provoking predictable responses in him. On the other hand, it would be equally misleading to state that his sole purpose is to count, if not the streaks of the tulip, at least the meanderings of the brook. To put it facetiously, one might say that he notices both the wood and the trees.

The narrator of the poem, who is also the beholder of the scene, traverses a gamut of emotions. He accepts the challenge of the hills with spontaneous glee, and, once on the hilltop, his exhilaration and ecstasy are tempered with not unduly sophisticated moral overtones. The poem ends on a catharsis-like note of calm and serene satisfaction, which is due to the fact that, by then, the narrator has put his message across. It should be noted that hardly any poet refers to the descent from the hill at all.

The beholder is at pains to share his experience with others. This appears, for example, from his repeated invitations to somebody else – and since the beholder is alone on the hilltop, this somebody else can only be the reader, or, more generally, mankind – to "look" or "see", or "there behold". The narrator's exclamations contain an appeal to make the same observations as he does himself and, by inference, agree with his deductions. The sense data and the ensuing moralization are liable to generalization. The beholder "reads" the landscape, and he "understands" it as well. There is a suggestion that he is speaking on behalf of mankind.

The position of the objects of the scene is significant for the conveyance of the moral: they co-operate in pairs, but also all together, which provides the account with an inherent centripetality. "Space is moral," said Pope, and the panorama displays that harmonious blend of freedom and order which was pleasurable to the Neo-Classicists.

A prominent feature of orthodox Neo-Classicism is its preoccupation with, and cult of, the general. The interest of philosopher and moralist alike in *quod semper, ab omnibus, et ubique* is perceptible behind the landscapists' moralizing, just as it finds a counterpart in the generalizations of the poets' literary formulations. The landscape poets implicitly or explicitly convey the inadvisability, indeed the potential danger, of riding one's own hobby-horse, and they do it so often that it cannot help striking a modern reader. Incipient economic changes made for greater self-centred ambition and, consequently, social mobility and unrest. The result was, almost inevitably, a change in moral values. And there is little doubt that the repeated insistence on order, stability and sedate peacefulness that we meet with especially in the first decade of the 18th century is a reaction to the licentiousness and debauchery that is made manifest in many Restoration dramas.

Order, Stability, and Harmony were the much sought-after supporting pillars of the social, political, and religious systems. However, they were only ancillaries to the overriding concept of Reason.

Neo-Classical pronouncements on reason are as high-flown and elusive as the attributes with which other ages have provided the name of God. But it is important to remember that there was also a non-rational strain in Neo-Classicism: it admitted *je ne sais quoi*, it cultivated decorum, and it enthroned taste as the ultimate arbiter – and the age lived quite well with those seeming contradictions. It is symptomatic that two works with diametrically opposed tenets, Rapin's poetics and Longinus' book on the sublime were published within a very short time of each other and became tremendously popular almost overnight.

The variegated landscape is a symbol serving as the conveyor of a political, moral, and religious message. The thoughts that are provoked in the observer are only vicariously concerned with nature. The poem becomes an all-embracing analogy – the order shown by the panorama should, ideally, be extended to be valid for life in general. The implication is that what is eg social is – or ought to be – a reflection or a derivation of what is shown by nature.

The Neo-Classicists saw a picture of harmony and equilibrium from their hilltops. It is true that to some extent they selected and arranged localities and features that provided the answers they wanted to be given. What they saw beneath them was a co-operating and well-functioning microcosmos. The ingredients had attained a stage of *concordia discors* showing that the Great Architect had created a harmonious and good place. The discordant elements included on the way served a purpose, they are meaningful finger-prints on the part of the Great Architect: perfection is a smooth merging and a heightened elimination of imperfections. Thus, the Neo-Classical landscape poem becomes a picture in more than one sense, for it is also a verbalized illustration of what many Neo-Classicists conceived of as the ideal society.

The poem describes a prototype of a society where everyone knows and keeps their place – even the sun is in its wonted position and does not seem to move. The taller and the stronger feel a responsibility for their less privileged fellow creatures: the trees "o'erarch" the lower plants so as to protect them against too much sunlight. The society is not static (lakes are not a prominent ingredient of the poems), but its pace is sedate, as is indicated by the "soft-gliding brooks". Inequality is not frowned upon: the lower bushes do not envy the taller trees, and as it is in nature, so it ought to be in an ideal society. Disrupting factors (eg weeds) are given short shrift. Prospects are necessary, but are never allowed to get out of control (unlike James Thomson's "boundless prospects"). Social and political dreams should never be allowed to run wild, and illusions are reined in: a clearly indicated horizon will see to that. If the society can be held to have reached a state of perfection, what changes would be desirable or imaginable? Accordingly, the goal of the slow movement of the brooks is hardly ever referred to.

The orchestration is didactic: the interdependence of all the participants is emphasized; they do not exist as substances only, but also as attributes to some other substance in the scene. Again the parallel with social conditions is obvious.

The Neo-Classicists were fond of syntheses, and they wanted to bridge the gap between nature and morality, indeed they derived morality from their comprehensive conception of "nature". An intimate relationship was believed to exist between cosmology and philosophy. Subject and object are separate, but by the use of analogies, metaphors and identical qualifiers, poets establish an area of common ground between inanimate and animate. Analogies were freely made between natural phenomena and social and human conditions. In the closing lines of *Cooper's Hill*, Denham uses the disastrous consequences of a river overflowing its banks as a warning not to let social passions run riot.

Just as the landscape poems are very nearly static, the moral they inculcate is cautious and conservative. The poems are discreetly patriotic and preach the virtue of tranquil contentment with things as they are; the poets are obviously anxious to preserve the *status quo*. There is a good deal of Ovid's *bene vixit qui bene latuit* implied in the descriptions. It is a model of a limited society, it is a Utopia because the overall structure is perfect and everything functions smoothly. The word change has a very limited occurrence in the poems. But the ideal state that is presented is anything but concrete: the destination of the brooks and rivulets is hardly ever referred to, no changes of the law are suggested to improve the plight of the poor, no political measures that could remedy the small defects of the system are mentioned, no concrete grievance within any area is analysed. The poems are not pamphlets, and their real message seems to be *Verweile doch, du bist so schön*.

A cautious age preferred to work with a filtered, fairly civilized slice of *natura naturata*. The conclusion of the poet's contemplation – often the ending of the poem – is that the order, stability and harmony that prevail in the panorama beneath him are an illustration of the edifice of the Great Architect. Accordingly, the hierarchies and interdependences that made a landscape scene a harmonious whole could profitably be copied in the way man arranged the structure of *his* design and the conduct of his life.

However, a faint undertone of anguish is perceptible in poets' responses to the idyllic vistas. Poets are aware that their Utopia is beset with lurking dangers. Contemporary Restoration Drama had shown inappropriate manifestations of unrestrained abandonment and debauchery. Poets avoided looking towards the future – that would have shown them the transitoriness of their "perfect place". The Neo-Classical landscape poem is also an escapist genre.

7

The doctrine of the Sisterhood of the Arts appealed to fundamental sides of the Neo-Classical *Zeitgeist*. The rationalist strain was gratified by the possibility of applying the analytical procedures of science to art, and of one art to another. Veneration for selected icons of Antiquity made it natural for them to embroider on an idea that in Horace is no more than one among many *obiter dicta*. Although the originator himself had not spent many lines on the idea and not considered the parallel from an *artistic* point of view, the Neo-Classicists were so much in awe of him that they took the parallel as gospel truth. They dislodged the maxim from its Horatian context and gave it an idiosyncratic interpretation.

The acquisition and possession of land increasingly became a status symbol, the value of which was considerably enhanced by the owners' multifarious "arrangements" of the rural areas, a fact that was also meant to show man's dominance over nature.

The concept of taste, which came to be one of the criteria of good breeding, revealed that various aspects of *natural naturata*, such as a "heightened" landscape, actually conveyed pleasure.

Neo-Classicists loved looking at pictures, and their landscapes were pictures in more than one sense of the word – they were "mirrors of life", and they permitted a felicitous union of *prodesse* and *delectare*.

The predilection of the age for establishing clear-cut divisions and for inscribing arbitrary distinctions into a halo of seemingly incontrovertible validity is reflected in Locke's analyses of the mind as well as the uniformity amidst variety read into the landscape features by the poets.

The conception of nature that we meet in the Neo-Classical landscape poem in some respects heralds the attitude of the Romanticists: blissful harmony is found away from the hustle and bustle of towns and cities, the possibility for the individual – be he a lonely beholder or a solitary wanderer – to establish a peculiar relationship with *natura naturata*, or selected segments of it, the feeling that nature is a worthy object of contemplation in its own right, accompanied with a sense that "here is more than meets the eye", the conviction that it was possible to acquire a deeper understanding of life when you were surrounded by trees, bushes and "mossy banks".

However, there are differences: the Neo-Classicists stopped before contemplation led to immersion. Whereas the Romanticists explored nature for the benefit of the poets, claiming to find personal enrichment and an existential "meaning" in nature – in Wordsworth's case it was a question of healing – which they did their utmost to extend to mankind at large, the Neo-Classicists were not preachers in the same insistent sense: They saw nature as a cog in the great wheel and did not feel above the common herd in the same way as many Romanticists did.

Both ages looked at *natura naturata* with an observant, respectful, and empathetic eye and can thus, each in their own way, be characterized as lovers of nature. But the cathartic effect on them was different: Neo-Classicism knows no visionary seers pretending to be the "unacknowledged legislators of mankind", to use

Shelley's formulation from *A Defence of Poetry*. Neo-Classicism was content to recognize that, when added up, the digits made a sum that came right. Their marvellous discovery was that the Great Architect – and unlike some Romanticists they do not shy back from sometimes using the word God – had made what was complicated immediately comprehensible to mankind.

The Neo-Classical landscape poem is a child of its age in that, though sometimes tending towards the mechanical, it is limpid like the waters of its own brooks, and it is not inimical to, or incompatible with, some degree of unforced elegance. The genre became the vehicle of an integrated, albeit earth-bound, interpretation of life in which harmony was shown to exist between macrocosmos and microcosmos.

BIBLIOGRAPHY

Primary sources

Anderson, Robert (ed.), *The Complete Edition of the Poets of Great Britain*, Volume the Seventh. London 1795. Title Page: *The Works of the British Poets, Containing Parnell, Garth, Rowe, Addison, Hughes, Sheffield, Prior, Congreve, Blackmore, Fenton, Granville, Yalden.*

Arber, Edward (ed.), *Webb: A Discourse of English Poetrie* (1586). London 1870.

Audra E. & Williams, Aubrey (eds.), *Pope: Pastorals. Windsor-Forest.* Twickenham Edition, vol. I. London & Yale 1961.

Ault, Norman (ed., completed by John Butt), *Pope: Minor Poems.* Twickenham Edition, vol. IV. London & Yale 1954.

Baillie, John, *Essay on the Sublime.* London 1747.

Banks, Theodore Howard (ed.), *The Poetical Works of Sir John Denham.* Oxford University Press 1938.

de Beer, E.S., (ed.), *The Diary of John Evelyn*, now first printed in full from the manuscripts belonging to Mr. John Evelyn. Vols. I-VI. Oxford 1955.

Bellori, Giovanni Pietro, *Le vite de pittori, scultori et architetti moderni.* Rome 1680.

Bennett, C.E. (transl.), *Horace: The Odes and Epodes.* Loeb's Classical Library. London 1914.

Beresford, John (ed.), *Poems of Charles Cotton.* London 1923.

Blunt, Anthony (ed.), *Nicolas Poussin: Lettres et propos sur l'art.* Paris 1964.

Blunt, Sir Thomas Pope, *Essays on Several Subjects.* London 1697.

(anon.), *Boeticorum Liber. Or, A New Art of Poetry, Containing the best Receipts for Making all Sorts of Poems, according to the Modern Taste. In Two Canto's.* London 1732. Printed in Thomas B. Gilmore (ed.), *Early 18th Century Essays on Taste.* New York 1972.

Boileau-Despréaux, *Oeuvres*. 3 volumes. Paris 1758.
Bond, John, *Quinti Horatii Flacci Poemata*. London 1606.
Le Bossu, R.P., *Traité du Poëme épique*. Sixième édition. La Haye 1714.
Boyle, Robert, *Works*. 4 vols. London 1744.
Boynton, Henry W. (ed.), *The Complete Poetical Works of Pope*. Cambridge, Mass. 1931.
Bramstone, James, *The Man of Taste. Occasion'd by an Epistle of Mr Pope's on that Subject. By the Author of the Art of Politics*. London 1733.
Bray, William (ed.), *Diary and Correspondence of John Evelyn, F.R.S.* London 1850.
Brink, C.O., *Horace: Ars poetica*. Cambridge University Press 1971.
Brome, James, *Travels over England, Scotland, and Wales, etc.* London 1700.
Brown, Baldwin (ed.), *Vasari: On Technique, being the introduction to the three arts of design, architecture, sculpture & painting, prefixed to the lives of the most excellent painters, sculptors, and architects*. By Giorgio Vasari, painter and architect of Arezzo. Transl. Louisa S. Maclehose. Introd. and notes by Professor G. Baldwin Brown. Dover Publications, New York 1960.
Browne, Alexander, *Ars Pictoria: or an Academy of Drawing, Painting, Limning, Etching*. 2nd ed. Corrected & Enlarged by the Author. London 1675.
Browne, Isaac Hawkins, *On Design and Beauty*. London 1744.
Bullen, A.H. (ed.), *England's Helicon. A Collection of Lyrical and Pastoral Poems: Published in 1600*. London 1899.
Burnet, Gilbert (Bishop of Salisbury), *Dr. G. Burnet's Tracts in two volumes, vol. I Containing 1. His Travels. 2. Animadversions on the Reflexions upon the Travels. 3. Three Letters of the Quietists, Inquisition and State of Italy. Vol. II: 4. His translations of Lactantius of the Death of Persecutors. 5. His Answer to Mr. Verilles, etc.* London 1689.
Burnet, Thomas, *Telluris theoria sacra: orbis nostri originem et mutationes generales, quas aut iam subiit, aut olim subiturus est, complectens*. 2 vols., Londoni 1681. English translation: *The Theory of the Earth: containing an account of the Original of the Earth and of all the general changes which it hath already undergone, or is to undergo, till the consummation of all things*. 2 vols., London 1684-90.
Buxton, John (ed.), *Poems of Michael Drayton*. London 1953.

Buxton, John (ed.), *Poems of Charles Cotton*. The Muses' Library. London 1958.

Bysshe, Edward, *The Art of English Poetry*. London 1702. 2nd ed., London 1705 (the edition used in this book).

Chambray, Fréart de, *An Idea of the Perfection of Painting*. Transl. J.E. (John Evelyn) London 1668.

Claude, Anne, comte de Caylus, *Vies des premiers peintres du roi*. Paris 1751.

Claude, Anne, comte de Caylus, *Vies des artistes du XVIIIe siècle. Discours sur la peinture et la sculpture. Salons de 1751 et de 1753*. Ed. par André Fontaine. Paris 1910.

Colombier, Pierre du, *Lettres de Poussin, publiées avec une introduction*. Paris 1829.

Cook, Albert S. (ed.), *The Art of Poetry. The Poetical Treatises of Horace, Vida, and Boileau, with the Translations of Howes, Pitt, and Soames*. Boston 1892.

Crousaz, Jean-Pierre, *Traité du Beau*. Amsterdam 1724.

Cunningham, Allan (ed.), *James Thomson: The Seasons and The Castle of Indolence*. London 1841.

Darbishire, Helen (ed.), *Milton's Poetical Works*. Two vols., vol. I, Oxford 1952, vol. II, Oxford 1955.

Defoe, Daniel, *A Tour through England and Wales*. Everyman ed., 1928.

Denham, Sir John, *Poetical Works*. Bell's Edition, Edinburgh 1780.

Dolce, Ludovico, *Dialogo della pittura intitolato l'Aretino*. Florence 1735 (first edition, Venice 1557).

Drant, Thomas, *Horace his arte of poetrie, pistles, a. satyrs, Englished and to the Earle of Ormounte by T. Drant addressed*. London 1567.

Drury, G. Thorn (ed.), *The Poems of Edmund Waller*. Vols. 1-2. The Muses' Library London 1901.

Dryden, John, *A Parallel between Poetry and Painting*. London 1695.

Dryden, John, *Dufresnoy's De arte graphica translated into English*, 2nd ed., corrected and enlarged. London 1718.

Dubos, J.-B., *Réflexions critiques sur la Poësie et sur la Peinture*. 3 vols., vols. I-II, Utrecht 1732, vol. III, Paris 1733.

Durham, William Highley (ed.), *Critical Essays of the Eighteenth Century, 1700-1725*. Yale University Press 1915, New York 1961.

Elledge, Scott (ed.), *18th Century Critical Essays*. 2 vols., New York 1961.

Faral, Edmond, *Les arts poétiques du XIIe et du XIIIe siècle*. Bibliothèque de l'école des hautes études publiée sous les auspices du Ministère de l'Instruction publique. Sciences historiques et philosophiques. Recherches et documents sur la technique littéraire du Moyen Age. Paris 1923.

Félibien, André, *Entretiens sur les Vies et sur les Œuvres des Plus Excellens Peintres Anciens et Modernes*. Seconde édition, Paris 1625.

Félibien, André, *L'Idée du Peintre Parfait*. London 1707.

Félibien, André, *Nicolas Poussin. Lettres précédées de la vie de Poussin*. Paris 1945.

Félibien, André, *Entretiens sur la vie et sur les ouvrages de Nicolas Poussin*. Genève 1947.

Feuilleret, Albert (ed.), *The Works of Sir Philip Sidney*. Vols. 1-4. Cambridge University Press 1962.

The Free-Thinker, or Essays on Ignorance, Superstition, Bigotry, Enthusiasm, Craft, &C Intermix'd with several Pieces of Wit and Humour. 3 vols., 2nd ed., London 1733.

Fry, Roger (ed.), *The Discourses of Sir Joshua Reynolds*. London 1905.

Gildon, Charles, *The Complete Art of Poetry*. London 1718.

Gilfillan, George (ed.), *The Poetical Works of Edmund Waller and Sir John Denham*. Edinburgh 1857.

Gilfillan, George (ed.), *The Poetical Works of Armstrong, Dyer, and Green*. Edinburgh 1858.

Gilmore, Thomas B. (ed.), *Early 18th Century Essays on Taste*. Scholars' Facsimiles and Reprints. Delmar, New York 1972.

Graham, Richard, *A Short Account of the most eminent painters, both ancient and modern*. London 1695.

Granville, George, *The Genuine Works in Verse and Prose of the Right Honourable George Granville, Lord Lansdowne*. London 1737.

Grayson, Cecil (ed.), *Leon Battista Alberti: On Painting and on Sculpture*. The Latin texts of *De pictura* and *De Status*. Ed. with translations, introduction, and notes. London 1972.

Grosart, Alexander B., (ed.), *The Complete Works of Joshua Sylvester*. 2 vols. Edinburgh 1880.

Grosart, Alexander B., (ed.), *The Complete Works in Verse and Prose of Abraham Cowley*. The Chertsey Worthies' Library, vols. 1-2. Edinburgh University Press 1881.

The Guardian, 1713.

(anon.), *The Happy Life. An Epistle to the Honourable Lieutenant General Wade*. London 1733. Printed in Thomas B. Gilmore (ed.), *Early 18th Century Essays on Taste*. New York 1972.

Hardie, Martin (ed.), *Edward Norgate: Miniatura, or The Art of Limning*. Oxford 1919.

Harris, J.H., *Three Treatises. The First Concerning Art. The Second Concerning Music, Painting and Poetry. The Third Concerning Happiness*. London 1744.

Haydocke, Richard (transl.), *Lomazzo: A Tracte containing the Artes of Curious Paintinge, Carvinge, and Buildinge*. 1598. Gregg International Publishers Ltd 1970.

Herford, C. & Simpson, Peter (eds.), *The Works of Ben Jonson*. Vol. 8: *The Poems. The Prose Works*. Oxford 1947.

Home, Henry, Lord Kames, *Elements of Criticism*. 3 vols., Edinburgh 1762.

Hooker, Edward Niles (ed.), *The Critical Works of John Dennis* Vol. I, Baltimore 1939, Vol. II, Baltimore 1943.

Howell, James, *Dendrologia, Dodona's Grove, or the vocall Forrest*. London 1640.

Humphreys, Samuel, *Cannons. A Poem Inscrib'd to his Grace the Duke of Chandos*. London 1728.

Hutcheson, Francis, *Inquiry into the Original of our Ideas of Beauty and Virtue*. In two treatises, 2nd ed., London 1725.

Johnson, Samuel, *Lives of the English Poets*. 2 vols. World's Classics series. Oxford University Press 1946.

Jonson, Ben, *Q. Horatius Flaccus: his Art of Poetry, Englished by Ben Jonson. With other workes of the author never printed before*. J. Okes f. Ben Jonson London 1640.

Jouanny, Ch. (ed.), *Correspondance de Nicolas Poussin, publiée d'après les originaux*. Paris 1911.

J.S.D.S.P., *Taste. An Essay*. Second ed., London 1739. Printed in Thomas B. Gilmore (ed.), *Early 18th Century Essays on Taste*. New York 1972.

Junius, Franciscus, *The Painting of the Ancients*. London 1638.

Ker, W.P., (ed.), *Essays of John Dryden*. 2 vols., Oxford 1900.

Kiessling, Adolf, *Q. Horatius Flaccus: Briefe, erklärt von Adolf Kiessling*. Siebente Auflage, bearbeitet von Richard Heinze. Berlin 1961.

Killigrew, Anne, *Poems* (1686). Introduction by Richard Morton. Gainesville, Florida 1967.

Lamb, W.R.M. (ed.), *The Discourses of Sir Joshua Reynolds F.R.A.* With Introduction and Portrait. London 1924.

Lambert, Mme de la Marquise de, *Œuvres.* Tome I-II. Paris 1748.

Lamy, Bernard, *La Rhétorique ou l'Art de Parler.* Cinquième Edition. Amsterdam 1712.

Latham, Robert & Matthew, William (eds.), *The Diary of Samuel Pepys.* A new and complete transcription, vols. 1-9. London 1971-76.

Lionardi, Alessandro, *Dialogi di Messer Alessandro Lionardi, delle inventione poetica.* Venice 1554.

Locke, John, *Works.* 3 vols., London 1714.

Locke, John, *Works.* 3 vols., London 1727.

Locke, John, *Works.* 3 vols., London 1801.

Longinus, Dionysius, *Peri Hupsous, or Dionysius Longinus, of the Height of Eloquence rendred out of the originall by J(ohn) H(all), Esq.* London 1652.

Longinus, Dionysius, *An Essay on the Sublime.* Translated from the Greek. London 1698.

Mack, Maynard (ed.), *Alexander Pope: An Essay on Man.* The Twickenham Edition, Vol. III, i. London & New Haven 1950, repr. 1970.

Malone, Edmund (ed.), *The Critical and Miscellaneous Prose Works of John Dryden.* 3 vols. London 1800.

Margoliouth, H.M. (ed.), *The Poems and Letters of Andrew Marvell.* Oxford 1923, repr. 1952.

Marmontel, Jean-François, *Poétique française.* Tome I-II. Paris 1763.

McCurdy, Edward (ed.), *Leonardo da Vinci's Notebooks.* London 1906.

Miner, Earl (ed.), *The Works of John Dryden.* Vols. I-XVIII. The California Edition of Dryden. University of California Press 1972 et seq.

Monier, P., *The History of Painting, Sculpture, Architecture, Graving, etc.* London 1699.

Monk, S.H., *Sir William Temple: Five Miscellaneous Essays.* Ann Arbor 1963.

Morris, Brian & Withington, Eleanor (eds.), *The Poems of John Cleveland.* Oxford 1967.

Moxon, T.A. (ed.), *Aristotle's Poetics. Demetrius on Style. Horace's Ars Poetica, etc.* Everyman's Library 901. London 1943.

Newton, Isaac, *The Mathematical Principles of Natural Philosophy, translated into English by Andrew Motts.* 1729. Introduction by I. Bernard Cohen. London 1968.

Norgate Edward, *Miniature: or, The art of limning*. London 1649.

Noyes, George (ed.), *The Poetical Works of Dryden*. Cambridge, Massachusetts 1950.

O Hehir, Brenda, *Expans'd Hieroglyphicks. A Critical Edition of Sir John Denham's 'Cooper's Hill'*. University of California Press 1969.

Oldham, John, *The Works of Mr John Oldham. Together with his Remains*. London 1692.

Orlandi, Giovanni, *Leon Battista Alberti: L'architettura (De re aedificatoria)*. Testo latino e traduzione a cure di Giovanni Orlandi. Introduzione e note di Paolo Portoghesi. Vols. 1-2. Milano 1966.

Osborn, James (ed.), *Joseph Spence: Anecdotes, Observations, and Characters of Books and Men*. 2 vols., Oxford 1966.

Page, T.E. (ed.), *Q. Horatii Flacci Carminum. Liber II*. London 1913.

Page, T.E. (ed.), *Q. Horatii Flacci Carminum. Liber III*. London 1923.

Parnell, Thomas, *Poetical Works*. London 1796.

Peacham, Henry, *The Art of Drawing with a Pen & Limning in Water Colours*. London 1606.

Peacham, Henry, *The Compleat Gentleman, fashioning him absolute in the most necessary and commendable Qualities concerning Minde or Bodie*. London 1622. Third impression much inlarged, especially in the art of Blazonry, by a very good hand. London 1661.

Peacham, Henry, *The Compleat Gentleman...To which is added The Gentleman's Exercise*. London 1661. Ed. Virgil B. Heltzel. Published for the Folger Shakespeare Library by Cornell University Press. Ithaca N.Y. 1962.

Peake, Charles (ed.), *Poetry of the Landscape and the Night*. London 1967.

Pelletier, Jaques, *Art poétique*, publié par André Boulanger d'après l'édition unique. Paris 1930.

Piles, Roger de, *Œuvres*. Tome I-IV. Amsterdam 1767.

Poole, Joshua. *The English Parnassus*. London 1657, 1677.

Quincy, Quatrième de (ed.), *Nicolas Poussin. Collection de lettres*. Paris 1924.

Raffel, Burton (ed. & transl.), *Horace: The Art of Poetry*. State University of New York Press 1974.

Rand, Benjamin (ed.), *An Essay concerning the Understanding, Knowledge, Opinion and Assent*. (The original draft of the *Essay Concerning Human Understanding*). Cambridge, Massachusetts 1931.

Rapin, René, *Oeuvres*. 3 vols., La Haye 1725.

Recueil de diverses pièces sur la philosophie, la religion naturelle, les mathématiques, & C, par Mesrs. Leibnitz, Clarke, Newton et autres auteurs célèbres. Amsterdam 1720.

Reeves, James & Seymour-Smith, Martin (eds.), *The Poems of Andrew Marvell.* London 1969.

Reynolds, Myura (ed.), *The Poems of Anne, Countess of Winchilsea.* University of Chicago Press 1903.

Richardson, Jonathan, *Two Discourses.* London 1719.

Robertson, Jean (ed.), *Sir Philip Sidney: The Countess of Pembroke's Arcadia (The Old Arcadia).* Oxford 1973.

Poems by the Earl of Roscommon. To which is added An Essay on Poetry. By the Earl of Mulgrave, now Duke of Buckingham. Together with Poems by Mr. Richard Duke. London 1717.

Roskill, Mark W., *Dolce's 'Aretino' and Venetian Art Theory of the Cinquecento.* Published for the College Art Association of America by New York University Press 1968.

Russell, D.A. (transl.), *Longinus: De Sublimitate.* Oxford 1965.

Saintsbury, George (ed.), *Minor Poets of the Caroline Period.* Vols. I-III. Oxford 1905 et seq.

Sambrook, James (ed.), *James Thomson: The Seasons and The Castle of Indolence.* Oxford 1972.

Sargeaunt, John (ed.), *The Poems of John Dryden.* With an introduction and textual notes. Oxford University Press 1948.

Savage, Richard, *The Poetical Works.* Edinburgh 1794.

Scaliger, Julius Caesar, *Poetices Libri Septem.* Editio Secunda. Apud Petrum Santandreanum 1581.

Scott, John, *Critical Essays on Some of the Poems of Several English Poets.* London 1785.

Schmitz, Robert M., *Pope's 'Windsor Forest' 1712.* Washington University Studies, New Series, Language and Literature, No. 21, Saint Louis 1952.

Segar, M.G. (ed.), *The Poems of Ambrose Philips.* London 1937.

Selby, F. (ed.), *Bacon's Essays.* London 1948.

Shaftesbury, Anthony Ashley Cooper, third Earl of, *A Letter Concerning Enthusiasm to my Lord ++++.* London 1708.

Shaftesbury, Anthony Ashley Cooper, third Earl of, *Characteristics of Men, Manners, Opinions, Times.* 3 vols., London 1714.

Shenstone, William, *Poetical Works.* London 1737.

Shepherd, Geoffrey (ed.), *Sir Philip Sidney: Apology for Poetry, or The Defence of Poetry*. London 1965.

Sherburn, George (ed.), *The Correspondence of Alexander Pope*. Vols. I-IV. Oxford 1956.

Smith, G. Gregory (ed.), *Elizabethan Critical Essays*. 2 vols. Oxford 1904, repr. 1937.

Smith, G. Gregory (ed.), *The Spectator*. 4 vols. Everyman Edition, London 1945, repr. 1970.

Smith, G. C. Moore (ed.), *The Early Essays and Romances of Sir William Temple*. Oxford 1930.

Smith J.C. & de Selincourt, E. de (eds.), *The Poetical Works of Edmund Spenser*. Oxford University Press 1947.

Spence, Joseph, *Polymetis, or An Enquiry concerning the Agreement between the Works of the Roman Poets, & the Remains of the Ancient Artists, being an Attempt to illustrate them mutually from one another*. The Second Edition, corrected by the Author. London 1755.

Spencer, Jeffry, *Heroic Landscape*. London 1984.

Spencer, John R. (ed.), *Leon Battista Alberti: On Painting*. Yale University Press 1956.

Spingarn, J.E. (ed.), *Critical Essays of the 17th Century*. Oxford University Press 1908, repr. 1957.

Sprat, Thomas, *The History of the Royal-Society of London. For the Improving of Natural Knowledge*. London 1667.

Steeves, Edna Leake (ed.), *Peri Bathous, or The Art of Sinking in Poetry*. New York 1952.

Switzer, Stephen, *Ichnographia Rustica, or the Nobleman, Gentleman, and Gardener's Recreation, containing Directions for the General Distribution of a Country Seat, into Rural and Extensive Gardens, Parks, Paddocks, &C, and a General System of Agriculture, illustrated with a great Variety of Copper-Plates, done by the best Hands, from the Author's Drawings*. 3 vols., London 1718.

Thomas, M.G. Lloyd (ed.), *The Poems of John Philips*. Oxford 1927.

Thorpe, James (ed.), *Rochester's Poems on Several Occasions (1680)*. Princeton University Press 1950.

Tickell, Thomas, *The Poetical Works of Thomas Tickell*. With the Life of the Author. London, n.d.

Trapp, Joseph, *Praelectiones poeticae*. London 1711. Transl. into *Lectures on Poetry*. London 1742.

Tutchin, John, *Selected Poems 1685-1700*. Introduction by Spiro Peterson. William Andrew Clark Memorial Library, University of California, Los Angeles 1964. Augustan Reprint Society Publications No. 110.

Varchi, Benedetto, *Lezzioni, lette, nel'Academia Fiorentina sopra diverse Materie, Poetiche e Filosofiche*. Fiorenza 1590.

Vinci, Léonard de, *Traité du Paysage*. Traduit par Peladan. Paris 1910.

Waller, A.R. (ed.), *Abraham Cowley: Poems, Miscellanies, The Mistress, Pindarique Odes, Davideis, Verses written on Several Occasions*. Cambridge University Press 1905.

Waller, A.R. (ed.), *Essays, Plays, and Sundry Verses by Abraham Cowley*. Cambridge University Press 1906.

Waller, Edmund, *The Poetical Works*. From Mr. Tention's quarto edition of 1729. With the Life of the Author. London 1816.

Warrington, John (ed.), *The Diary of Samuel Pepys*. Revised and reset, 3 vols., London & New York 1953.

Welsted, Leonard, *The Works in Verse and Prose by Leonard Welsted, Esq*. London 1787.

West, Gilbert, *Stowe. A Poem, The Gardens of the Right Honourable Richard Lord Viscount Cobham, Address'd to Mr. Pope*. London 1732.

Whittaker, E.T. (ed.), *Newton: Opticks, or a Treatise of the Reflections, Refractions, Inflections, and Colours of Light*. New York 1931.

Wickham, Edward (ed.), *Q. Horatii Flacci Opera*. Scriptorum Classicorum Biblioteca Oxoniensis. Oxford 1963.

Wilkins, John, *An Essay towards a Real Character and a Philosophical Language*. London 1668.

Williams, Gordon (ed.), *The Third Book of Horace's Odes*. Oxford 1969.

Williams, Harold (ed.), *Jonathan Swift: Journal to Stella*. Vols. 1-2. Oxford 1948.

Willock, G.D. & Walker, A. (eds.), *George Puttenham: The Arte of English Poesie*. Cambridge University Press 1936.

Worlidge, John, *Systema Agricultura*. 4th ed., London 1687.

Wotton, William, *Reflections upon Ancient & Modern Learning. To which is now added A Defense thereof, in Answer to the Objections of Sir W. Temple and Others. With Observations upon the Tale of a Tub. Also a Dissertation upon the Epistles of Themistocles, Socrates, Euripides &C, and the Fables of Aesop by R. Bentley D.D*. 3rd edition corrected. London 1725.

Secondary sources

Abrams, M.H., *The Mirror and the Lamp*. Oxford University Press 1953. New York 1958.

Abrams, M.H., *Natural Supernaturalism*. New York 1971.

Allen, B. Sprague, *Tides in English Taste*. 2 vols. Harvard University Press 1937.

Alpers, Paul, *What is Pastoral?* University of Chicago Press 1996.

Anderson Howard & Shea, John (eds.), *Esssays in Honor of Samuel Holt Monk. Studies in Criticism and Aesthetics*. University of Minnesota Press 1967.

Appelton, Jay, *The Experience of Landscape*. London & New York 1975.

Ashbery, John, '*And ut pictura poesis is her name*'. *The plastic arts and the avant-garde*. Comparative Literature 1998.

Atkins, J.W.H., *English Literary Criticism, 17th and 18th Centuries*. London 1951, 1954, 1957.

Atkinson, Geoffrey, *Le sentiment de la nature et le retour à la vie simple (1660-1740)*. Genève-Paris 1960. Société des Publications romanes et françaises 66.

Aubin, Robert A., '*Grottoes, Geology, and the Gothic Revival*'. Studies in Philology, vol. 31, 1934.

Aubin, Robert A., *Topographical Poetry in XVIII Century England*. New York 1936.

Ault, Norman, *New Light on Pope*. London 1949.

Babcock, Robert W., '*The Idea of Taste in the Eighteenth Century*'. PMLA vol. L, 1935.

Baker, C.H. Collins & Constable, W.G., *English Painting of the 16th and 17th Centuries*. Firenze & Paris 1930.

Baldwin, Charles Sears, *Renaissance Literary Theory and Practice* (1939). Gloucester, Massachusetts 1959.

Barat, Emmanuel, *Le Style Poétique et la Révolution Romantique*. Paris 1904.

Barrell, John, *The Idea of Landscape and the Sense of Place 1730-1840. An Approach to the Poetry of John Clare*. Cambridge University Press 1972.

Bate, Walter Jackson, '*The Sympathetic Imagination in Eighteenth Century Criticism*'. Journal of English Literary History XII, 1945.

Bate, Walter Jackson, *From Classic to Romantic. Premises of Taste in Eighteenth Century England*. Cambridge, Massachusetts 1946; 2nd ed., New York 1961.

Baxandall, *Giotto and the Orators. Humanists' Observation of Painting in Italy and the Discovery of Pictorial Composition 1350-1450.* London 1951.

Bek, Lise, *'Motivkatalog eller litterært topos'.* Festskrift til Else Kai Sass. Copenhagen 1973.

Benson, Donald R., *"Ideas' and the Problem of Knowledge in Seventeenth Century English Aesthetics'.* English Miscellany XIX, 1968.

Biese, Alfred, *The Development of the Feeling for Nature in the Middle Ages and the Modern Times.* London 1905.

Binyon, Laurence, *English Poetry in its Relation to Painting and the Other Arts.* Proceedings of the British Academy 1917-18. "Third Annual Lecture on Art in its Relation to Civilization". Henriette Hertz Trust, Read June 5, 1918.

Bland, D.S., *'Poussin and English Literature'.* The Cambridge Journal vol. IV, No. 2, November 1952.

Blunt, Anthony, *Artistic Theory in Italy 1450-1600.* Oxford 1940.

Blunt, Anthony, *'The Heroic and the Ideal Landscape in the Works of Nicolas Poussin'.* Journal of the Warburg and Courtauld Institutes, vol. 7, 1944.

Bond, Donald F., *'The Neo-Classical Psychology of the Imagination'.* ELH, vol. 4, No. 4 December 1937.

Borinski, K., *Die Antike in Poetik und Kunsttheorie.* Leipzig, vol. I 1914, vol. II, 1924.

Bowra, Sir Maurice, *Heroic Poetry.* London 1952.

Boyd, John D., *The Function of Mimesis and its Decline.* Cambridge, Massachusetts 1968.

Braitmaier, Friedrich, *Geschichte der poetischen Theorie und Kritik von den Diskursen der Maler bis auf Lessing.* Frauenfeld 1889.

Bray, René, *La formation de la doctrine classique en France.* Paris 1927.

Bredsdorff, Thomas, *Digternes natur.* Copenhagen 1975.

Bredvold, Louis I., *The Intellectual Milieu of John Dryden. Studies in some Aspects of 17th Century Thought.* University of Michigan Press 1934.

Brett, Raymond Laurence, *'The Aesthetic Sense and Taste in the early Eighteenth Century'.* Review of English Studies, vol. XX, 1944.

Bronson, Bertrand H., *'Personification Reconsidered'.* ELH, vol. 14, No. 3. September 1947.

Bronson, Bertrand H., *'When was Neoclassicism?'* in: Howard Anderson & John Shea (eds.). *Essays in Honor of Samuel Holt Monk. Sudies in Criticism and Aesthetics.* University of Minnesota Press 1967.

Bryan, John Ingram, *The Feeling for Nature in English Pastoral Poetry.* Tokyo 1908.

Buchwald, Emilie, *'Gainsborough's 'Prospect, Animated Prospect''* in: Howard Anderson & John Shea (eds.), *Essays in Honor of Samuel Holt Monk. Studies in Criticism and Aesthetics.* University of Minnesota Press 1967.

Budick, Sanford, *Poetry of Civilization. Mythopoetic Displacement in the Verse of Milton, Dryden, Pope, and Johnson.* New Haven & London 1974.

Bundy, Murray Wright, *The Theory of Imagination in Classical and Medieval Thought.* University of Illinois Studies in Language and Literature 1927.

Bury, John Bagnell, *The Idea of Progress.* London 1920, repr. 1958.

Bush, Douglas, *Prefaces to Renaissance Literature.* Harvard University Press 1965.

Butcher, S.H., *Aristotle's Theory of Poetry and Fine Art.* London 1895.

Buxton, John, *Elizabethan Taste.* London 1963.

Carritt, E.F., *A Calendar of British Taste, from 1600 to 1800, being A Museum of Specimens and Landmarks chronologically arranged.* London 1948.

Chalker, John, *The English Georgic.* London 1969.

Chambers, Douglas, *The Reinvention of the World: English Writing 1650-1750.* London, Arnold 1996.

Chester, F. Chapin, *Personification in 18th Century English Poetry.* Columbia University Press 1955.

Chastel, André, *'Poussin et la Postérité'.* Actes du Colloque Poussin II. Paris 1960.

Clark, A.F.B., *Boileau and the French Classical Critics in England 1660-1830.* Paris 1925.

Clark, D.L., *Rhetoric and Poetry in the Renaissance.* New York 1922.

Clark, H.F., *'Eighteenth Century Elysiums. The Role of 'Association' in the Landscape Movement'.* Journal of the Warburg and Courtauld Institutes IV, 1943.

Clark, H.F., *The English Landscape Garden.* London 1948.

Clark, Sir Kenneth, *The Gothic Revival.* London 1928, 3rd ed., 1962.

Clark, Sir Kenneth, *Landscape into Art*. London 1949.

Clément, N.H., '*Nature and the Country in 16th and 17th Century French Poetry*'. PMLA, Vol. XLIV, No. 4, December 1929.

Close, A.J., '*Commonplace Theories of Art and Nature in Classical Antiquity and in the Renaissance*'. Journal of the History of Ideas, vol. 30 1969.

Clough, Wilson D., '*Reason and Genius – an Eighteenth Century Dilemma*'. Philological Quarterly. XXIII 1944.

Cohen, Ralph, '*Thomson's Poetry of Space and Time.*' In Howard Anderson & John Shea (eds.), *Essays in Honor of Samuel Holt Monk. Studies in Criticism and Aesthetics*. University of Minnesota Press 1967.

Collingwood, R.C., *The Principles of Art*. Oxford 1938.

Collingwood, R.C., *The Philosophy of History*. Oxford 1946.

Courtney, William Prideaux, *Dodsley's Collection of Poetry*. London 1910.

Cragg, Gerald R., *Reason and Authority in the 18th Century*. Cambridge University Press 1964.

Crane, Donald S., Bredvold, Louis I., Bond, Richmond P., Friedmann, George and Lands, Louis A., *English Literature 1600-1800. A Bibliography of Modern Studies Compiled for the Philological Quarterly*. Princeton University Press 1926 et seq.

Crane, R.S. (ed.), *Critics and Criticism*. University of Chicago Press 1952.

Crane, R.S., '*English Neoclassical Criticism: An Outline*' in R.S. Crane (ed.), *Critics and Criticism*. University of Chicago Press 1952.

Danto, Arthur C., *The Transfiguration of the Commonplace*. Harvard University Press 1981.

Dauzat, Albert, *Le sentiment de la nature et son expression artistique*. Paris 1914.

Davie, Donald, *The Language of Science and the Language of Literature 1700-1740*. London & New York 1963.

Davis, Cicely, '*Ut pictura poesis*'. Modern Language Review XXX, 1935.

Deane, Cecil V., *Aspects of 18th Century Nature Poetry*. Oxford 1935.

Dobai, Johannes, *Die Kunstliteratur des Klassizismus und der Romantik in England*. Band I, 1700-1750, Bern 1974.

Douglas, David, C., *English Scholars 1660-1730*. 2nd enlarged edition. London 1951.

Draper, John W., '*Aristotelian Mimesis in 18th Century England*' PMLA, vol. XXXVI, No. 3 September 1921.

Draper, John W., *Eighteenth Century British Aesthetics. A Bibliography*. Heidelberg 1931, repr. Amsterdam 1970.

Drennon, Herbert, '*Scientific Rationalism and James Thomson's Poetic Art*'. Studies in Philology, vol. 31, 1934.

Durling, Dwight D., *Georgic Tradition in English Poetry*. Columbia University Press 1935

Dutton, George B., '*The French Aristotelian Formalism and Thomas Rymer*'. PMLA, vol. XXIX, New Series, vol. XXII. Baltimore 1914.

Ehrhard, John, *L'idée de nature en France dans la première moitié du 18ᵉ siècle*. Paris 1963.

Eliot, T.S., *Selected Essays*. London 1946.

Elledge, Scott, '*The Background and Development in English Criticism of the Theories of Generality and Particularity*'. PMLA LXII 1947.

Faust, Joan, *The "Art" of Engagement: Ut pictura poesis Once more*. The International Journal of the Humanities 2003.

Fehr, B., '*The Antagonism of Forms in the 18ᵗʰ Century*'. English Studies Nos. 18 & 19 Amsterdam 1937 & 1938.

Folkierski, Wladislaw, *Entre le Classicisme et le Romantisme. Etude sur l'Esthétique et les Esthéticiens du XVIIIe siècle*. Paris 1925.

Folkierski, Wladislaw, '*Ut pictura poesis, ou l'étrange fortune du De Arte Graphica de Du Fresnoy en Angleterre*'. Revue de Littérature Comparée 1953.

Folkierski, Wladislaw, '*L'état présent des recherches sur les rapports entre les lettres et les arts figuratifs au 18ᵉ siècle*'. Atti del Quinto Congresso Internazionale di lingue e letterature moderne. Firenze 1955.

Fontaine, André, *Les doctrines d'art en France de Poussin à Diderot*. Paris 1909.

Fowler, Alistair, *Renaissance Realism: Narrative Images in Literature and Art*. Oxford University Press 2003.

Fraenkel, Eduard, *Horace*. Oxford 1957.

Francastel, Pierre, *Peinture et Société. Naissance et destruction d'un espace plastique de la Renaissance au Cubisme*. Paris 1965.

Friedländer, Max J., *Die Niederländischen Maler des 17. Jahrhunderts*. Berlin 1923.

Friedländer, Walter, *Nicolas Poussin*. München 1914.

Friedländer, Walter, *Nicolas Poussin. A New Approach*. New York 1965.

Friedländer, Walter, *Claude Lorrain*. Berlin 1921.

Friedmann, Raymond (ed.), *Surfiction*. Chicago 1975.

Frost, William, *Dryden and the Art of Translation*. Yale University Press 1955.

Frye, Northrop, '*Towards defining an Age of Sensibility*'. ELH, vol. 23, No. 1 March 1956.

Gallaway, Francis, *Reason, Rule, and Revolt in English Classicism*. New York 1940.

Gay, Peter, *The Enlightenment*. 2 vols., London 1966.

Geikie, Archibald, *Landscape in Literature*. London 1905.

Genouy, Hector, *L'élément pastoral dans la poésie narrative et le drame en Angleterre de 1579 à 1640*. Montpellier 1928.

Gilbert, K.E. & Kuhn, H., *A History of Esthetics*. New York 1939.

Gneiting, Teone Tone, '*Pictorial Imagery and Satirical Inversion in Pope's 'Dunciad'*. Eighteenth Century Studies, vol. 8, No. 4, Summer 1975.

Goad, Caroline, *Horace in the English Literature of the 18th Century*. Yale University Press 1918.

Goldstein, Harvey D., '*Ut poesis pictura: Reynolds on Imitation and Imagination*'. ECS 1, 1968.

Gombrich, E.H., *Art and Illusion. A Study in the Psychology of Pictorial Representation*. London 1960.

Gombrich, E.H., '*Moment and Movement in Art*'. Journal of the Warburg and Courtauld Institutes, XXVI 1964.

Gombrich, E.H., *Norm and Form. Studies in the Art of the Renaissance*. London & New York 1966.

Goodman, Nelson, *Languages of Art*. Indianapolis 1960.

Goodman, Nelson, *Ways of Worldmaking*. Indianapolis 1978.

Grant, Maurice Harold, *A Dictionary of English Landscape Painters from the 16th Century to the early 20th Century*. Leigh-on-Sea 1952; 2nd Ed., 1961.

Greene, Theodore Meyer, *The Arts and the Art of Criticism*. Princeton University Press 1947.

Greever, Garland, '*The Two Versions of 'Grongar Hill'*'. Journal of English and German Philology XVI. Baltimore 1915.

Grimal, Pierre, *Essai sur l'art poétique d'Horace*. Paris 1968.

Haas, C.E. de, *Nature and the Country in English Poetry of the first half of the 18th Century*. Amsterdam 1928.

Haferkorn, Reinhard, *Gotik und Ruine in der englischen Dichtung des 18. Jahrhunderts*. Leipzig 1924.

Hagstrum, Jean, *The Sister Arts*. University of Chicago Press 1958.

Hale, J.R., 'The Influence of Salvator Rosa in English Literature of the Eighteenth Century'. PMLA, LXIV 1949.

Halewood, William, 'The Reach of Art in Augustan Poetry'. in: Howard Anderson & John Shea (eds.), Essays in Honor of Samuel Holt Monk. Studies in Criticism and Aesthetics. University of Minnesota Press 1967.

Hamilton, K.G., The Two Harmonies: Poetry and Prose in the Seventeenth Century. Oxford 1963.

Hansen, Niels Bugge, That Pleasant Place. Copenhagen 1973.

Hard, Frederick, 'Richard Haydocke and Alexander Browne: Two Half-Forgotten Writers on the Art of Painting'. PMLA LV, No. 3, September 1940.

Harrison, Bernard, Inconvenient Fiction: Literature and the Limits of Theory. Yale University Press 1991.

Hathaway, Baxter, The Age of Criticism: The Late Renaissance in Italy. Cornell University Press 1962.

Havens, Raymond D., 'Changing Taste in the 18th Century: A Study of Dryden's and Dodsley's Miscellanies'. PMLA, XLIV, June 1929.

Haydn, Hiram, The Counter-Renaissance. New York 1950.

Haynes, Kenneth, English Literature and Ancient Languages. Oxford University Press 2003.

Hazard, Paul, La crise de la conscience européenne (1680-1715). Vols I-III. Paris 1935.

Henkel, Arthur & Schöne, Albert (eds.), Emblemata: Handbuch zur Sinnbildkunst des XVI und XVII Jahrhunderts. Erganzte Neuausgabe. Stuttgart 1976.

Hernadi, Paul, Beyond Genre, New Directions in Literary Classifications. Cornell University Press 1972.

Herrmann, Luke, British Landscape Painting of the 18th Century. London 1973.

Hibbard, G.R., 'The Country House Poem of the 17th Century'. Journal of the Warburg and Courtauld Institutes, vol. XIX 1956.

Hind, Arthur Mayger, A History of Engraving and Etching, from the 15th Century to the Year 1914. London 1923.

Hipple, W.J. Jr., The Beautiful, the Sublime, and the Picturesque in 18th Century British Aesthetic Theory. Illinois 1957.

Hipple, W.J. Jr., 'Philosophical Language and the Theory of Beauty in the 18th Century'. In: Howard Anderson & John Shea (eds.), Essays *in Honor of Samuel Holt Monk. Studies in Criticism and Aesthetics.* University of Minnesota Press 1967.

Hoffman, Arthur W., *John Dryden's Imagery.* University of Florida Press 1962.

Hollander, John, *The Untuning of the Sky. Ideas of Music in English Poetry 1500-1700.* Princeton University Press 1961.

Hoskins, W.G., *The Making of the English Landscape.* Pelican 1975.

Houghton, Walter E. Jr., 'The English Virtuoso in the Seventeenth Century'. Journal of the History of Ideas III, January 1942.

Howard, William Guild, 'Ut pictura poesis'. PMLA, New Series XVII 1909.

Hubbard, Henry W. & Kimball, Theodore, *An Introduction to the Study of Landscape Design.* New York 1917.

Humfrey, Belinda, *John Dyer.* University of Wales Press on behalf of the Welsh Arts Council 1980.

Hunt, John Dixon (ed.), *Encounters. Essays on Literature and the Visual Arts.* London 1971.

Hunt, John Dixon, *Gardens and the Picturesque. Studies in the History of Landscape.* London 1996.

Hussey, Christopher, *The Picturesque. Studies in a Point of View.* London & New York 1927.

Irlam, Shaun, *Elations: The Poetics of Enthusiasm in 18th Century England.* Stanford University Press 1999.

Jensen, H. James, 'Comparing the Arts in the Age of Baroque'. Eighteenth Century Studies Vol. VI, No. 3, Spring 1973.

Jensen, H. James, 'A Note on Restoration Aesthetics'. Studies in English Literature 1500-1900, vol. XIV, No. 3. Summer 1974.

Jones, R.F., 'Science and English Prose Style in the Third Quarter of the 17th Century'. Journal of the History of Ideas, I 1940.

Johnson, James William, *The Formation of English Neo-Classical Thought.* Princeton University Press 1967.

Kermode, Frank, Fender, Stephen and Palmer, Kenneth, *English Renaissance Literature.* Introductory Lectures, London 1974.

Klein, Hannelore, *There's no Disputing about Taste. Untersuchungen zum englischen Geschmacksbegriff im achtzehnten Jahrhundert.* Neue Beiträge zur englischen Philologie. Herausgegeben von Edgar Martner, Band 7, Münster 1967.

Korninger, Siegfried, *Die Naturauffassung in der englischen Dichtung des 17. Jahrhunderts*. Wiener Beiträge zur englischen Philologie LXIV. Wien & Stuttgart 1956.

Korshin, Paul J., *From Concord to Dissent. Major Themes in English Poetic Theory 1640-1700*. The Scholar Press, Menston, Yorkshire 1973.

Kristeller, Paul G., 'The Modern System of Arts. A Study in the History of Aesthetics'. Journal of the History of Ideas XII (1951) & XIII (1952).

Laforgue, Pierre, *Ut pictura poesis. Baudelaire, la peinture et le romantisme*. Presses Universitaires de Lyon 2000.

Lebègue, Raymond, *Horace en France pendant la Renaissance*. Humanisme et Renaissance Tome III, 1936.

LeCoat, Gerard G., 'Comparative Aspects of the Theory of Expression in the Baroque Age'. Eighteenth Century Studies, vol. V, No. 12, 1971-72.

Lee, Rensselaer, 'Ut pictura poesis. The Humanistic Theory of Painting'. Art Bulletin 1940.

Lerner, Laurence, *The Uses of Nostalgia: Studies in Pastoral Poetry*. London 1972.

Lipking, Lawrence, *The Ordering of the Arts in 18th Century England*. Princeton University Press 1970.

Lovejoy, Arthur D., 'The Parallel of Deism and Classicism'. Modern Philology, XXIX 1932.

Lovejoy, Arthur, *Essays in the History of Ideas*. Baltimore 1948, 1952. New York 1955.

Lovejoy, Arthur, 'Nature as Aesthetic Norm'. *Essays in the History of Ideas*. New York 1955.

Mace, Dean Tolle, 'Ut pictura poesis: Dryden, Poussin and the parallel of poetry and painting in the 17th century'. In: J. Dixon Hunt (ed.), *Encounters. Essays on Literature and the Visual Arts*. London 1971.

Macintire, Elizabeth Jellife, 'French Influence on the Beginnings of English Classicism'. PMLA, vol. XXVI. New Series, vol. XIX 1911.

Mack, Maynard, *The Garden and the City. Retirement and Politics in the Later Poetry of Pope 1731-43*. University of Toronto Press 1969.

MacLean, Kenneth, *Locke and English Literature of the 18th Century*. New York 1962.

MacLean, Norman, 'From Action to Image'. In: R.S. Crane (ed.), *Critics and Criticism*. Chicago 1952.

MacLean, Norman, 'Personification, not Poetry'. ELH, vol. 23, No. 1, March 1956.

Malins, Edward, *English Landscaping and Literature 1660-1840*. Oxford University Press 1966.
Manwaring, Elizabeth Wheeler, *Italian Landscape in 18th Century England*. Oxford University Press 1925, repr. London & Liverpool 1965.
Markiewicz, H., *Ut pictura poesis. A History of the Topos and the Problem*. London 1987.
Marinelli, Peter V., *Pastoral*. London 1971.
Matz, Robert, *Defending Literature in Early Modern England: Renaissance Literary Theory in a Social Context*. Cambridge Studies in Renaissance Literature and Culture. Cambridge University Press 2000.
Mccoy, Dorothy Schuchman. *Tand Convention. A Study of Periphrasis in English Pastoral Poetry from 1557-1715*. Studies in English Literature vol.V. Mouton, The Hague 1965.
McKillop, Alan, *The Background of Thomson's 'Seasons'*. University of Minnesota Press 1942.
McNamara, Katherine, *Landscape architecture. A classified Bibliography with Author Index, compiled in the Library of the School of Landscape Architecture and City Planning, Harvard University*. Harvard University School of Landscape Architecture 1934.
Medicus, Fritz, 'Das Problem einer vergleichenden Geschichte der Künste'. In: Ermatinger (ed.), *Philosophie der Naturwissenschaft*. Berlin 1930.
Miliburn, D. Judson, *The Age of Wit 1650-1750*. New York & London 1966.
Miner, Earl, 'The 'Poetic Picture, Painted Poetry' of 'The Last Instructions to a Painter'', Modern Philology, vol. LXIII, No. 4, May 1966.
Miner, Earl, *The Metaphysical Mode from Donne to Cowley*. Princeton University Press 1969.
Miner, Earl, *17th Century Imagery*. University of California Press 1971.
Monk, Samuel Holt, *The Sublime*. New York 1935.
Monk, Samuel Holt, 'A Grace beyond the Reach of Art'. Journal of the History of Ideas, Vol. V, No. 2, April 1944.
Mornet, Daniel, *Histoire de la littérature française classique 1660-1700*. Paris 1940.
Mourges, Odette de, *Metaphysical, Baroque, and Précieux Poetry*. Oxford 1953.
Munteano, B., 'Le Problème de la peinture en poésie dans la littérature française du XVIIIe siècle. Atti del Quinto Congresso Internazionale di lingue e letterature moderne. Florence 1955.

Nicolson, Marjorie Hope, *Newton Demands the Muse: Newton's 'Opticks' and 18th Century Poetry*. Princeton University Press 1946.

Nicolson, Marjorie Hope, *The Breaking of the Circle. Studies in the Effect of the New Science upon 17th Century Poetry*. Northwestern University Press, Illinois 1950.

Nicolson, Marjorie Hope, *Science and Imagination*. Ithaca N.Y. 1956.

Nicolson, Marjorie Hope, *Mountain Gloom and Mountain Glory: The Development of the Aesthetics of the Infinite*. New York 1959.

Nivelle, Armand, *Kunst- und Dichtungstheorien zwischen Aufklärung und Klassik*. Berlin & New York 1971.

Novitz, David, '*Roger de Piles and Antiquity*'. Journal of Aesthetics and Art Criticism Vol. xxxiv, No. 2, Winter 1975.

Nugel, Barnfried, *A New English Horace. Die Übersetzungen des horazischen Ars Poetica in der Restaurationszeit*. Münster 1971.

Ogden, Henry V.S., *A Bibliography of Seventeenth Century Writings on the Pictorial Arts in English*. The Arts Bulletin, XXIX, September 1947.

Ogden, Henry V.S. '*Thomas Burnet's 'Telluris Theoria Sacra' and Mountain Scenery*'. ELH, vol. 14, No. 3, September 1947.

Ogden, Henry V.S. & Ogden, Margaret S., *English Taste in Landscape in the 17th Century*. Ann Arbor 1955.

Ogilvie, Robert Maxwell, *Latin and Greek: A History of the Influence of the Classics on English Life from 1680 to 1918*. Hamden, Connecticut: Archon Books 1964.

O Hehir, Brendan, *Harmony from Discords. A Life of Sir John Denham*. Berkeley, Los Angeles 1968.

Olson, Elder, '*The Argument of Longinus' 'On the Sublime'*'. In: R.S.Crane (ed.), *Critics and Criticism*. Chicago 1952.

Omasreiter, Ria, *Naturwissenschaft und Litteraturkritik im England des 18. Jahrhunderts*. Erlanger Beiträge zur Sprach- und Litteraturkritik, Band 41. Nürnberg 1971.

Panofsky, Erwin, *Meaning in the Visual Arts*. New York 1955.

Panofsky, Erwin, *Idea. A Concept in Art Theory*. Columbia University Press 1968.

Papajewski, Helmuth '*Die Bedeutung der Ars Poetica für den englischen Neo-Klassizismus*'. Anglia 1961.

Paulhan, Fr., *L'esthétique du paysage*. Paris 1913.

Paulson, Ronald, '*Gainsborough's Landscape Drawings*'. Review Essay, Eighteenth Century Studies, vol. 6, No. 1, Fall 1972.

Paulson, Ronald, *'Townscape and Landscape Painting'*. Review Essay, Eighteenth Century Studies, vol. 3, No. 8, Spring 1975.

Peake, Charles (ed.), *Poetry of the Landscape and Night in the 18th Century*. London 1967.

Phelps, William Lyon, *The Beginnings of the English Romantic Movement. A Study in 18th Century Literature*. Boston 1893.

Praz, Mario, *Studies in 17th Century Imagery*. Vols 1-2. London 1939, 2nd ed., considerably increased, Rome 1964.

Price, Martin, *To the Palace of Wisdom. Studies in Order and Energy from Dryden to Blake*. Southern Illinois University Press 1964.

Price, Martin, *'The Picturesque Moment'*. In: Hilles & Bloom (eds.), *Sensibility to Romanticism. Essays Presented to Frederick A. Pottle*. Oxford University Press 1965.

Price, Martin, *'The Sublime Poem, Pictures and Powers'*. Yale Review 58, 1968-69, Winter 1969.

Quayle, Thomas, *Poetic Diction*. London 1924.

Richmond, H.M., *Renaissance Landscapes. English Lyrics in a European Tradition*. The Hague and Paris 1973.

Robertson, J.G., *Studies in the Genesis of Romantic Theory in the 18th Century*. Cambridge University Press 1923.

Rocheblave, Samuel, *'L'art français au XVIIe siècle dans ses rapports avec la littérature'*. Chapter XII of L. Petit de Juileville, *Histoire de la Langue et de la Littérature françaises des origines à 1900*. Tome V, Paris 1898.

Roper, Alan, *Dryden's Poetic Kingdoms*. London 1965.

Rose, H.J., *The Eclogues of Vergil*. University of California Press 1942.

Rosenberg, Alfred, *Longinus in England bis zum Ende des achtzehnten Jahrhunderts*. Weimar 1917.

Rosenmeier, Henrik, *'Ut pictura poesis. Some Elements of Description and Composition in 17th Century English Poetry'*. Analecta Romana Instituti Danici VII, Copenhagen 1974.

Rosmarin, Adena, *The Power of Genre*. University of Minnesota Press 1985.

Routh, James, *The Rise of English Classical Criticism*. Tulane University Press, New Orleans 1915.

Ruthven, K.K., *The Conceit*. 'The Critical Idiom' Series. Methuen, London 1969.

Røstvig, Maren-Sofie, *The Happy Man. Studies in the Metamorphoses of a Classical Ideal.* Vols. 1-2. Oslo Studies in English, Oslo 1958, 2nd ed. Oslo 1962.

Saintsbury, George, *A History of Criticism and Literary Taste in Europe.* Vols. 1-2. New York 1902.

Saisselin, R.G., *Taste in 18th Century France.* Syracuse University Press 1965.

Saisselin, R.G., '*Some Remarks on French 18th Century Writings on the Arts.*' Journal of Aesthetics, Winter 1966.

Salerno, Luigi, '*Seventeenth Century English Literature on Painting.*' Journal of the Warburg and Courtauld Institutes 1951.

Schneller, Herbert, '*Correspondences between Music and the Sister Arts according to the Eighteenth Century Aesthetic Theory.*' Journal of Aesthetics and Art Criticism XI 1953.

Scoular, Kitty W., *Natural Magic. Studies in the Presentation of Nature from Spenser to Marvell.* Oxford 1965.

Selden, Raman, '*Objectivity and Theory in Literary Criticism.*' Essays in Criticism, vol. XXIII, No. 3, July 1973.

Shephard, Paul, *Man in Landscape. A Historic View of the Esthetics of Nature.* New York 1967.

Simonsuuri, Kirsti, *Homer's Original Genius. Eighteenth Century Notions of the Early Greek Epic (1688-1798).* Cambridge University Press 1979.

Smith, D. Nichol, *Some Observations on 18th Century Poetry.* Toronto 1937.

Souriau, Etienne, *La Correspondance des Arts.* Paris 1947.

Spencer, Jeffry B., *Heroic Nature. Ideal Landscape in English Poetry from Marvell to Thomson.* Northwestern University Press 1973.

Spingarn, J.E., *A History of Literary Criticism in the Renaissance.* London 1899.

Staiger, Emil, *Grundbegriffe der Poetik.* Zürich 1946.

Stephen, Leslie, *History of English Thought in the Eighteenth Century.* London 1902.

Stevens, Wallace, '*The Relations between Poetry and Painting.*' In: *The Necessary Angel. Essays on Reality and the Imagination.* New York 1951.

Stewart, Stanley, *The Enclosed Garden. The Tradition and the Image in 17th Century Poetry.* University of Wisconsin Press & London 1966.

Stratman, Gerd, *Englische Aristokratie und klassizistische Dichtung. Eine literatur-soziologische Studie*. Erlanger Beiträge zur Sprach- und Kunstwissenschaft, Band 21, Nürnberg 1965.

Sutherland, James, *A Preface to 18th Century Poetry*. Oxford 1948.

Tayler, Edward William, *Nature and Art in Renaissance Literature*. Columbia University Press 1964.

Teyssèdrae Bernard, *Roger de Piles et les débats sur le coloris au siècle de Louis XIV*. Paris 1957.

Thomson, J.A.K., *Classical Influences on English Poetry*. London 1951.

Thorpe, Clarence de Witt, 'Two Augustans cross the Alps. Dennis and Addison on Mountain Scenery.' Studies in Philology, vol. 32, 1938.

Tieghem, Paul van, *Le Préromantisme. Etudes d'histoire littéraire européenne*. 3 vols. Paris 1924-47.

Tillyard, E.M.W., *The Miltonic Setting*. Cambridge University Press 1932.

Tinker, Chauncey Brewster, *Painter and Poet*. Harvard 1938.

Tobin, James Edward, *Eighteenth Century English Literature and its Cultural Background. A Bibliography*. New York 1967.

Topazio, Virgil W., 'Art Criticism in the Enlightenment'. Studies on Voltaire and the 18th Century, Vol. XXVII 1963.

Tuve, Rosemund, *Elizabethan and Metaphysical Imagery*. Chicago 1946.

Tuveson, Ernest, 'Shaftesbury and the Age of Sensibility'. In: Howard Anderson & John Shea (eds.), *Essays in Honor of Samuel Holt Monk. Studies in Criticism and Aesthetics*. University of Minnesota Press 1967.

Vieth, David M., *Attribution in Restoration Poetry. A Study of Rochester's Poems of 1680*. Yale University Press 1963.

Vitry, Paul, *De C.A. Dufresnoy Pictoris Poemate quod 'De Arte Graphica inscribitur'*. Paris 1901.

Voitle, Robert, 'The Reason of the English Enlightenment'. Studies on Voltaire and the 18th Century, vol. XXVII 1963.

Wallerstein, Ruth, *Studies in 17th Century Poetic*. University of Wisconsin Press 1950.

Walton, Geoffrey, *Metaphysical to Augustan: Studies in Tone and Sensibility in the Seventeenth Century*. London 1955.

Wasserman, Earl, *The Subtler Language*. Baltimore 1959.

Wasserman, Earl (ed.), *Aspects of the 18th Century*. Baltimore 1965.

Waterhouse, Ellis K., 'Poussin et l'Angleterre jusqu'en 1740'. Actes du Colloque Poussin I (ed. André Chastel). Paris 1960.

Watson, J., *Picturesque Landscape and English Romantic Poetry*. Hutcheson Educational 1970.

Wecter, Dixon, '*Burke's Theory Concerning Words, Images, and Emotions*'. PMLA, vol. LV, 1940.

Weinberg, Bernard, '*Castelvetro's Theory of Poetics*'. In: R.S. Crane (ed.), *Critics and Criticism*. University of Chicago Press 1952.

Weinberg, Bernard, *A History of Literary Criticism in the Italian Renaissance*. Vols. 1-2. University of Chicago Press 1961.

Weinbrot, Howard D., *The Formal Strain. Studies in Augustan Imitation and Satire*. Chicago & London 1969.

Wellek, René, '*The Parallelism between Literature and the Arts*'. English Institute Annual 1941.

Wellek, René, *Discriminations: Further Concepts of Criticism*. Yale 1970.

Westfall, Richard S., *Science and Religion in 17th Century England*. Yale University Press 1958.

Wilkinson, L.P., *Horace and his Lyric Poetry*. Cambridge University Press 1946.

Willey, Basil, *The Eighteenth Century Background. Studies on the Idea of Nature in the Thought of that Period*. London 1940, repr. 1953, 1962.

Williams, Ralph M., *Poet, Painter, and Parson. The Life of John Dyer*. New York 1956.

Williams, Raymond, *The Country and the City*. London 1973.

Wilmotte, Maurice, *Etudes critiques sur la tradition littéraire en France*. Paris 1909.

Wimsatt, W.K. Jr., '*Samuel Johnson and Dryden's Du Fresnoy*'. Studies in Philology, Vol. XLVIII, No. 1, January 1951.

Winslow, '*Re-Evaluation of Pope's Treatment of Nature.*' University of Wyoming Publications IV, July 1938.

Wittkower, R., '*Imitation, Eclecticism, and Genius*'. In: Earl Wasserman (ed.), *Aspects of the 18th Century*. Baltimore 1965.

Wood, Theodore E.B., *The Word 'Sublime' and its Context 1650-1760*. Mouton, The Hague & Paris 1972.

Yates, Frances, *The Art of Memory*. London 1966.

NOTES

Introduction

1 Paul Hazard, *La crise de la conscience européenne*, vol. II, p. 296.

Chapter 2

1 *Works*, p. 403.
2 Ll. 13-14. Robert Anderson (ed.), *The Works of the British Poets*, vol. vii, p. 223.
3 *The Ordering of the Arts in 18th Century England*, p. 38.
4 A Parallel... Malone (ed.), The Critical and Miscellaneous Prose Works of John Dryden, vol. III, p. 321.
5 Malone, op. cit., vol. III, p. 294.
6 Malone, op. cit., vol. III, p. 295.
7 *De art graphica..., translated by John Dryden*, 2nd ed., p. 104.
8 Malone, op. cit., vol. III, p. 352.
9 *Heroic Landscape*, pp. 16-18.
10 Carritt, *A Calendar of British Taste...*, p. 50.
11 Ault, *New Light on Pope*, pp. 68-69.
12 August 31, 1713. Sherburn (ed.), *The Correspondence of Alexander Pope*, vol. I, p. 125.
13 Sherburn, op. cit., vol. I, p. 74.
14 After writing this passage, I have seen that an identical observation has been made by Teone Tone Gneiting in an article in *Eighteenth Century Studies*, summer 1975, vol. 8, No. 4, pp. 420-430: '*Pictorial Imagery and Satirical Inversion in Pope's Dunciad*'.
15 Sherburn, op. cit., vol. II, p. 330.
16 *Réflexions critiques.... Œuvres* (1732), vol. II, p. 82.
17 *Works* (1801), vol. III, p. 275.
18 *Peinture et Société*, p. 17.
19 Ruth Wleerstein, *Studies in 17th Century Poetic*, p. 16.
20 *Mnemosyne*, p. 45.
21 *Dialogue Four, Of Tragedy & Comedy, how to draw the Plot & form the Characters &C of both.*

22 The essay is printed in Malone (ed.), *The Critical and Miscellaneous Prose Works of John Dryden,* vol. II, pp. 34 et seq.
23 Malone, op. cit., vol. II, p. 37.
24 Herford & Simpson (eds.), *The Works of Ben Jonson,* vol. VIII, p. 611.
25 Edna Leake Stevens (ed.), *The Art of Sinking in Poetry,* p. 21.
26 Saintsbury (ed.), *Minor Caroline Poets,* vol. III, pp. 277 et seq.
27 *Trattato,* I, 15.
28 Malone (ed.), *The Critical and Miscellaneous Prose Works of John Dryden,* vol. III, p. 304.
29 *Réflexions critiques,* 1732, vol. I, p. 216.
30 *Réflexions critiques,* vol. I, p. 154.
31 *Poems on Several Occasions With Some Select Essays in Prose,* vol. II, pp. 157 et seq.
32 Herford and Simpson (eds.), *The Works of Ben Jonson,* vol. viii, p. 609.
33 *Theory of Painting,* p. 10.
34 *Characteristics,* vol. III, pp. 375-76.
35 Malone (ed.), *The Critical and Miscellaneous Prose Works of John Dryden,* vol. III, pp. 314 et seq.
36 For a typical instance, see Congreve's *Ode to Kneller.* Robert Anderson (ed.), *The Works of the British Poets,* vol. vii, pp. 558-59.

Chapter 3

1 Ed. Moxon, Dent, Everyman 1943, p. 5.
2 Op. cit., p. 51.
3 Ibid.
4 Op. cit., p. 51.
5 Moxon, op. cit., p. 31.
6 Roger de Piles, *Cours de peinture par principes,* 1708. Charles Batteux, *Les Beaux Arts Réduits à un même Principe,* 1746.
7 Geoffrey Shepherd (ed.), *Sidney's Apology for Poetry,* p. 101.
8 See Arthur Lovejoy's seminal article 'Nature as Aesthetic Norm' in *Essays in the History of Ideas,* New York 1955, pp. 69-71.
9 *The Advancement and Reformation of Modern Poetry.* E.N. Hooker (ed.), *The Critical Works of John Dennis,* vol. II, p. 202.
10 Lovejoy, op. cit., p. 73.
11 *The Author's Apology for Heroic Powetry and Poetic Licence. Prefixed to The State of Innocence and the Fall of Man, an Opera.* Ker (ed.), *Essays of Dryden,* vol. I, pp. 183-84.
12 *Essay on Criticism,* l. 73.
13 *Essay on Criticism,* l. 105.
14 *Œuvres,* vol. ii, p. 110.
15 *Œuvres,* vol. ii, pp. 109-110.
16 *Essay on Criticism,* l. 362.
17 *Oeuvres,* vol. II, p. 123.
18 Korshin, *From Concord to Dissent,* p. 44.
19 *Réflexions sur la Poëtique et sur les ouvrages des Poètes anciens et modernes. Œuvres,* vol. II, p. 148.
20 *Elémens de peinture pratique. Oeuvres,* tome III, p. 363.

21 *Essay on Criticism*, l. 153.
22 *Essay on Man*, III, p. 169.
23 E.S. de Beer (ed.), *The Diary of John Evelyn*, vol. IV, p. 127.
24 IV, l. 50.
25 *Prèface aux Conférences de l'Académie Royale de Peinture et de Sculpture*, repr. in *Entretiens sur les vies et sur les ouvrages des plus excellens peintres*. Trévoux, 1725.
26 *Characteristics*, vol. III, p. 378.
27 *Entretiens...*, p. 310.
28 *Ars poetica*, l. 89.
29 *Poetics* (ed. Moxon), pp. 58-60.
30 Peter Hägin, *The Epic Hero*, pp. 35-36.
31 Malone, op. cit., vol. III, p. 316.
32 *The Hermit*, ll. 13-14. Anderson (ed.), *The Works of the British Poets*, vol. VII, p. 19.
33 I, 98. Kitty W. Scoular, *Natural Magic...*, p. 27.
34 *Ars poetica*, ll. 333-34.

Chapter 4

1   For a detailed treatment of the *locus amoenus* tradition, see the stimulating book by Niels Bugge Hansen, *That Pleasant Place*. Copenhagen 1973.
2   *Poems on several Occasions*, vol. I, pp. 111-12.
3   M.C. Sear (ed.), *The Poems of Ambrose Philips*, p. 3.
4   *The English Parnassus*, p. 144.
5   *The Complete Art of Poetry*, vol. II, pp. 158-60.
6   Audra & Williams (eds.), *Pope's Pastoral Poetry*, vol. I, p. 24.
7   Audra & Williams, op. cit., vol. I, p. 28.
8   Laurence Lerner, *The Uses of Nostalgia*, Ch. I passim.
9   *Pliny's Letters* (tr. Melmoth), Book IV, 6. Vol. I, pp. 377-97.
10 Ll. 69-70. Helen Darbishire (ed.), *Milton* vol. II, p. 140. The spelling and the line numbers are those of Miss Darbishire's edition.
11 E.C. Carritt, *A Calendar of British Taste...*, p. 70.
12 A.R. Waller (ed.), *Essays, Plays and Sundry Verses by Abraham Cowley*, p. 395.
13 Saintsbury (ed.), *Minor Poets of the Caroline Period*, vol. I, p. 558.
14 George Gilfillan (ed.), *The Poetical Works of Edmund Waller and Sir John Denham*, pp. 75-78.

Chapter 5

1   Ogden & Ogden, *English Taste in Landscape in the 17th century*, p. 1.
2   Op. cit., p. 6.
3   Op. cit., p. 7.
4   Op. cit., p. 7.
5   A.R. Waller (ed.), *Essays, Plays, and Sundry Verses by Abraham Cowley*, p. 42.
6   M.G. Seger (ed.), *The Poems of Ambrose Philips*, p. 3.

7   *Tracts*, I, 5.
8   E.N. Hooker (ed.), *The Critical Works of John Dennis*, vol. I, p. 111.
9   L. 71.
10 Robert Anderson (ed.), *The Works of the British Poets*, vol. VII, p. 638.
11 *Creation*, Book IV. Robert Anderson, op. cit., vol. VII, p. 622.
12 *Works* (1801), vol. I, p. 195.
13 *Of the Conduct of the Understanding*. *Works* (1801), vol. III, p. 238.
14 *Pharsalia*, I, 98. Kitty W. Scoular, *Natural Magic*, p. 27.
15 Saintsbury (ed.), *Minor Poets of the Caroline Period*, vol. I, p. 563.
16 *Works* (1801), vol. I, pp. 138-39.
17 *The Making of the English Landscape*, p. 141.
18 Op. cit., p.177.
19 *Elémens de Peinture pratique* (1684). *Oeuvres*, vol. III, p. 407.

Chapter 6

1   Røstvig, *The Happy Man*, vol. I, p. 168.
2   *Works*, p. 294.
3   *Oeuvres*, vol. II, p. 158.
4   *The Author's Apology for Heroic Poetry and Poetic Licence. Prefixed to The State of Innocence and the Fall of Man, an Opera*, 1677. Ker (ed.), *Essays of Dryden*, vol. I, p. 181.
5   *Traité du Poëme Epique* (Sixième édition), p. 485.
6   Op. cit., p. 235.
7   Op. cit., p. 447.
8   Op. cit., p. 451.
9   *Art poétique*, Chant III, ll. 55-60.
10 *Works*, p. 251.
11 *The Works of Mr. John Oldham*, vol. I, p. 3.
12 *Works*, p. 250.
13 *Ars poetica*, ll. 445-48.
14 *Traité du Poëme Epique*, p. 451.
15 *Oeuvres en trois volumes*, vol. II, p. 166.

Chapter 7

1   *The New Organon*, transl. Fulton H. Anderson. M.H. Abrams, *Natural Supernaturalism*, p. 62.
2   *Essay on Man*, I, l. 267.
3   Ll. 245-46.
4   *The Works of Locke* (1801), vol. I, p. 3.
5   *The Works of Locke* (1714) vol. I, p. 1.
6   *The Works of Locke* (1801), vol. I, p. 14.
7   *The Works of Locke* (1801), vol. I, p. 57.
8   *The Works of Locke* (1801), vol. I, p. 77.
9   Ibid.

10 *The Works of Locke* (1801), vol. III, p. 63.
11 Op. cit., vol. III, p. 64.
12 *Creation*, Book V. Robert Anderson (ed.), *The Works of the British Poets*, vol. VII, p. 627.
13 *Poems on Several Occasions*, vol. I, pp. 111-12.
14 *The Genuine Works in Verse and Prose of...George Granville*, vol. I, p. 123.
15 *Spectator*, 411.
16 *Characteristics...*, vol. II, p. 395.
17 Pope, *Essay on Man*, II, l. 32.
18 *Spectator*, 411.
19 Whittaker, *Newton's Opticks*, p. 369.
20 *Vasari on Technique*, transl. Louisa Maclehose, p. 197.
21 G.P. Lomazzo, *A Tracte...*, transl. Richard Haydock, p. 16.
22 Ll. 41-42. *The Genuine Works...of George Granville*, vol. I, p. 119.
23 Maynard Mack, *The Garden and the City*, p. 21.
24 Maynard Mack (ed.), *Alexander Pope: An Essay on Man*. The Twickenham Edition, vol. iii, p. i.
25 *Ichnographia Rustica*, vol. III, p. 109.
26 Op. cit., vol. III, p. 6.

Chapter 8

1 Saintsbury (ed.), *Minor Poets of the Caroline Period*, vol. II, p. 10.
2 *Minor Poets of the Caroline Period*, vol. I, p. 7.
3 Book I, Canto I, ll. 142 et seq.
4 Saintsbury, op. cit., vol. I, p. 106.
5 Saintsbury, op. cit., vol. I, p. 108.

Chapter 9

1 *The Philosophy of History*, pp. 4-5.
2 L. 19.
3 *Works* (1801), vol. I, p. 1.
4 *The Mathematical Principles of Natural Philosophy*, transl. Andrew Motte, I, p. 12.
5 Ll. 361-62.
6 Ll. 84-85. George Gilfillan (ed.), *The Poetical Works of Edmund Waller and Sir John Denham*, p. 76.
7 The letter describing his crossing of the Alps. Clarence de Witt Thorpe, *Two Augustans crossing the Alps*, pp. 465-66.
8 Vol. II, p. 158.
9 *To Mr Constantine, On his Paintings*, l. 8. *Poems*, vol. I p. iii.
10 *Works* (1801), vol. I, p. 3.
11 Op. cit., vol. I, p. 198.
12 Spence, *Anecdotes*, vol. I, p. 255.

13 *The Moralists. Characteristics...*, vol. II, p. 285.
14 *Cours de peinture par principes. Oeuvres*, vol. II, pp. 185 et seq.
15 Stanza LXXVI.
16 *Ichnographia rustica*, vol. I, p. 192.
17 II, ll. 121-22.
18 Book I, l. 563.
19 John Wilson Foster, 'Topography in 18th Century Poetry', p. 248.
20 *The Genuine Works of...Granville*, vol. I, p. 80.
21 Translation of Homer. Audra & Williams (eds.), *Pope, Pastoral Poetry...*, vol. I, p. 134.
22 *A Poem written to commemorate Mrs. Elizabeth Hughes, who died in 1714. Poems,*vol. II, p. 98.
23 *Spectator*, 411.
24 *Ichnographia rustica*, vol. III, p. 78.
25 Ibid.
26 Clarence de Witt Thorpe, 'Two Augustans Cross the Alps', p. 475.
27 *Inquiry into the Original...*Treatise II: *Concerning Moral Good and Evil*, pp. 113-14.
28 H.V.S. Ogden, 'Thomas Burnet's Telluris Sacra and Mountain Scenery', pp. 146-47.
29 *Oeuvres diverses*, vol. II, p. 172.
30 Book I, ll. 35 et seq.
31 Myra Reynolds (ed.), *The Poems of Anne, Countess of Winchilsea*, p. xxxiv.
32 Robert Anderson (ed.), *The Works of the British Poets*, vol. VII, p. 601.
33 Ll. 330 et seq.
34 Saintsbury (ed.), *Minor Poets of the Caroline Period*, vol. I, p. 554.
35 *To Mr. Henry Lawes*, ll. 25-30. Saintsbury, op. cit., vol. I, p. 518.
36 *To the Royal Society*, stanza 9. Occasional Verses 1663-68. Grosart (ed.), *The Complete Works in Verse and Prose of Abraham Cowley*, vol. I, p. 169.
37 *Spectator*, 632.
38 *Oeuvres*, vol. II, p. 174.
39 *To the Palace of Wisdom*, p. 388.
40 May 8, 1713. Vol. I, p. 210.
41 *The Picture of Dorian Gray*, Preface. Penguin ed., p. 6.

Chapter 10

1 *The Poetical Works of Thomas Tickell*. Cooke Edition, p. 43.
2 Tickell, op. cit., pp. 105 et seq.
3 *Poems*, vol. I, pp. 106-07.
4 *Poems*, vol. II, pp. 100-01.
5 Friday, February 27, 1718. *The Free-Thinker*, vol. II, pp. 201 et seq.
6 Myra Reynolds (ed.), *The Poems of Anne, Countess of Winchilsea*, p. 266.
7 Reynolds, op. cit., p. 34.
8 Ll. 60-3; Reynolds, op. cit., p. 35.
9 O Hehir, *Expans'd Hieroglyphicks*, p. 35.
10 Ibid.
11 *Natural Magic*, p. 234.

12 *Expans'd Hieroglyphicks*, p. 244.
13 Op. cit., p. 254.
14 *Expans'd Hieroglyphicks*, p. 244.
15 Op. cit., p. 268.
16 Op. cit., p. 345.
17 *Cooper's Hill Latine Redditum*.
18 *Works*, Book II, p. 82.
19 *Oxford*, l. 245. *The Poetical Works of Thomas Tickell*, p. 72.
20 *Oxford*, ll. 279-80. *Poetical Works*, p. 73.
21 *Epistle Dedicatory to The Rival Ladies* (performed late in 1663, or early in 1664). To the Right Honourable Roger, Earl of Orrery. Malone (ed.), *The Critical and Miscellaneous Prose Works of John Dryden*, vol. I, Part 2, p. 12.
22 Myra Reynolds (ed.), *The Poems of Anne, Countess of Winchilsea*, p. xxxiv.
23 E.N. Hooker (ed.), *The Critical Works of John Dennis*, vol. II, p. 136.
24 *Denham. Lives of the Poets*, vol. I, p. 59.
25 Bysshe, *The Art of English poetry*, p. 25.
26 *The Poetical Works of Thomas Tickell*, pp. 66-67.
27 P. 160.
28 *The Sister Arts*, p. 210.
29 Norman Ault, *New Light on Pope*, p. 81.
30 Norman Ault (ed.), *Pope's Minor Poems*, vol. iv, pp. 14-15.
31 Ibid.
32 Audra & Williams (eds.), *Pope: Pastoral Poetry, and An Essay on Criticism*. Twickenham ed., vol. I, p. 135.
33 *Heroic Nature. Ideal Landscape in English Poetry...*, p. 214.
34 George Gilfillan (ed.), *The Poetical Works of Armstrong, Dyer, and Green*, p. 204.

Chapter 11

1 A.R. Waller (ed.), *Essays, Plays, and Sundry Verses by Abraham Cowley*, p. 247.
2 Ibid.
3 Ibid.
4 *La crise de conscience européenne*, vol. II, p. 61.
5 Richard F. Jones, 'Science and Criticism in the Neo-Classical Age of English Literature', pp. 396-97.
6 Robert Anderson (ed.), *The Works of the British poets*, vol. VII, p. 639.
7 A.R. Waller (ed.), *Abraham Cowley: Poems, Miscellanies...*, p. 450.
8 Malone (ed.), *The Critical and Miscellaneous Prose Works of John Dryden*, vol. III, p. 351. Page references in this section, unless otherwise stated, are to vol. III of Malone's work.
9 Mornet, *Histoire de la littérature francaise classique*, p. 16.
10 *Cinquième dialogue*. Mornet, op. cit., p. 159.
11 *Essay on Criticism*, ll. 653-54.
12 *Norm and Form*, p. 89.
13 *A Discourse Upon Comedy. In Reference to the English Stage. In a Letter to a Friend*. W.H. Durham (ed.), *Critical Essays of the 18th Century 1700-1725*, p. 277.
14 Durham, op. cit., p. 285.

15 Monk (ed.), *Five Miscellaneous Essays by Sir William Temple*, p. 182.
16 *Characteristics*, vol. I, p. 146.
17 E.N. Hooker (ed.), *The Critical Works of John Dennis*, vol. I, p. 210.
18 May 7, 1713. Røstvig, *The Happy Man*, 2nd ed., vol. I, p. 205.
19 *Réflexions critiques...*, vol. II, p. 178.
20 Rie Omasreiter, *Naturwissenschaft und Literaturkritik im England des 18. Jahrhunderts*, p. 118.
21 Hannelore Klein, *There is no Disputing about Taste*, pp. 9-10.
22 *La formation de la doctrine classique*, p. 137.
23 Mornet, *Histoire de la littérature française classique*, p. 154.
24 Mornet, op. cit., p. 121.
25 *The Genuine Works...*, vol. I, p. 48.
26 E.N. Hooker, *The Critical Works of John Dennis*, vol. I, p. 127.
27 *Réflexions critiques...*, vol. II, p. 2.
28 *Essay Upon Unnatural Flights in Poetry. The Genuine Works...*, vol. I, p. 118.
29 Second edition, *Corrected & Enlarg'd*, p. x.
30 Op. cit., p. 38.
31 Op. cit., p. 44.
32 Op. cit., p. 75.
33 Rosenberg, *Longinus in England bis zum Ende des 18. Jahrhunderts*, p. 1.
34 D.A.Russell (transl.), *Longinus: De Sublimitate*, pp. 39-42.
35 *Heroic Poetry and Poetic Licence* (1674/75). Ker (ed.), *Essays of Dryden*, vol. I, pp. 179-80.
36 *Oeuvres de Boileau-Despréaux*, vol. III, p. 24.
37 Ibid.
38 Russell (transl.), *De Sublimitate*, pp. 1-2.
39 *Œuvres de Boileau-Despréaux*, vol. III, p. 24.
40 Ibid.
41 Hooker, *The Critical Works of John Dennis*, vol. II, pp. 380-81.
42 Waller (ed.), *Essays, Plays, and Sundry Verses by Abraham Cowley*, p. 256.
43 *Heroic Poetry and Poetic Licence*. Ker (ed.), *Essays of Dryden*, vol. I, p. 179.
44 Ker, op. cit., vol. I, p. 490.
45 *Characteristics*, vol. I, pp. 242-43.
46 Op. cit., vol. I, p. 243.
47 *Theory of Painting*, p. 136.
48 Op. cit., p. 124.
49 *The Works in Verse and Prose of Leonard Welsted, Esq.*, p. 354.
50 *Elémens de Peinture pratique*, 1684. *Œuvres* tome III, p. 381.
51 *Spectator*, 413.
52 *The Works in Verse and Prose of Leonard Welsted, Esq*, p. 128.
53 Op. cit., p. 129.
54 *The Works in Verse and Prose...*, p. 131.
55 *Poems on Several Occasions*, vol. II, p. 157.
56 Op. cit., vol II, p. 330.
57 Ibid.
58 Op. cit., vol. II, p. 335.

Chapter 12

1. James Sambrook (ed.), *James Thomson: The Seasons and The Castle of Indolence*, pp. 38-39.
2. Sambrook, op. cit., p. 74.
3. Sambrook, op. cit., pp. 75-76.
4. Sambrook, op. cit., p. 6.
5. Sambrook, op. cit., pp. 15-16.
6. Sambrook, op. cit., 15-16.
7. Sambrook, op. cit., pp. 106-07.

Conclusion

1. *De officiis*, I, 87.
2. Op. cit., I, 130.
3. iv, 31.
4. *De pictura veterum*, Book I, ch. 4.
5. Op. cit., Book III, ch. 5.
6. Roskill (ed.), *Dolce's 'Aretino' and Venetian Art Theory of the Cinquecento*, p. 23.
7. *Claude Lorrain*, p. 12.
8. Carritt, *A Calendar of British Taste*, p. 109.
9. Ll. 142-46.
10. Saintsbury (ed.), *Minor Poets of the Caroline Period*, vol. I, p. 563.
11. A.R. Waller (ed.), *Essays, Plays, and Sundry Verses by Abraham Cowley*, p. 409.
12. 'Enter the Frame' in Raymon Federman (ed.), *Surfiction*.

INDEX

Addison 13, 78-79, 107, 122, 192
   Spectator essays 36, 106, 182, 196
Aeneid 39, 58, 68
Apelles 128
Aristotle 14, 24, 28-30, 33, 37-39, 41, 66-67, 165, 167, 172, 176-177, 189-190, 196
   Poetics 29, 39
ars celare artem 36, 45

Bacon 74
Batteux, *Les beaux arts réduits...* 31
Baumgarten, Alexander 27
beholder 18, 20, 24, 41, 48, 51, 56, 61, 73, 76-77, 85-86, 88, 92-93, 95, 97-99, 104, 106-108, 110, 117-118, 123, 125, 128, 137, 142-143, 148, 153, 155, 158, 161, 164, 182, 189, 201, 203-204, 207-208, 210, 212, 219-220, 222-224, 227-228, 232
la belle nature 31, 66, 171
Bellori 23, 170-172, 218
Berkeley 98
bienséance/decorum 34, 179, 183, 192-193
Blackmore 21, 60, 77, 111, 167-168
   Creation 111-112
Boileau 7, 66-67, 69, 175-176, 179, 187-190
   Art poétique 176, 187
Bossu 39, 66-68, 70, 173, 181
Bosworth, William 106
Brown, Lancelot ("Capability Brown") 84
Le Brun 12
La Bruyère 18
Burnet, Gilbert 58
Burnet, Thomas 108, 115
Bysshe, Edward 137, 140

canon/rules 11, 27, 29, 33, 42, 44, 66-67, 70, 165-179, 181-183, 187, 190, 193-194
Caryll 16, 17
Cato the Elder 223
Chamberlayne, William 58, 89-90, 94, 96
   Pharonnida 89-92, 96
Chambray 12
Cicero 34, 217
clair-obscur/chiaroscuro 103, 128, 148, 155
Claude glass 79, 81, 151
Cleveland, John 89
comedy 40, 177, 180
concordia discors, uniformity amidst variety 42, 59, 61, 83, 93, 103, 110, 128, 133, 148-149, 156, 192, 218, 226, 229, 232
Congreve 16
Corregio 17
Cotton, Charles 222
Cowley 35, 51-52, 57, 78, 113, 138, 146, 151, 165-166, 168, 189, 226
   Solitude 51

Dacier 173, 183
delight/instruct, *delectare/prodesse, dulce/utile* 111, 131, 169, 173, 183-185, 188, 196, 226, 232
Denham 34, 58, 63, 96, 113, 132-141, 147-148, 152, 161, 214, 230
   Cooper's Hill 7, 53, 63, 68-69, 89, 105, 131-132, 135-141, 147-148, 161, 230
   The Brook 93, 110, 122, 141, 163
Dennis, John 32, 100, 139-140, 152, 175, 184, 191

Advancement and
  Reformation... 178
Crossing the Alps 188
Remarks on Prince Arthur 58, 183
Descartes 165, 226
design/disposition 9, 13, 41, 43, 51, 62, 70, 77-78, 82, 85, 101, 117, 139, 142, 144-145, 150, 152, 169, 196, 203, 215, 219, 226, 231
the designer 83-84, 131
dispositio, see design
Dolce, Ludovico 219
  L'Aretino 37
Dryden 14, 16, 23, 32, 67, 108, 132, 138, 180, 187, 190, 197
  A Parallel... 40, 184, 218
  To Sir Godfrey Kneller 58
  Translation of Dufresnoy 25, 169-174
Dubos 18, 23, 179, 197
  Réflexions critiques... 184
Dufresnoy 219
  De arte graphica 13, 14
Dyer
  Grongar Hill 111, 147, 152-154, 156-159
  The Country Walk 97, 161-163, 207
  The Ruins of Rome 164

ecphrasis 209
elocution/*elocution* 38, 41, 219
emblem 51
engraving 15
epic 18, 24, 29, 37, 39-41, 67-68, 70, 167, 177, 220
Evelyn 36

Farquhar 177
Félibien 37
Fénelon 18, 19
Flatman, Thomas 22
The Free-Thinker 19, 79, 125

garden 35
  English garden 84
  French garden 83-84
  landscape gardening 82, 114, 131
genius 14, 29, 33-34, 175, 179-180, 186-187, 195, 218

genre/"*kind*" 7, 11-13, 24, 37-40, 65, 67, 71, 85, 87, 138, 164, 169, 192, 217, 225, 231, 233
georgic 43
Gildon, Charles 46
  The Complete Art of Poetry 19
grace 34-36, 175, 178, 180
Granville, George, Lord
  Lansdowne 78, 105, 148, 151, 183-184
  Essay upon Unnatural Flights... 81
  The British Enchanters 13
grotto 36, 96, 109, 111, 114-115, 145, 192, 221, 224
The Guardian 35, 100, 116, 179, 198

ha-ha fence 82
Hall, John 187, 190
Haydocke, Richard, Translation of Lomazzo 81
Herrick 138
Homer 17-18, 28, 30, 32, 34, 39, 45, 68, 165, 179, 207, 224
Horace 7, 11-13, 24, 28, 33, 38, 41, 62, 66-67, 69-70, 88, 98, 165, 175, 214, 217, 220, 231
  Ars poetica 7, 29, 33-34, 66, 69, 98, 165, 175
hortus conclusus 45, 47, 88
Howard, Sir Robert 180
Hughes, John 24, 45, 78, 100, 106, 123-124, 127-128, 197-198
Hutcheson, Francis:
  Inquiry into the Original... 107, 185

idea 29, 65, 172-173
imagination 20, 23, 33, 169, 196, 198, 208, 219
imitation 18-19, 29, 32, 38, 40, 65, 168-169, 171, 185, 197, 219, 221
instruct, see delight
invention/*invention* 13, 38, 41, 97, 193, 219

je ne sais quoi 34-35, 108, 172, 175, 180, 193, 195, 218, 229
Jervas, Charles 15-16
Dr Johnson 137, 140
Inigo Jones 219

Ben Jonson 21, 24, 177
    Penshurst 49, 57, 89, 91, 150, 213
judgement 33, 186, 218
Junius, Franciscus 218

"*kinds*", see genre
Kneller, Sir Godfrey 16

landscape gardening, see garden
Lawes, Henry 113
Leibnitz 7, 59
Leonardo da Vinci 23
Lessing 22, 44
limitation 81
Locke 18, 31, 60, 62, 75-76, 81, 165, 170, 185, 197
    Essay Concerning Human Understanding 75
locus amoenus 45-46, 57, 88, 91
Longinus 108, 189-190, 229
    Peri hupsous/On the Sublime 186-187
Lorrain, Claude 25, 101, 221
Lucan 42, 61

Marmion, Shakerly 89
Marvell
    Appleton House 50, 102
Michelangelo 37
Milton 138, 197
    Paradise Lost 50
    L'Allegro 49-50
mimesis 30, 86, 107, 131, 166, 168
mirror 23, 41, 50, 79, 111, 147, 151, 232
mock-heroic 39, 103

Newton 59, 74-75, 78, 165
    Opticks 79
    Principia 98
Norgate, Edward 56
Le Nôtre 83

Odyssey 39
Oldham, John 12
    Translation of Horace's *Ars poetica* 69
Otway 197
Ovid 230

Parnell, Thomas 42
pastoral 39-40, 45-48, 50, 57-58, 75, 85, 88-89, 95, 102, 154, 157, 202, 221, 224
Peacham, Henry
    The Art of Drawing... 55
peri bathous 21
Philips, Ambrose 46, 58
Philips, John 104, 109
Philips, Katherine 52, 61, 112-113, 225
Philostratus 171
Piles, Roger de 31, 35, 63, 88, 101, 116-117
    Translation of Dufresnoy 14
    Cours de peinture... 108
Plato 65, 115
Pliny 12, 48
poetic diction 47, 101, 103, 214, 224
Poole, Joshua 46, 137-138
    The English Parnassus 137, 144
Pope 15-16, 18, 74-75, 82, 101, 105, 113-115, 144-145, 147-151, 175, 206, 215, 225
    Windsor Forest 25, 112, 139-140, 147-148, 150, 152, 206, 215, 224
    Pastorals 46, 145
    Dunciad 17, 145
    Essay on Man 32, 35, 104
    Eliosa to Abelard 145-146
Poussin 15, 19, 70, 101, 145, 170
prodesse/delectare, see delight
prospect 16, 28, 31, 36, 46, 49, 51, 53, 58, 78, 91-93, 99, 104-107, 117, 125, 127, 130, 132, 134, 142-143, 154, 162, 202, 205-206, 208-209, 212, 230

Quintilian 34, 180

Raphael 17, 19, 37
Rapin 7, 11, 33-34, 37, 39, 66-67, 70-71, 179, 181, 183, 229
Ray, John 77, 108
Richardson, Jonathan 25, 66, 191
Rosa, Salvator 25, 110
Roscommon, Earl of (Wentworth Dillon) 66
    Translation of Horace's *Ars poetica* 69-70

Rubens 219
ruins 115-117
rules, see canon
Rymer, Thomas 67

Shaftesbury, third Earl of (Anthony Ashley Cooper) 25, 37, 78, 182
  Soliloquy, or Advice to an Author 190
  Sensus Communis 178
Shelley 233
Shenstone 84, 105
Sidney, Sir Philip 31
The Spectator 84, 114, 182
Spence, Jeffrey 101, 152
Steele 12
still-life 37, 41, 48, 221
the sublime 108-109, 186-187, 189-192, 222
surveying 48-49, 52, 57, 70, 99
Swift 16
Switzer, Stephen 103, 106
  Ichnographia rustica 84-85

Tasso 197
taste 7, 180-183, 193, 323
Temple, Sir William 36, 83, 178
the Thames 63, 112-113, 121-123, 132-133, 137, 147, 150-151, 204-206

Theocritus 179, 227
Thomas, Dylan 157
Thomson, James 230
  The Seasons 8, 201-203, 205-215, 225
Tickell, Thomas 121-123, 138
  Oxford 117, 142-144
tragedy 23, 29, 31, 39-41, 88, 167, 180

uniformity amidst variety, see *concordia discors*
unities 25, 28, 87, 178
utile/dulce, see delight

Vergil 14, 30, 32-33, 39, 43, 58, 68, 132, 172, 179, 197, 226
verisimilitude 20, 34, 56, 62
Vida 13, 39, 41, 219
virtuosi 15

Waller, Edmund 99, 138
  Instructions to a Painter 18
  On St. James' Park 52, 89, 102
weeds 36, 81, 117-118, 230
Welsted, Leonard 125, 191, 194-195
Wilde, Oscar 118
Winchilsea, Lady 109, 129-130, 139
Wordsworth 216, 323
Worlidge, John 78